Communications
in Computer and Information Science

T0238014

Junjie Wu   Haibo Chen
Xingwei Wang (Eds.)

Advanced Computer Architecture

10th Annual Conference, ACA 2014
Shenyang, China, August 23-24, 2014
Proceedings

 Springer

Volume Editors

Junjie Wu
National University of Defense Technology
410073 Changsha, China
E-mail: junjiewu@nudt.edu.cn

Haibo Chen
Shanghai Jiao Tong University
200240 Shanghai, China
E-mail: haibochen@sjtu.edu.cn

Xingwei Wang
Northeastern University
110819 Shenyang, China
E-mail: wangxw@mail.neu.edu.cn

ISSN 1865-0929   e-ISSN 1865-0937
ISBN 978-3-662-44490-0   e-ISBN 978-3-662-44491-7
DOI 10.1007/978-3-662-44491-7
Springer Heidelberg New York Dordrecht London

Library of Congress Control Number: 2014945568

Typesetting: Camera-ready by author, data conversion by Scientific Publishing Services, Chennai, India

Printed on acid-free paper

Springer is part of Springer Science+Business Media (www.springer.com)

Preface

Welcome to the proceedings of 10th Annual Conference of Advanced Computer Architecture (ACA 2014), which was held in Shenyang, China! The emergence of big data and the continued popularity of cloud computing create grand challenges and prolific opportunities for computer architecture and systems research, ranging from high-performance computer architecture, multicore architecture, compilers, reconfigurable computing and so on. These topics also formed the theme of ACA 2014. The two-day technical program of ACA 2014 provided an excellent venue for presenting recent advances in research and practic by researchers in China.

To ensure the quality of the program and to stimulate interactive discussions, we assigned each submission to at least three Program Committee (PC) members and selected papers based on their review scores as well as on the potential of the paper to generate discussions during the conference. Further, to provide a chance for interesting papers with controversial reviews, we introduced a "conditional accept" with a shepherd this year. We held an online PC meeting from April 25 to May 1 to reach consensus on each submission. We directly accepted papers with all positive reviews. Papers with support from at least two PC members and only one weak reject, were accepted conditionally and assigned a PC member with high review confidence as the shepherd. In total, we accepted 15 papers directly and four papers conditionally. After careful revision, the four papers were approved by the shepherds.

We would like to express our thanks to all authors who submitted papers to ACA 2014, and our congratulations to those whose papers were accepted. ACA is an event that has taken place for 19 years. In addition to the authors, we would also like to show our appreciation to this year's dream-team PC. The 36 PC members did a great job in returning constructive reviews in time and in having active participation in the online PC discussions. This ensured the timely delivery of results to the authors.

Finally, we would like to thank our honorary general chair Prof. Xuejun Yang, our general chairs Prof. Yong Dou and Prof. Ge Yu, the Technical Committee on Computer Architecture of China Computer Federation and Northeastern University of China for their support in making this event happen. Our thanks also goes to Springer for its assistance in publishing the proceedings. Their help made ACA 2014 a great success.

August 2014

Haibo Chen
Xingwei Wang
Junjie Wu

Organization

ACA 2014 was hosted by the China Computer Federation.

Organizers

Technical Committee on Computer Architecture of CCF
Northeastern University

Honorary Chair

Xuejun Yang   National University of Defense Technology

General Chairs

Yong Dou   National University of Defense Technology
Ge Yu   Northeastern University

Program Chairs

Xingwei Wang   Northeastern University
Haibo Chen   Shanghai Jiao Tong University

Program Committee

Hong An   University of Science and Technology
Qiang Cao   Huazhong University of Science and Technology
Tianshi Chen   ICT, China Academy of Sciences
Wenzhi Chen   Zhejiang University
Yunji Chen   ICT, China Academy of Sciences
Yaozu Dong   Intel Inc.
Dongrui Fan   ICT, China Academy of Sciences
Yinhe Han   ICT, China Academy of Sciences
Fengru He   Open University of Guangdong
Mengshu Hou   University of Electronic Science and
                                    Technology
Jie Jia   Northeastern University
Tao Li   Nankai University

Xiaoyao Liang	Shanghai Jiao Tong University
Yingwei Luo	Peking University
Sheng Ma	National University of Defense Technology
Jian Ouyang	Baidu Inc.
Li Shen	National University of Defense Technology
Jinsong Wang	Tianjing University of Technology
Tao Wang	Peking University
Wei Wang	Tongji University
Yu Wang	Tsinghua University
Chenggang Wu	ICT, China Academy of Sciences
Chengtao Wu	Shanghai Jiao Tong University
Song Wu	Huazhong University of Science and Technology
Yubin Xia	Shanghai Jiao Tong University
Yibo Xue	Tsinghua University
Guihai Yan	ICT, China Academy of Sciences
Zhibin Yu	SIAT, China Academy of Sciences
Fengzhe Zhang	Huawei Technologies Inc.
Kuangjiu Zhou	Dalian University of Technology
Weihua Zhang	Fudan University
Xingjun Zhang	Xian Jiao Tong University
Yu Zhang	University of Science and Technology

Steering Committee

Yong Dou	National University of Defense Technology
Zhengzhou Ji	Harbin Institute of Technology
Xingwei Wang	Northeastern University
Dongsheng Wang	Tsinghua University
Minyou Wu	Shanghai Jiao Tong University
Gongxun Zhang	Nanjing University of Science and Technology
Junjie Wu	National University of Defense Technology

Local Arrangements Chair

Ruiyun Yu	Northeastern University

Publication Chair

Junjie Wu	National University of Defense Technology

Web Chair

Yu Wang	Northeastern University

Publicity Chair

Chenggang Wu   ICT, China Academy of Sciences

Sponsorship Chair

Xiushuang Yi   Northeastern University

Finance Chair

Fanrong Meng   Northeastern University

Table of Contents

Processors and Circuits

High Performance Computing

GPUs and Accelerators

Cloud and Data Centers

Energy and Reliability

Intelligence Computing and Mobile Computing

Fusion Coherence: Scalable Cache Coherence for Heterogeneous Kilo-Core System

Songwen Pei[1,2,3], Myoung-Seo Kim[3], Jean-Luc Gaudiot[3], and Naixue Xiong[4]

[1] Department of Computer Science and Engineering,
University of Shanghai for Science and Technology, Shanghai 200093, China
[2] State Key Laboratory of Computer Architecture, Institute of Computing Technology,
Chinese Academy of Sciences, Beijing 100190, China
swpei@usst.edu.cn
[3] Department of Electrical Engineering and Computer Science,
University of California, Irvine, California 92697, USA
{songwenp,myoungsk,gaudiot}@uci.edu
[4] School of Computer Science, Colorado Technical University, Springs, Colorado 80907, USA
nxiong@coloradotech.edu

Abstract. Future heterogeneous systems will integrate CPUs and GPUs on a single chip to achieve high computing performance as well as high throughput. In general, it would discard the current discrete pattern and will build a uniformed shared memory system avoiding explicit data movement among CPUs and GPUs connected by high throughput NoC.

We propose a scalable cache coherence solution *Fusion Coherence* for Heterogeneous Kilo-core System Architecture by integrating CPUs and GPUs on a single chip to mitigate the coherence bandwidth side effects of GPU memory requests as well as overhead of copying data among memories of CPUs and GPUs. The Fusion Coherence coalesces L3 data cache of CPUs and GPUs based on a uniformed physical memory, further integrates a region directory and cuckoo directory into two levels of cache coherence directory without modifying cache coherence protocol. According to the experimental results with a subset of Rodina benchmarks, it is effective to decrease the overhead of data transfer and get an average execution speedup by 2.4x. The highest speedup is approximate to 4x for data-intensive applications.

Keywords: Fusion Coherence, Fusion Directory, Two-level Cache Directories, Heterogeneous Kilo-core System, Cache Coherence.

1 Introduction

Moore's Law continues with technology scaling, emerging 3D stacking technology, increasing transistor capacity and number per square inches, so it is probable to implement thousands of cores on a single chip. The evolutionary approach is to continue the trend with a few large cores, and a large shared cache [1]. The integration capacity will still double in every two years, and implementing coherent cache hierarchies becomes increasingly difficult in the age of thousands of cores processor.

J. Wu et al. (Eds.): ACA 2014, CCIS 451, pp. 1–15, 2014.

At the mean time, data-parallel accelerators such as general-purpose graphics processing unit (GPGPU) computing is emerging as a high-throughput many core accelerator. The availability of heterogeneous multicore systems such as AMD Fusion [2], Intel Haswell [3], Nvidia Denver[4] and ARM big.LITTLE[5] suggests that multicore systems with heterogeneous processing elements are becoming the mainstream in the field of future processor design. Especially, as the rapid development of manufacture technology, it becomes probable to make heterogeneous kilo-core system by integrating the general-purpose (non-graphics or data flow) computing units and GPGPU on a single chip in the near future.

In current paradigms of both discrete and integrated GPUs, there are relatively large overheads associated with data transfer, kernel launch, cache coherence and synchronization[6]. Taking an example shown in [6], the physical transferring latency of a 128KB *memcpy* from host to device occupies on 70% of the whole overhead of data moving, either in discrete GPU system or integrated system. It will be mostly benefited from eliminating the overhead of data transferring along with increasing the scale of computing units. Besides, the cost of data transfer is overweighed to execution on discrete GPU architecture on Radeon HD5870. But, the performance is expected to be improved by Heterogeneous System Architecture (HSA) over Trinity APU[7]. HSA is a uniformed computing framework cooperated by industries and academies. It provides a single address space accessible to both CPU and GPU to avoid data copying, user-space queuing to minimize communication overhead, and preemptive context switching for better quality of service across all computing elements in the system[7]. Gregg et al[8] verified that the time to transfer data between CPU and GPU cores is huge and inspired us to reduce the overhead of communication in heterogeneous architectures. Besides, Daga et al.[9]showed that AMD APU's performance is better than hybrid architecture integrated by CPU processors and discrete GPU cores over PCIe. Hwu et al.[10] also pointed out that the overhead of data transferring between CPU and discrete GPU is a bottleneck of hybrid processor. As the increasing scale of cores on a chip, the more communications and data movements among cores will be occurred, and the whole computing performance would be decreased while the power dissipation would be increased sharply if there is not a good solution for it. All of the prior work inspired us to eliminate the overhead of data transferring and highly scalable cache scheme by designing a fusion coherence for real heterogeneous system.

To this end, in order to eliminate huge overhead of transferring data and keep high efficiency of accessing cache between CPUs and GPUs, we propose the fused and scalable cache coherence solution-*Fusion Coherence* for heterogeneous kilo-core system based on a uniformed physical memory (UPM) framework [11] to coordinate data switch among GPUs and CPUs by directly cross accessing to memories of each other without explicit data copying. Within fusion coherence, a new fused cache directory called *Fusion Directory* takes advantages of cuckoo directory [12] and region directory [13].

The main contributions of this paper are:

◆ Fusion directory not only takes advantages of high harsh structure and regional directory, bust also decreases the overhead of communication among heterogeneous processing elements.

◆ Optimization for the cache coherence directory by supplementing states transmitting algorithm for classified cache data blocks with different tags.

◆ System performance is improved by the seamless coordination of fusion coherence and the uniformed physical memory system of heterogeneous kilo-core system.

We implemented *Heterogeneous Kilo-core System Architecture* (HKSA) on a cycle-level simulator based on Gem5[14] and GPGPU-Sim[15]. Furthermore, we evaluate fusion coherent cache by the heterogeneous simulator with 1024 cores integrating 256 CPU cores and 768 GPU cores on a single chip, and a 3-level hierarchical cache directory. We show that, the fused coherent cache is scalable and effective to support thousands of cores, and which sharply decreases the overhead of data transferring among cores.

The rest of this paper is organized as follows. Section 2 provides the related work and Section 3 presents the target architecture Heterogeneous Kilo-core System Architecture, and Section 4 proposes the fusion cache coherence and fusion directory structures. Section 5 provides an evaluation result of the fusion coherence. Finally, we conclude it and expect our future work.

2   Related Work

Snooping and directory-based cache coherence protocols are classical protocol in the past decades[16]. Snooping cache coherence protocols work well in small-scale systems, but it is not well scalable beyond a handful of cores due to their large bandwidth overheads, even with optimizations like snoop filters[17]. Directory-based cache coherence system uses a global directory to track the coherence state of individual cache blocks. Requests from a computing element or caches consult the global directory entry corresponding to the requested cache blocks to determine where the location of the up-to-date copies, and which kind of actions should be taken. In generally, directory-based protocols are better for large-scale CMPs due to introducing a coherence directory between the private and shared cache levels to track and control which caches share a line and serve as an ordering point for concurrent requests. However, while conventional directory-based protocols scale to hundreds of cores and beyond, implementing directories that can track hundreds of sharers efficiently has been problematic[18]. Traditional cache coherence directory includes duplicate-tag directories[19] maintaining a copy of all tags in the tracked caches and bringing energy-inefficient with a large number of cores, and sparse directories usually using a bit-vector to maintain each entry[20]. Hierarchical directories [21] implement multiple levels of sparse directories with each level tracking the lower-level sharers.

Protoza[22] is an adaptive granularity cache coherence which makes more effective spatial locality by avoiding to waste bandwidth and unnecessary coherence traffic for shared data. SPATL [23] decoupled the sharing patterns from bloom filters and eliminated the redundant sharers based on tagless cache directory, and finally they extended it to support 1024-core chips with less than 1%of the private cache space. Sanchez, et al. [18,24] proposed a scalable coherence directory for 1024-core CMP, but it's just a single-level cache directory and needed to track a fixed number of sharers, and their further work Jigsaw[25] was a scalable software-defined cache for smaller CMPs systems. WayPoint [17] is a scaling coherence to 1000-core architecture of Rigel[26], which added a broadcast-collective probe filtering for cache coherence scheme and minimized its on-die storage and maintaining overhead for directory protocols. Xu et al. [27] addressed composite cache coherence for thousand-core CMPs by leveraging merging optical on-chip interconnect technology. Their protocol benefited from advantages of both snoopy protocol and directory protocol, such as direct cache-to-cache accesses and cache probing. However, most of their work just focused on cache coherence for homogeneous many-core system, their schemes did not involve into multiple levels cache coherence between CPU cache and GPU cache.

Hechtman et al. [28] proposed a cache-coherence shared virtual memory for heterogeneous multicore chips, but they did not share last level CPU cache and GPU cache just depending on an inclusive L2 cache and they did not proposed an effective solution for heterogeneous thousand core system. Library cache coherence (LCC)[29] is a time-based hardware coherence that stores unexpired blocks to enforce sequential consistency on CMPs. Temporal coherence [30] is also a time-based cache coherence framework for GPU architectures aiming at Nvidia GPU architecture. Ubik[31] is an efficient cache sharing scheme to support strict QoS for latency-critical workloads. Basu et al [32] proposed a dual-grain CMP directory protocol by using snooping region coherence to maximize the effectiveness of precious on-chip directory state. HeLM [33] is a novel shared LLC management policy that takes advantage of the GPU's tolerance for memory access latency by passing the LLC, and the latency tolerance of a GPU application is determined by the availability of thread-level parallelism. However, it did not solve the cache coherence among CPU and GPU caches within a real heterogeneous processor on a single chip.

3   Target Architecture

3.1   Heterogeneous Kilo-core System Architecture(HKSA)

The *heterogeneous kilo-core system architecture* (HKSA) is an enhanced architecture framework for a thousand cores processor, which is inspired from Rigel[26]. HKSA is consist of 3-level computing elements, the heterogeneous CPUs and GPUs cluster are at the lowest level, as shown in the right lower corner of Fig.1, each cluster has 4 CPU cores and 12 GPU cores sharing exclusive L2 data cache among each type of interior cores. In default, each CPU core and GPU core has its private L1 instruction cache and L1 data cache independently which was not shown in the Fig. 1. Then, each cluster is a quarter of a tile, and each quarter shares their data by input/output queues over high throughput network on chip, thus each tile concludes 16 CPU cores and 48 GPU cores. Similar to Rigel architecture, there are 16 tiles connected by a high speed high radix asymmetric crossbar network[34]. Furthermore, the L3 Fusion cache is set up for storing uniformed CPU and GPU data. From the sight of software programmer, the L3 fusion cache not only supplies a logical uniformed address, but also supports uniformed physical cache structure. In other words, there will be no physical data copying among CPU data caches and GPU data caches due to the fusion data cache. All the data would be referred directly from GPU to CPU or vice versa.

We can get at least two advantages from this kind of cache structure: (1) It eliminates the overhead of data transferring among GPU cores and CPU cores; (2) It decreases the overhead of communication on chip and improves the efficiency of energy per square inches.

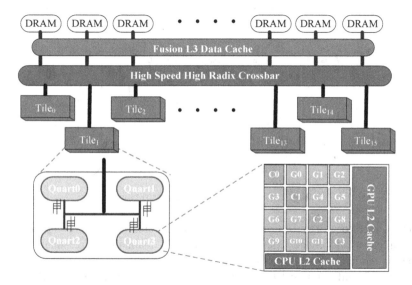

Fig. 1. Heterogeneous Kilo-core System Architecture(HKSA)

3.2   Hierarchical Cache Directory

As the number of cores grows, the aggregate directory must increase commensurately[11]. It means that the more directory slices should be set to accommodate more cores, and then the power dissipation grows quadratically as well as the aggregate directory area grows quadratically. Bit vectors are popularly used in traditional spare directory to track cache sharers, which grow linearly with core count, and lead to increasing of power dissipation and area quadratically as core counts increase[35]. Hierarchical directory uses coarse bit vectors at a primary location and exacts sub bit vectors at secondary location[36].

Cuckoo directory is a scalable distributed directory with nearly constant power and area utilization per core, regardless of core count, which avoids set conflicts of traditional spare directory and can achieve scalable power- and area-efficient CMP coherence[11]. Cuckoo directory structure is an alike set-associative structure, but it displaces victims to alternate non-conflicting ways instead of evicting a replaced victim from a small set of conflicting entries in terms of Cuckoo hash functions. Take a simple example, cuckoo hash uses two independent tables, indexed through two different hash functions. A new entry is always inserted in one of the two tables and displaces a valid entry[37]. The insertion process is ended until the final temporal displaced block is inserted into a vacant alternate location.

In order to solve the directory coherence on two levels of data cache, L2 data cache and L3 uniformed data cache, we propose a hierarchical Cuckoo directory scheme. As shown in Fig.2, a 4-way Cuckoo directory structure is designed for GPU L2 data cache and CPU L2 data cache respectively in a cluster.

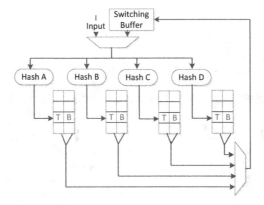

Fig. 2. 4-way Cuckoo directory structure

Cuckoo directory organization achieves up to 7x area reduction compared to the spare directory and Spare Hierarchical directory, maintaining reasonable energy dissipation while bring the area of the directory storage under 3% of the L2 area for the Shared-L2 configuration 1024 cores and under 30% of the L2 area for the private-L2 configuration with 1024 cores[11].

Region coherence was first proposed in 2005 to reduce the bandwidth required on snooping-based system[38-40]. And it was also extended to a directory-based cache[41]. In order to decrease the computing and communication overhead of cache directory, especially plenty of requests from GPU and CPU cores, we introduce the region directory as a global directory. Generally, a region is an aligned multi-block range of cache block. We define its capacity as 1K Bytes of 16 64-Byte blocks in default.

3.3   Heterogeneous Cache

Traditionally, coherence among CPUs and GPUs has been managed by software through explicit copies between address spaces. Explicitly copying shared data among CPUs and GPUs is either complicated for software programming models and programmers or time consuming over the heterogeneous hardware, such as the explicit API memory copying in the framework of CUDA. The programmer should firstly understand the detail of GPUs infrastructure and the application features, then use the memory copying function to move data from CPU memory to GPU memory. After the data is used by GPUs and the new result should be copied again from GPU memory to CPU memory.

To mitigate these issues and increase performance, Kelm, et al [42,43] proposed a cohesion scheme to migrating data between coherence domains without copying by coordinating software-managed coherence protocol and hardware-managed coherence protocol. Hechtman [44] tried to achieve memory consistency for throughput-oriented processors.

4   Fusion Cache Coherence

We build a hierarchical cache coherence schemes together with two level cache structures by taking advantages of cuckoo directory and region directory with tags respectively. The first level cache directory is cuckoo directory which is corresponding L2 data cache separately for GPU and CPU. The second one is region directory with tags for data original source, such as tiles identifier, GPU tags and CPU tags, which is corresponding L3 uniformed data cache.

4.1   Discrete L2 Data Cache

Due to the L2 data cache for CPUs cluster and GPUs cluster is separate, and we observed that the reused frequency of interior data blocks either in GPUs cluster or in CPUs cluster is high. So, in order to decrease the possibility of replaced blocks, we design a 4-way cuckoo directory for each CPUs and GPUs cluster, as shown in Fig.2.

4.2   Uniformed L3 Data Cache

Each quart has two corresponding Region Coherence Array(RCA), the one is RCA for CPU L2 data cache (RCAC) and the other one is RCA for GPU L2 data cache(RCAG). According to the HKSA, there would be 64 RCACs and 64 RCAGs respectively. The Fig.3 shows the abstract cache coherence architecture based on HKSA with region cache and region directory.

In order to effectively access uniformed data cache and uniformed physical memory system, we also propose the two phase parallel execution technology like [45] while we simulate applications based on HKSA simulator integrating Gem5 and GPGPU-Sim. At the first phase, all the instructions are executed for an interval of a few thousand cycles by ignoring resource contention and memory load. Thus, we can record the track of all memory accesses including cache accessing, main memory accessing, invalidation operations among cache structure, and tagging all data by where it was generated from, such as the vector {T, Q, C, G}. This can help CPUs or GPUs controllers making the final determines how to operate them according to the requirements of a write or read. At the second phase, the instructions are started over to be execute in parallel, and load or store data with the actual latency. Due to the all tracks of accessing memory and possible interactions among GPU computing units and CPU cores are recorded at the first phase, we can get more accurate simulation results and decrease the overhead of synchronization.

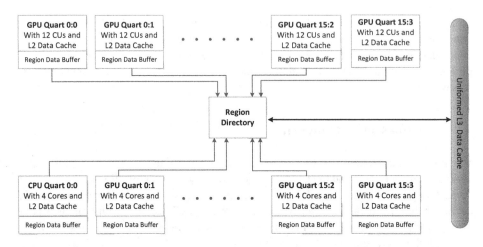

Fig. 3. Uniformed Data Cache Coherence with Region Directory

The coherence protocol is hierarchical coherence with a global region-level directory that has 7 bits for the sharing vector responding to 64 GPU quarts and 64 CPU quarts. The Region directory entry structure is shown in Fig.4.

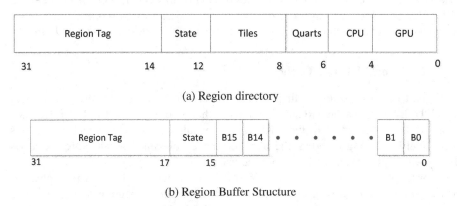

(a) Region directory

(b) Region Buffer Structure

Fig. 4. Region directory entry structure

4.3 Fusion Directory

The fusion cache directory structure is basically composed of Cuckoo Cache under the L2 data cache in a quart and a Region cache under the L3 uniformed data cache. The Cuckoo directory is helpful to lengthen the residence time of a block without replaced too frequently. It enhances the temporal locality of cache and decrease power dissipation by decreasing cache area per square inches. Moreover, the Region directory decreases the communication bandwidth among CPU cores and GPU computing units by bypassing the accessing directly from Main memory if there are many continual accessing a region of blocks. Besides, Region directory is a bridge of L3 uniformed data cache and other tiles. It coordinates the data switch among CPU data cache and GPU data cache over tiles. Similar to the heterogeneous system coherence in [13], each quart has two Region Buffers as shown in Fig.5. One is a GPU Region buffer containing region tags, permissions, and other metadata. The other is a CPU Region buffer

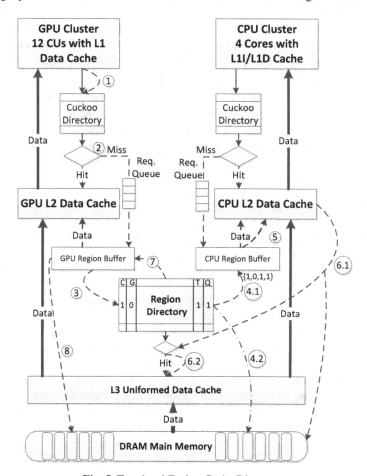

Fig. 5. Two-level Fusion Cache Directory

Fig.5 shows an example of an exclusive write request flows to memory system with three levels of cache. ①The GPU cluster issues a exclusive write request for address F, then looks up the cuckoo directory. If it misses in cuckoo directory, then ②the request is added into a corresponding Req. Queue connecting Region directory. The write request will be forward to GPU Region Buffer until it comes up to the top of the queue.

Otherwise, it hits that means the corresponding block of address F is located at GPU L2 data cache and the subsequent actions are similar to traditional writing operations. If the address F is part of a region $R(F)$, which is not included into GPU Region Buffer. ③Therefore, a region-exclusive request is sent to the region directory. If the tag of write request for $R(F)$ hits Region Directory, that means there exists at least one region, either interior the same quart or outside the quart, including block of corresponding address F. Therefore, the controller of Region directory compares the vectors, such as T, Q, C and G which respectively represents the vector for Tiles, Quart, CPU side and GPU side. For example, the vector of {T,Q,C,G} is {1,1,1,0}, that means there is a region in a CPU Region Buffer including block of address F in the same tile and quart. Therefore, ④⋅¹ the controller sends an invalidate probe to CPU Region Buffer. ⑤As soon as the CPU Region Buffer receives the invalidate probe request, it will invalidates all blocks, with valid state in the CPU L2 data cache, belong to the region $R(F)$. ⑥⋅¹The corresponding blocks in the region will be written back to main memory. By the way, if the blocks in the region are also in the L3 uniformed data cache, ⑥⋅²these blocks in the L3 uniformed data cache will be evicted. ⑦After then, the controller of Region Directory will notify GPU Region Buffer and grant it the permission to directly access main memory. ⑧The subsequent write requests for one of the blocks of the same region $R(F)$ from the GPU and they missed in GPU L2 data cache, then they can directly access to main memory without probing the other GPU computing units or CPU cores and asking for the permission to access to the blocks. This kind of mechanism will help to decrease the frequency of probing other computing units or cores and mitigate the bus load of communication. Furthermore, it supply an alternative path to directly access the uniformed cache or main memory without copying any data from CPU cache to GPU cache and break through the bottleneck of accessing opposite memory on heterogeneous systems. Especially, it can be easily scalable to thousands of cores, either for GPU computing units or CPU cores.

If the write requests are issued from CPU cluster, the procedure of accessing memory system is similar because of symmetrical memory system. As for memory requests flows of read instructions, it firstly looks up the local Cuckoo directory as well. If it hits, then L2 data cache returns the responding blocks. If not, then a request is forwarding to Region Buffer and tries to find the responding regions including the requested block's address. If the request reaches the Region directory and finds the regions in CPU Region buffer. Then comparing to the attribution vectors to judge whether the region is located in local quart or not and whether the L3 Uniformed Data Cache contains the same region blocks. If it does, then return the corresponding blocks to the original Region Buffer and update their states of the blocks reserving other quarts.

5   Experiments and Evaluation

5.1   Methodology and Simulation

We conduct the verification research by combing Gem5[14] and GPGPU-Sim[15] simulation, which are all built on a unmodified x86 64bits Linux 2.6. They simulated 256 in-order x86 CPU cores at 2G Hz and distributed into 16 tiles, and 768 GPU cores at 600MHz and also distributed into 16 tiles. The Gem5 CPU system obeys traditional MOESI cache coherence protocol, and the GPU caches are write-through and obey the VI-based cache coherence protocol. Table 1 shows the detail parameters of the simulation infrastructure.

Currently, we just use one benchmark suites to evaluate the fusion coherence based on heterogeneous kilo-core system. We mainly choose 10 benchmarks from Rodinia, which are back propagation (bp), breadth-first search (bfs), computational fluid dynamics solver (cfd), heart wall (hw), hotspot (hs), lavaMD2(lmd), LU decomposition (lud), MUMmergpu (mum), Needleman-Wunsch(nw), speckle reducing anisotropic diffusion (srad). The *bp* is a machine-learning algorithm for layered neural network, *cfd* is a solver for the 3D Euler equations for compressible flow, *hw* tracks the movement of a mouse heart over a ultrasound images, *hs* is a simulation for processor temperature, *lmd* calculates particle potential and relocation within a 3D space of molecular dynamics, *mum* implements an high throughput parallel alignment algorithm, *nw* is a optimization method for DNA sequence alignments, and *srad* implemtns a diffusion method for ultrasonic and radar images.

Table 1. Simulation Configuration Parameters

CPU	Total 256 uniformly distributed into 16 tiles, each tile has 16 CPU cores, and each Quart has 4 in-order CPU cores at 2GHz
CPU L1 Data Cache	64KB
CPU L1 Instruction Cache	64KB
CPU L2 Data Cache	2MB (16-way)
GPU	Total 768 computing elements(CEs) uniformly distributed into 16 tiles, each tile has 48 CEs, and each Quart has 12 CEs at 600MHz
GPU L1 Data Cache	64KB
GPU L1 Instruction Cache	64KB
GPU L2 Data Cache	8MB (32-way)
L3 Uniformed Data Cache	32MB (16-way)
DRAM	DDR3
Cuckoo Directory	2^{10} entries (8-way)
Region Directory	2^{18} entries (16-way)
Region Buffer	2^{15} entries (16-way)

5.2   Experimental Result

We present the experimental result for HKSA, and the experiments are compared with a basic infrastructure built with a discrete Nvidia Tesla T20 GPU and an Intel i5 CPU. The results include execution time speedup and latency of Load and Store compared to the basic infrastructure with discrete GPU.

As shown in the Fig.6, the average speedup is 2.4x and the maximum speedup is more than 4x. However, not all the applications achieve the high speedup, such as *bp*, *bfs*, *hw*, *lud* and *nw*. These applications are mainly computing-intensive, and spend a significant execution time on CPU core instead of transferring a large mount of data between CPU and GPU memory.

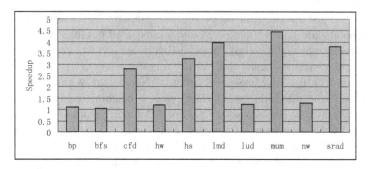

Fig. 6. Execution time speedup

As for those applications get high speedup, such as *cfd*, *hs*, *lmd*, *mum* and *srad*, according to our observation, the main reason is increasing the hit ratio on L3 uniformed data cache and decreasing the delay of load and store instructions due to directly accessing cross memory system under the support of two-levels of cache directories and uniformed physical memory system, especially the memory operations across CPU and GPU. Fig.7 shows the average delay of load and store instructions. The average delay of accessing memory within 10 benchmarks are decreased to 40%, the most significant decreasing lowers to 21% due to large mount of memory data copying among CPU and GPU in the baseline infrastructure.

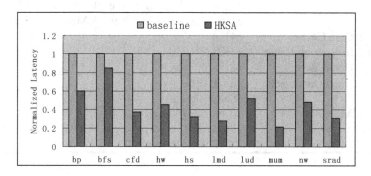

Fig. 7. Delay of accessing memory

6   Conclusions

We get some benefits from the design of fusion coherence by two-level directory and directly accessing uniformed L3 data cache, which sharply decrease the execution time and latency of accessing memory system because of bypassing L3 data cache guided by fusion directory, directly accessing memory space instead of copying data between each other and transmitting over system bus.

However, the future research would be conducted on the chip's area due to introducing fusion directory and uniformed L3 data cache, and the corresponding power dissipation. Furthermore, the effects of system bus and directory bandwidth would be investigated. In our opinions, the fusion coherence framework not only indicating fusion cache directories, but also the fusion L3 data cache are really helpful to build a new large scale of heterogeneous CPU and GPU system.

Acknowledgements. The authors would like to thank Shouq Alsubaihi and Ganghee Jang for their helps with supporting infrastructures, and Joel Hestness and Jason Power for their advices to build initial simulator. This work was partially funded by the Shanghai Key Lab of Modern Optical System, Engineering Research Center of Optical Instrument and System, Ministry of Education, and State Key Laboratory of Computer Architecture, Institute of Computing Technology under Grant No. CARCH201206. The Funding to Cultivate National Research Projects under Grant No.12XGQ07.

References

1. Borkar, S.: Thousand core chips: a technology perspective. In: Proceedings of the 44th Annual Design Automation Conference (DAC), San Diego, CA, pp. 746–749 (2007)
2. Brookwood, N.: AMD fusion family of APUs: enabling a superior, immersive PC experience, AMD white paper (2010) (available in January 2014)
3. Intel Corpaoration. Intel Haswell Microarchitecture, http://www.intel.com (available in January 2014)
4. Nvidia Corporation. Nvidia Project Denver, http://www.nvidia.com (available in January 2014)
5. ARM Corporation. Big.LITTLE Processing, http://www.arm.com (available in January 2014)
6. Lustig, D., Martonosi, M.: Reducing GPU offload latency via fine-grained CPU-GPU synchronization. In: IEEE Conference on HPCA (2013)
7. AMD. Heterogeneous System Architecture: A Technical Review, http://developer.amd.com/wordpress/media/2012/10/hsa10.pdf (available in January 2014)
8. Greeg, C., Hazelwood, K.: Where is the data? Why you cannot debate CPU vs. GPU performance without the answer. In: IEEE International Symposium on Performance Analysis of Systems and Software (ISPASS), Austin, TX, pp. 134–144 (2011)
9. Daga, M., Aji, A.M., Feng, W.: On the Efficacy of a Fused CPU+GPU Processor (or APU) for Parallel Computing. In: 2011 Symposium on Application Accelerators in High-Performance Computing, Knoxville, Tennessee, pp. 141–149 (2011)
10. Hwu, W.-M.: Rethinking computer architecture for throughput computing. In: 2013 International Conference on Embedded Computer Systems: Architectures, Modeling and Simulation (SAMOS), Keynote, Greece (2013)
11. Pei, S., Gaudiot, J.-L., et al.: Decoupled memory system for heterogeneous kilo-core high throughput processor. Tech Report, UC Irvine (2013)

12. Ferdman, M., Lotfi-kamran, P., Balet, K., et al.: Cuckoo directory: a scalable directory for many-core systems. In: Proceedings of IEEE 17th International Symposium on High Performance Computer Architecture (HPCA), San Antonio, TX, pp. 169–180 (2011)
13. Power, J., Basu, A., Gu, J., et al.: Heterogeneous system coherence for integrated CPU-GPU systems. In: Proceedings of the 46th Annual IEEE/ACM International Symposium on Microarchitecture (MICRO), Davis, CA, pp. 457–467 (2013)
14. Binkert, N., Beckmann, B., Black, G., et al.: The gem5 simulator. ACM SIGARCH Computer Architecture News 39(2), 1–7 (2011)
15. Bakhoda, A., Yuan, G.L., Fung, W.W.L., et al.: Analyzing CUDA workloads using a detailed GPU simulator. In: 2009 IEEE International Symposium on Performance Analysis of Systems and Software (ISPASS), Boston, MA, pp. 163–174 (2009)
16. Hennessy, J., Patterson, D.: Computer Architecture a quantitative approach, 5th edn., p. 333 (2012)
17. Kelm, J., Johnson, M., Lumettea, S., et al.: WayPoint: scaling coherence to 1000-core architectures. In: Proceedings of the 19th International Conference on Parallel Architectures and Compilation Techniques (PACT), Vienna, Austria, pp. 99–110 (2010)
18. Sanchez, D., Kozyrakis, C.: SCD: A scalable coherence directory with flexible sharer set encoding. In: Proceedings of the 2012 IEEE 18th International Symposium on High-Performance Computer Architecture (HPCA), New Orleans, LA, pp. 1–12 (2012)
19. Barroso, L., Gharachorloo, K., McNamara, R., et al.: Piranha: a scalable architecture based on single-chip multiprocessing. In: Proceedings of the 27th Annual International Symposium on Computer Architecture (ISCA), Vancouver, Canada, pp. 282–293 (2000)
20. Gupta, A., Weber, W., Mowry, T.: Reducing memory and traffic requirements for scalable directory based cache coherence schemes. In: Proceedings of the International Conference on Parallel Processing, ICPP (1990)
21. Yang, Q., Thangadurai, G., Bhuyan, L.: Design of an adaptive cache coherence protocol for large scale multiprocessors. IEEE Transactions on Parallel and Distributed Systems (TPDS) 3(3), 281–293 (1992)
22. Zhao, H., Shriraman, A., Kumar, S., et al.: Protozoa: Adaptive granularity cache coherence. In: Proceedings of the 40th Annual International Symposium on Computer Architecture (ISCA), Israel, pp. 547–558 (2013)
23. Zhao, H., Shriraman, A., Dwarkadsa, S., et al.: SPATL: Honey, I Shrunk the Coherence Directory. In: 2011 International Conference on Parallel Architectures and Compilation Techniques (PACT), Galveston, TX, pp. 33–44 (2011)
24. Sanchez, D., Kozyrakis, C.: The ZCache: decoupling ways and associativity. In: Proceedings of the 43rd Annual IEE/ACM Symposium on Microarchitecture (MICRO), Atlanta, GA, pp. 187–198 (2010)
25. Beckmann, N., Sanchez, D.: Jigsaw: scalable software-defined caches. In: Proceedings of the 22nd International Conference on Parallel Architectures and Compilation Techniques (PACT), pp. 213–224 (2013)
26. Johnson, D.R., Kelm, J.H., Crago, N.C., et al.: Rigel: a scalable architecture for 1000+ core accelerators. IEEE Micro 31(4), 30–41 (2011)
27. Xu, Y., Du, Y., Zhang, Y., et al.: A composite and scalable cache coherence protocol for large scale CMPs. In: Proceedings of the International Conference on Supercomputing, Tucson, Arizona, pp. 285–294 (2011)
28. Hechtman, B.A., Sorin, D.J.: Evaluating cache coherent shared virtual memory for heterogeneous multicore chips. In: 2013 IEEE International Symposium on Performance Analysis of Systems and Software (ISPASS), Austin, TX, pp. 118–119 (2013)

29. Lis, M., Shim, K.S., Cho, M.H., et al.: Memory coherence in the age of multicores. In: 2011 IEEE 29th International Conference on Computer Design (ICCD), Amherst, MA, pp. 1–8 (2011)
30. Singh, I., Shriraman, A., Fung, W.W.L., et al.: Cache Coherence for GPU Architecture. In: 2013 IEEE 19th International Symposium on High Performance Computer Architecture (HPCA), Shenzhen, China, pp. 578–590 (2013)
31. Kasture, H., Sanchez, D.: Ubik: Efficient Cache Sharing with Strict QoS for Latency-Critical Workloads. In: Proceedings of the 19th International Conference on Architectural Support for Programming Languages and Operating Systems (ASPLOS), pp. 1–14 (2014)
32. Basu, A., Beckmann, B.M., Hill, M.D., et al.: CMP Directory Coherence: One Granularity Does Not Fit All. TR1798, http://minds.wisconsin.edu/handle/1793/66144 (available in January 2014)
33. Mekkat, V., Holey, A., Yew, P.C., et al.: Managing shared last-level cache in a heterogeneous multicore processor. In: Proceedings of the 22nd International Conference on Parallel Architectures and Compilation Techniques (PACT), pp. 225–243 (2013)
34. Abeyratne, N., Das, Q., Li, Q., et al.: Scaling towards kilo-core processors with asymmetric high-radix topologies. In: Proceedings of the 19th IEEE International Symposium on High Performance Computer Architecture (HPCA), Shenzhen, China, pp. 496–507 (2013)
35. Cesier, L.M., Feautrier, P.: A new solution to coherence problems in mulicache systems. IEEE Transactions on Computers 27 (1978)
36. Guo, S.L., Wang, H.X., Xue, Y.B., et al.: Hierarchical cache directory for CMP. Journal of Computer Science and Technology 25(2) (2010)
37. Pagh, R., Rodler, F.F.: Cuckoo Hashing. Algotithms 51 (2004)
38. Moshovos, A.: RegionScout: Exploiting Coarse Grain Sharing in Snoop-Based Coherence. In: Proceedings of the 32nd Annual International Symposium on Computer Architecture (ISCA), pp. 234–245 (2005)
39. Zebchuk, J., Safi, E., Moshovos, A.: A Framework for Coarse-Grain Optimizations in the On-Chip Memory Hierarchy. In: Proceedings of the 40th Annual IEEE/ACM International Symposium on Microarchitecture (MICRO), pp. 314–327 (2007)
40. Alisafaee, M.: Spatiotemporal Coherence Tracking. In: Proceedings of the 45th Annual IEEE/ACM International Symposium on Microarchitecture (MICRO), Vancouver, BC, pp. 341–350 (2012)
41. Beckmann, B.M., Basu, A., Reinhardt, S.K.: Region Privatization in directory-based cache coherence. U.S.Patent Application Publication, US2013/0073811a1 (2013)
42. Kelm, J.H., Johnson, D.R., Tuohy, W., et al.: Cohesion: a Hybrid Memory Model for Accelerators. In: Proceedings of the 37th Annual International Symposium on Computer Architecture, Saint-Malo, France, pp. 429–440 (2010)
43. Kelm, J.H., Johnson, D.R., Tuohy, W., et al.: Cohesion: An Adaptive Hybrid Memory Model for Accelerators. IEEE Micro 31(1), 42–55 (2011)
44. Hechtman, B.A., Sorin, D.J.: Exploring Memory Consistency for Massively-Threaded Throughput-Oriented Processors. In: Proceedings of the 40th Annual International Symposium on Computer Architecture (ISCA), Tel-aviv, Israel, pp. 201–212 (2013)
45. Sanchez, D., Kozyrakis, C.: ZSim: Fast and Accurate Microarchitectural Simulation of Thousand-Core Systems. In: Proceedings of the 40th Annual International Symposium on Computer Architecture (ISCA), Tel-aviv, Israel, pp. 475–486 (2013)

ACRP: Application Customized Reconfigurable Pipeline

Guanwu Wang, Lei Liu, and Sikun Li

College of Computer, National University of Defense Technology Changsha, China, 410073
GuanwuWang1986@gmail.com

Abstract. Reconfigurable architectures have become popular in recent years in the high performance computing field, because of their reconfigurable characteristic and abundant computing resources. These architectures combine the high performance of ASICs with the flexibility of microprocessors. A novel architecture named Application Customized Reconfigurable Pipeline (ACRP) is proposed for domain-specific applications in this paper. According to analyze and abstract the domain computing character, an application Customized Functional Unit (CFU) is designed to execute the frequent instruction sequence efficiently. The CFU is shared with the hardware pipeline which is composed of some Simple Process Elements (SPEs). The experimental results show that ACRP can exploit the CFU-, pipeline- and data-level parallelism efficiently with the area constraint.

Keywords: reconfigurable architecture, reconfigurable pipeline, SIMD, Application customized.

1 Introduction

Reconfigurable architectures combine the high performance of ASICs with the flexibility of the microprocessors because of the abundant hardware resources and the reconfigurable interconnection network. Reconfigurable computing is a major research direction of the high performance computing nowadays. Reconfigurable architectures are divided into CGRA (Coarse Grained Reconfigurable architecture) and FGRA (Fine Grained Reconfigurable architecture) according to operation grain of the process elements. Compared to FGRA, the CGRA achieves higher performance, lower power and shorter configuration time but lower flexibility. CGRA is a significant research direction of the reconfigurable computing.

The past few years, many reconfigurable architectures are proposed with their mapping methods[1]. CGRA generally is composed of abundant PEs (Processing Elements) and a reconfigurable interconnect network which connects those PEs. According to the type of the interconnect network, CGRA can be divided into the array architecture and the linear architecture. In this paper, we concentrate on linear architecture named the reconfigurable pipeline. Due to the area constraints, the PEs in CGRA are often quite simple. The PEs typically contains a reconfigurable functional

---

* Supported by National Natural Science Foundation of China under grant No. 61076020.

J. Wu et al. (Eds.): ACA 2014, CCIS 451, pp. 16–30, 2014.
© Springer-Verlag Berlin Heidelberg 2014

unit and a small local memory, which can perform the byte operation or half byte operation efficiently. The CGRA typically is domain-specific, e.g. DSP. The large number of PEs available in CGRA can be utilized to exploit the parallelism in the domain-specific application, while the reconfigurable interconnect network provides the required flexibility for the domain-specific application.

Another domain-specific calculating acceleration method is the ASIP (Application-Specific Instruction-set Processor). ASIP makes analysis of the computing characteristics, abstracts the frequent instructions sequence, customizes a new FU to perform that instructions sequence efficiently, and generate a CI (Customized Instruction) that the compiler can identify. The compiler is responsible for identifying the CI and mapping the CI to the original FU to improve the performance. In this work, we introduce the application customized idea to the CGRA. Due to the area constraint, CGRA's PE is usually very simple. So we first design an application customized function unit (CFU) of a certain domain application, and share the CFU with a simple hardware pipeline which is composed of some simple process elements. We call this architecture ACRP (Application Customized Reconfigurable Pipeline).

The contributions of this paper include:

1. An ACRP framework is proposed. The ACRP framework is customized for a specific domain and this reconfigurable architecture is composed of two types of PEs, SPE and CFU.
2. The customized instruction selection problem is analyzed. This problem arises when the CFU is employed to exploit the parallelism with the module scheduling algorithm.
3. Prototype: Two types of ACRPs, DSP-ACRP for DSP domain and SHA-ACRP for the secure hash algorithm, are implemented for verifying our architecture.

The rest of the paper is organized as follows: in Sect. 2, the existing work in the field of reconfigurable architecture and their mapping methods. Sect. 3 introduces the ACRP framework. Sect.4 presents a case study of ACRP mapping, while experimental results are presented in Sect. 5. Finally, conclusions are outlined in Sect. 6.

2   Related Work

Accompany the development of this age, the embedded domain application brings up a higher standard for computer architecture, including higher performance, higher flexibility and lower power. Reconfigurable computing is one important method to satisfy the requirements. The first devices that had been used for reconfigurable computing were the FPGAs (Field Programmable Gate Arrays). An FPGA consists of a matrix of programmable logic cells, executing bit-level operations, with an interconnect network. FPGA is very popular for the implementation of complex bit level operations, while is inefficient for coarse-grained operations due to the high cost of reconfiguration in performance and power. FPGA belongs to FGRA. To overcome the bottleneck of performance, the research tended to CGRA. Compared to FGRA, the CGRA reduces the delay, power and configuration time at the expense of flexibility. Surveys of reconfigurable systems can be found in [1] and [2].

CGRA consists of a lot of PEs which execute the byte operations or half byte operations efficiently. Due to the coarser granularity, CGRA reduces the delay, power and configuration time at the expense of flexibility. In the past few years, many CGRAs have been proposed with their mapping methodologies. According to the type of interconnect network, CGRA can be divided into the array architecture and the linear architecture. In the array architecture, the PEs are organized in a 2D array with horizontal and vertical connections which support communication with horizontal and vertical PEs. Tanks to the lavish interconnections, the array architecture is better at exploiting the parallelism than the linear architecture but more complicated and larger area. Considering the introduction of the complicated CFU, in this paper, we focus on the linear architecture. The linear architecture usually organizes the PEs in pipeline structure, so we call the linear architecture RP (Reconfigurable Pipeline). RP is suitable for pipelined execution stream-based applications with static or dynamic reconfiguration.

RaPiD (Reconfigurable Pipelined Datapath) [4] and PipeRench [3] have a linear array structure. RaPiD's PE is a basic cell consists of diverse computing resources like ALUs, RAMs, multipliers and registers. These resources are irregularly distributed on one dimension and are mostly reconfigured in a static way using bus segments, multiplexers, and bus connectors.

PipeRench relies on dynamic reconfiguration, allowing the reconfiguration of a processing element in each execution cycle. It consists of stripes composed of interconnects and PEs with registers and ALUs. The reconfigurable fabric allows the configuration of a pipeline stage in every cycle, while concurrently executing all other stages.

RP is good for applications that can be executed in the form of linear pipeline. However, mapping of an application that performs 2D data processing or forks into multiple branches onto RP will be inefficient and require many global interconnects. Although the application domains are limited, mapping application onto the RP is simple because of the structure's linear characteristics. In addition, the configuration time is small and the configuration bus bandwidth requirement is trivial due to the incremental reconfiguration characteristic of the RP [7]. Moreover, we can copy several RPs to exploit the data parallelism. In [8] an SIMD (Single Instruction Multiple Data) reconfigurable architecture is proposed to map some iterations of a kernel to one array in SIMD style.

Most of the CGRAs have a 2D array structure. Array architectures have more PEs with the lavish interconnections and are good for applications that perform 2D data processing. The array architectures can exploit the inherent parallelism in the kernel of applications. At the same time, it also brings up the mapping difficulty, large configuration time and large configuration bus bandwidth requirement.

ADRES (Architecture for Dynamically Reconfigurable Embedded System) [5] is a VLIW architecture tightly coupled with a reconfigurable array of PEs. ADRES has two views: VLIW view and reconfigurable matrix view. The reconfigurable matrix part works as a co-processor of the VLIW and so their executions never overlap with each other. The reconfigurable is responsible for executing the data-intensive code while the VLIW is good for the control-intensive code. ADRES firstly introduces the modulo schedule method of VLIW flied to reconfigurable architecture to exploit loop-level parallelism, and develops a compiler framework named DRESC (Dynamically Reconfigurable Embedded System Compiler) [6]. So the iterations of a loop can continuously fire in a regular interval named II (Initial Interval). DRESC generates a mapping PE randomly for an operation, and judges whether meets the data routing requirement. DRESC uses the simulated annealing algorithm to avoid the local maximum problem.

The DSE flow presented in [9] considers resource sharing and pipelining in a heterogeneous reconfigurable architecture. It assumes that an area critical resource is not directly contained in each PE but is shared among a set of PEs. The area critical resources can be pipelined not to slow down the clock and at the same time to enhance their utilization.

3   ACRP Framework

In this section, we will introduce our ACRP framework in three aspects. 1) The number and type of the PEs, 2) the interconnect network, 3) the data memory and memory access bus. We define the ACRP as a CGRA that consists of multiple SPE (Simple Processing Element) reconfigurable pipelines and some CFUs. Figure 1 illustrates the ACRP framework. We can see that 1) there are two types of PEs: SPE and CFU. The SPE is a simple processing element for executing the arithmetic operations and the CFU is a customized processing element to execute the expensive operation for domain applications. 2) SPEs is organized in 1D structure, the result of one SPE can be used by another SPE in the next cycle. Some CFUs are shared with the SPE pipeline. 3) To exploit the data parallelism, we can place several RPs which are independent for each other. 4) The ACRP's local memory is typically a multi-bank scratchpad memory which the data arrays used by the ACRP are placed in for fast access. The SPEs of hardware pipeline share a memory access bus while the CFUs share another memory access. 5) All the PEs and interconnect network is controlled by the configuration in configuration memory. The ACRP can be reconfigured dynamically when needed.

PE is the least computing unit in CGRA. Due to the large number of PEs, CGRA architectures can provide massive amounts of parallelism and high computational capability. With the area constraints, the PE in CGRA typically is very simple. SPE in the ACRP is similar to the PE in the typical CGRA, as illustrated in the right part of Fig. 1. SPE is a two-input, one-output ALU for executing the simple arithmetic, logic, shifting operations. SPE contains a small set of private registers for constants and temporary variables, as well as an output register. Two multiplexer are responsible for supplying the inputs. Inputs of the ALU come from the local memory access bus, SPEs that are connected with, local register file or CFUs, where outputs of the ALU are also routed to. The SPE is controlled by the configuration register to select the inputs, change the operation and specify the output.

In this work, we introduce the domain-specific calculating acceleration method for ASIP to CGRA. The CFU is a specific functional unit to execute the complicated instruction or simple instruction sequence for a specific domain application. But how to abstract the calculate characteristic and how to design a CFU are beyond the scope of this article. Without violating the area constraints, ACRP organize the SPEs into a linear structure. The CFUs are shared by the linear structure. To exploit the data parallelism, we can copy several ACRPs which combine reconfigurable architecture with SIMD processing.

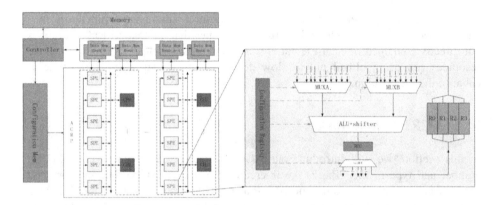

Fig. 1. The ACRP framework

Fig.1 illustrates a CGRA with two ACRPs that consists of 6 SPEs and 2 CFUs. 6 SPEs are organized into a linear structure. Every SPE can communicate with the other 5 SPEs. The linear structure is best for the pipelined stream-based application. But the drawback is not suitable for mapping the 2D data processing application and the branch code. However, the ACRP is domain-specific, e.g. DSP domain kernels are mostly stream-based.

Two CFUs are shared by the SPE reconfigurable pipeline. The architecture designer firstly makes an analysis of the computing characteristics, abstracts the complicated instruction or frequent instructions sequence, customizes a new FU to perform that instructions sequence efficiently, and generates a CI that the compiler can identify. The compiler is responsible for identifying the CI and mapping the CI to the original FU to improve the performance. In this work, we don't discuss how to abstract the calculate characteristic and how to design a CFU but the effect of introducing a CFU to CGRA. For the DSP domain, we introduce a MAC-CFU which can execute the multiply-add operation. For the secure hash algorithm domain, we design a HE-CFU which can perform the F functions of MD5 and SHA.

The memory system of ACRP contains configuration memory, data memory and the local register file in the PE. The configuration memory stores all the configurations for the ACRPs, which control operating of the ACRPs. The data memory is responsible for storing the source data and operation results. The local register file is used for the constants and temporary variables. When the capacity of the memory is not enough, the ACRP need to load data from the external memory leading to extra delay.

Fig.1 is a framework of the ACRP. According to the domain application, we can design the different CFU, specify the parameters of architecture for executing the kernel of domain application efficiently, e.g. the operand width, SPE operation latency and so on.

4   Case Study

The mapping methodologies of a CGRA are the major research problem in reconfigurable computing domain. In this section, a case study is presented for describing the new problem of mapping an application to the ACRP.

Mapping an application to a CGRA always contains three sub problems: mapping the operation to a certain PE, routing the operation's result to the successive operation and scheduling every operation to execute at a certain cycle.

The case study relates to how to map the 4-taps FIR algorithm of DSP domain to the DSP-ACRP. DSP-ACRP is a simplified ACRP for DSP domain including 5 SPEs and 1 CFU. The PE operand width is 32 bits. Every SPE is connected with his adjacent SPE and the CFU is shared by the SPEs. SPEs can execute multiplication and addition in 1 cycle, while the CFU named MAC-CFU can perform the multiplication, addition and multiply-add operation in 1 cycle. In this case study, we assume that the additional hardware resources e.g. the memory access bus, are enough and conflict-free.

FIR (Finite Impulse Response) is a filtering algorithm that widely used in the DSP domain. Fig. 2(d) illustrates the kernel of the 4-taps FIR C code and Fig. 2(c) is the DFG (Data Flow Graph) of this kernel. We can see that the 4-taps FIR contains 4 multiplications and 3 additions. The goal of mapping FIR to CGRA is mapping these 7 operations to certain PEs, routing the operation's result to his successive operation and scheduling operations to execute at the certain cycle with the hardware constraint and the dependent constraint.

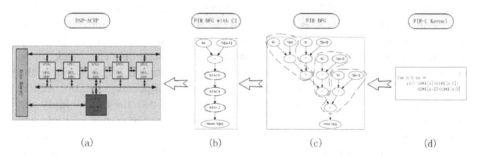

(a)   (b)   (c)   (d)

Fig. 2. A case study for mapping FIR to DSP-ACRP

By now, the best known mapping algorithm for CGRA is the edge-centric modulo scheduling [10]. We also use this modulo scheduling for mapping application to

ACRP to exploit the loop level parallelism. Besides a SIMD mapping method is used to exploit the data level parallelism.

Modulo scheduling makes the iteration initiate before the last iteration completely finished in the regular interval II to exploit the loop level parallelism. The II is determined by the hardware dependence and the loop-carried dependence [11]. In this case study, we assume the hardware is enough and conflict-free. At the same time, there is no loop-carried dependency in FIR. So the II of 4-taps FIR is 1, in other words, the iteration can initiate next to the last iteration.

The ACRP compiler first transfers the C code to the intermediate DFG like the traditional compiler for microprocessor. The DFG is a directed acyclic graph called G= (V, E). The V is the set of nodes which represent the operations and E is the set of edges that represent the data dependency. The operations in V are the basic arithmetic operations.

Due to the CFU which can execute the complicated operation, the ACRP compiler faces a new problem called the CI selection problem. Before mapping the DFG to ACRP directly, the ACRP compiler adds a CI covering phase. Firstly, ACRP compiler identifies the instruction sequences or complicated instructions that can be substituted for the CI. How to identify the instruction sequence is an instruction matching problem and beyond the scope of this paper. There may be several these instruction sequences, so the compiler must decide which of these instruction sequences are replaced, which called the CI selection problem.

In this case study, the MAC-CFU can execute the multiply-add operation. To maximize the performance, the MAC-CFU prefers to execute the multiply-add operation rather than the multiplication or addition operation. The compiler identifies three multiply-add operations in 4-taps FIR as illustrated in Fig.2(c). In Fig.2(c), the instructions sequences which can be replaced by the multiply-add operation are surrounded by the red dotted line. The intermediate DFG is transferred to a new one that contains CIs, as illustrated in Fig. 2(b). The II is computed from this new DFG again. When mapping kernel to CGRA using modulo scheduling, it may be considered as the hardware resources are duplicated II times in the time dimension to which the whole kernel must map. There are three multiply-add operations, but only one MAC-CFU in DSP-ACRP. So when mapping the DFG contains three multiply-add operations, II at least is 3, as illustrated in Fig.3(c). In Fig. 3, the horizontal axis is the PEs of ACRP and the vertical axis is time. '*' represents the multiplication, '+' is the addition, and 'mac' stands for the multiply-add operation. The black circle represents the recursion of modulo scheduling every II times. When mapping the DFG contains three multiply-add operations and one multiplication to DSP-ACRP, the multiplication firstly is mapped to the SPE0 at cycle 1, then the first multiply-add operation is mapped to the CFU0 at cycle 2. When mapping the second multiply-add operation, there is no PE left for this CI while II is 1. So II must increase to 2 and the second CI is mapped to CFU0 at cycle 3. The third CI is the same as the second one. At last, II is 3 and the modulo scheduling result is illustrated in Fig. 3 (c).

There are other different mapping choices. A DFG contains 2 multiply-add operations, 2 multiplications and 1 addition of the 4-taps FIR is selected for mapping to the ACRP. The modulo scheduling result is illustrated in Fig. 3(b) and II is 2.

The best mapping choice of 4-taps FIR is mapping the DFG contains 1 multiply-add operation, 3 multiplications and 2 additions. The modulo scheduling result of this best choice is illustrated in Fig. 3(a) and II is 1. The placing operations and routing results of this best choice is illustrated in Fig. 2(a), which is represented by the red dotted line. If we do not introduce the CFU to RP, the modulo scheduling result is illustrated in Fig. 3(d) and the II is 2. In this mapping, we instead the CFU0 of SPE5 since the hardware should be roughly equal.

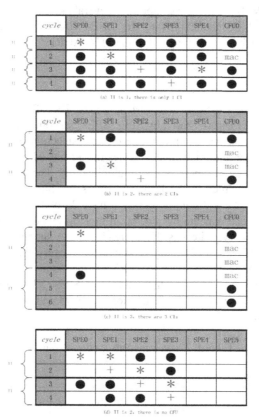

Fig. 3. Different mapping scheduling of CI selection problem

II makes a great impact on the performance and resources utilization. When mapping the DFG contains 1 multiply-add operation, 3 multiplications and 2 additions, the best performance is obtained as illustrated in Fig. 3(a), the throughput of which is 97 MOPS (Millions Outputs per Second), and the hardware resources utilization is 100%. In Fig. 3(b), the throughput is 49 MOPS and hardware resources utilization rate is 42%. The throughput is 33 MOPS and hardware resources utilization is 22% in Fig. 3(c) which is one third of the best condition. In Fig. 3(d), the throughput is 49 MOPS and hardware utilization is 58%. As we have seen, the best condition is 3 times higher than the worst one. The CI selection problem is extremely important for the ACRP mapping.

5   Experiment

We have implemented two ACRPs for DSP domain and secure hash algorithm, named DSP-ACRP and SHA-ACRP. The proposed reconfigurable architecture with the CFU has been designed at the RT-level with verilog. The ACRPs have been synthesized with Design Compiler [15] using technology of SMIC[16] 0.13μm. ModelSim[17] is used for RTL-level and gate-level simulation. The simulation frequency is 100MHZ. We have applied several kernels of Livermore loops benchmark [18] and DSPstone [19] to the DSP-ACRP. And the MD5 and SHA algorithms in MiBench [20] are mapped to the SHA-ACRP.

5.1   Synthesis Results

The DSP-ACRP contains 6 SPEs and 2 MAC-CFUs. The SPEs is organized into the linear structure. Two CFUs are shared by SPEs. SPEs can communicate with each other by direct connection and the latency of the direct connection is 0 cycle. Every SPE contains an adder and a multiplier, and executes the 32 bits addition, subtraction, logic operations, shift operations and 16 bits multiplication. The CFU can execute the multiply-add operation which the multiplier is 16bits and the addend is 32 bits, 16bits multiplication and 32 bits addition, so the CFU have 2 16bits input ports and 1 32bits input port. Every PE can execute the operation in 1 cycle. All SPEs share 2 memory read buses and 1 memory write bus. Every read bus can supply one 32bits data in 1 cycle. At last, the configuration memory is 64 words and every configuration is 32 bits.

The architecture parameters of SHA-ACRP are the same as the DSP-ACRP's, but the instruction set of the CFU and the number of SPEs. The CFU of SHA-ACRP named HE-Logic32 can execute the F functions in MD5 and SHA. There are 8 SPEs for simple operation.

Table 1. The components synthesis results

component	Area(mm^2)	Latency(ns)
ALU32	0.01276	1.34
MUL16	0.02079	3.39
MAC16	0.02683	3.86
MUX32-8	0.00703	0.21
MUX16-8	0.00361	0.21
HE-Logic32	0.00383	1.20

Table 1 lists the synthesis results of some components. The synthesis results are obtained before placement and routing phase. The synthesis software is Design Compiler using technology of SMIC 0.13μm. operation condition is worst. We can see the area and latency increase because of the CFU qualitatively.

5.2   Effect of the CFU

For this experiment, we consider the effect of the CFU. The experimental architectures are DSP-ACRP and SHA-ACRP described in previous section. The reference reconfigurable architecture for DSP-ACRP named DSP-RP is a reconfigurable pipeline without CFUs, which contains 8 SPEs. The hardware resources of DSP-RP are roughly equal to the DSP-ACRP which contains 6 SPEs and 2 CFUs. The reference reconfigurable architecture for SHA-ACRP is SHA-RP with 10 SPEs. In this experiment, we assume that the memory access bandwidth is unlimited and the system frequency is 100MHZ. Table 2 lists the test kernels.

Table 2. Benchmarks and their descriptions

benchmarks	*descriptions*
5-FIR	5-taps FIR algorithm
25-FIR	25-taps FIR algorithm
MMV1	Matrix (8×8) Multiply Vector(8×1) optimized
MMV2	Matrix (8×8) Multiply Vector(8×1) unoptimized
Hydro	Hydro fragment algorithm
Over	Porter-Duff over Operator
MD5	Message Digest Algorithm V5
SHA	Secure Hash Algorithm

Fig. 4 shows the performance comparison for mapping the test kernels of DSP on the two architectures respectively. In Fig. 4, throughput increases because of CFUs. There are three reasons for this performance increase. The first reason is decreasing the II by the CFUs which increases the hardware resources, e.g. 5-FIR, 25-FIR. In this case, a sharp increase is got. The decrease of the critical path is the second reason. The throughput increase for second reason is lower than that in the first condition. The last reason is mapping two or more kernels onto the architecture at one time to exploit the data parallelism. In the last case, the performance increases exponentially. Some performance increases are caused by two or more previous reasons. For example, the mapping results of Hydro and Over improve by the second and third reasons.

MMV1 is the multiplication of 8×8 matrix and 8×1 vector which is optimized by the tree height reduction, and the MMV2 is the multiplication unoptimized. The structure of MMV1's DFG is a binary tree, and the critical path is 4. MMV2's DFG is a linear structure and the critical path is 8. From the experimental results, the throughput of MMV1 is 32 MOPS when mapping to the DSP-RP, while the MMV2's is 47MOPS. Although the critical path of MMV2 is longer than that of MMV1, but the II of MMV2 is 2 and the II of MMV1 is 3. This experiment shows that the reconfigurable linear structure is more suitable for the linear DFG.

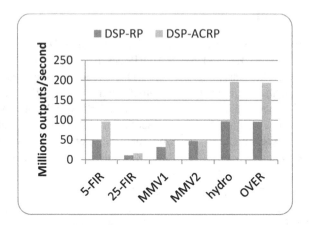

Fig. 4. Performance comparison with and without CFUs for DSP

In the contrast group of mapping the MMV2 to DSP-RP and DSP-ACRP, the performance does no change though the CFU is used. This is explained by the fact that the critical path does not decrease.

Hydro kernel is very simple. The Hydro only contains 5 operations, and its critical path is 4. When mapping to DSP-RP and DSP-ACRP, both II is 1. But it is possible that two iterations are mapped onto the DSP-ACRP at one time because of the hardware resources increase. So performance of DSP-ACRP in this case is double that of DSP-RP. It is much the same when mapping the Over kernel to DSP-ACRP which also contains 5 operations.

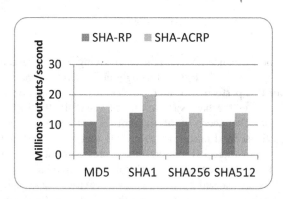

Fig. 5. Performance comparison with and without CFUs for SHA

In the preceding experiments, hardware resources determine the II which is greatly important for performance. There is another condition that the loop-carried dependence determines the II. In the secure hash encryption domain, the iteration's output is the input of the next iteration. So the iteration has to initiate until the last iteration finished. Fig. 5 shows the performance comparison with and without CFUs for SHA.

Compared to the DSP-ACRP, in SHA-ACRP the loop-carried dependent determines the II. In this experiment, the performance improvement is 27% to 45% because the critical paths of four kernels decrease and II of all four kernels are equal to the critical path. The improvement in SHA-ACRP is more than that in DSP-ACRP due to the decrease of the critical path. This is because the HE-Logic is more efficient than the MAC-CFU.

5.3   Performance in Respect to the CFU Number

Fig. 6 illustrates the impact of CFU number on the performance when mapping the kernel to DSP-ACRP. The CFU is customized according to the computing characteristics of the domain. The cause of performance improvement is not only the optimization of the frequent instruction sequences but also the decrease of the critical path, II and exploitation of data parallelism.

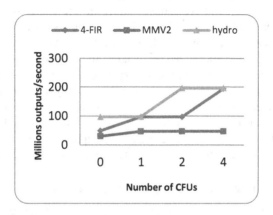

Fig. 6. Performance relative to the CFU number

In this experiment, the experimental architecture is DSP-ACRP described in previous section. There are 6 SPEs and every SPE can communicate with each other. System operates at 100MHZ. We assume that the memory access bandwidth is unlimited. The results refer to 4 different scenarios concerning the CFU number: 0, 1, 2 and 4.

Fig. 6 shows that the throughout improves with the increase of CFUs. There are two reasons for performance improvement. The first reason is the decrease of II with the increase of CFUs, and another one is exploitation of data parallelism. In the experiment refer to 4-FIR, the II is 2 without CFUs and throughout is 49MOPS. With 1 CFU, the II becomes into 1 and the throughout increases to 97MOPS. But when there are 2 CFUs, the II does not change and the second CFU is idle. At last, we can map two iterations to the ACRP with 4 CFUs, so the throughout increase to 194MOPS.

Even more, Fig. 6 shows that blindly increasing the hardware may not lead to constant performance improvement. For example, in the MMV2 experiment, MMV2 is a little complicated for this DSP-ACRP. The II is 3 without CFUs and throughout is 30MOPS. With 1 CFU, the II becomes into 2 and the throughout increases to 47MOPS. But until the CFU number increases to 4, the performance does not change.

5.4   Effect of the Memory Access Bandwidth

We have analyzed the performance effect of the hardware resources and loop-carried dependent. The other factors include connectivity, memory access bus bandwidth, local data memory capacity and so on.

In the previous experiments, we assume the memory access bandwidth is unlimited and the hardware resources are enough. But it is not true in practice. The ACRP is good for the stream-based application. These applications always deal with mass data. The data array usually is placed in the local scratchpad memory. So the memory access bus bandwidth is greatly important to the ACRP performance. Actually the memory bus bandwidth is an expensive resource. In this experiment, we analyze the effect of memory bus bandwidth for DSP-ACRP. Otherwise the CFUs are unable to function efficiently.

The experimental architecture DSP-ACRP is represented in the previous section. In this architecture, DSP-ACRP contains 6 SPEs and 2 CFUs. The 6 SPEs share the memory read bus, while the 2 CFUs have another one. The memory read bus bandwidth is the total operands that read from the memory in one cycle. In ACRP, the CFU executes the complicated CI. The CI usually has more inputs requirement, so we design another memory bus shared by the CFUs. In this experiment, we analyze the performance in respect to memory read bus bandwidth of the SPEs instead of the CFU's.

Table 2 shows that the effect of the memory access bandwidth. In this experiment, bandwidth unlimited means that the system can supply all the data that ACRP required in one cycle, while bandwidth limited case is that every cycle two data can be read from the local memory and one data can be written to the local memory. In table 3, PP is short for Parallel Pipeline and MOPS represents the throughput. Number of memory operations means the read and write operations in the kernels.

Table 3. Effect of the memory access bandwidth

Kernels	# of mem OPs	Bandwidth unlimited (∞/∞)			Bandwidth limited (2/1)		
		II	PP	MOPS	II	PP	MOPS
5-FIR	5/1	1	1	96	1	1	96
MMV1	16/1	2	1	48	3	1	31
MMV2	16/1	2	1	47	2	1	47
Hydro	3/1	1	2	196	2	1	47
Over	3/1	1	2	194	1	1	97

When mapping the MMV1 to DSP-ACRP, each iteration requires 16 data and writes one data to memory. In the unlimited bandwidth condition, II of the MMV1 is 2 and the throughput is 48MOPS, but when the bandwidth is limited, the II increase into 3 and throughput reduces to 31MOPS. The DFG of MMV1 is binary-tree structure, and there are 8 multiplications in the first level of the binary-tree. Every multiplication needs 2 data at one time, but the bandwidth is limited. So the II has to increase to 3, which leads to performance degradation. In Hydro and Over cases, every iteration requires 3 data and writes one data. In the unlimited bandwidth condition, two iterations can be mapped into DSP-ACRP at one time, so the PP in bandwidth unlimited case of Hydro is 2. However, when the bandwidth is limited, only one iteration can be mapped at one time, so the PP in bandwidth limited case of Hydro decreases to 1. In summary, the memory bandwidth makes a great impact on ACRP performance.

Fig.7 shows the performance in respect to the memory bandwidth. With the memory bandwidth increase, the throughput of Hydro grows linearly. But the performance has an upper bound. Blindly increasing of the bandwidth also cannot break through the upper bound. The MMV1 is an example.

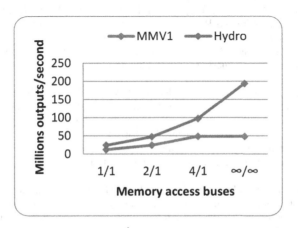

Fig. 7. Performance relative to the memory bandwidth

6   Conclusions

In this work, a novel reconfigurable architecture named ACRP is proposed for specific domain. The ACRP contains two types of PE, SPE and CFU. The SPEs which execute basic operations are organized into a linear structure. And the CFU is customized according to the domain computing characteristic, which specially executes the frequent instruction sequence of the domain. The CFUs are shared by the SPEs to observe the area constraint.

Moreover some experiments are made to verify the ACRP. The experiments include hardware synthesis, effect of the CFU, performance in respect to the CFU number and effect of the memory access bandwidth. These experiments show the acceleration effect of the CFUs, and verify that ACRP can exploit the parallelism in CFU level, pipeline level and data level. At last, some key factors which include CFU number and memory bandwidth for the ACRP performance are analyzed.

References

1. Choi, K.: Coarse Grained Reconfigurable Array: Architecture and Application Mapping. IPSJ Transactions on System LSI Design Methodology 4, 31–46 (2011)
2. Compton, K., Hauck, S.: Reconfigurable Computing: a Survey of System and Software. ACM Computing Surveys 34(2), 171–210 (2002)
3. Coldstein, S.C., Schmit, H., Moe, M., Budiu, M., Cadambi, S., Taylor, R.R., Laufer, R.: PipeRench: A Coprocessor for Streaming Multimedia Acceleration. In: ISCA (1999)
4. Ebeling, C., Cronquist, D.C., Franklin, P., Secosky, J., Berg, S.G.: Mapping applications to the RaPiD configurable architecture. In: Proceedings of the 5th IEEE Symposium on FPGA-Based Custom Computing Machines, April 16-18, p. 106 (1997)
5. Mei, B., Vernalde, S., Verkest, D., DeMan, H., Lauwereins, R.: ADRES: An Architecture with Tightly Coupled VLIW Processor and Coarse-Grained Reconfigurable Matrix. In: Cheung, P.Y.K., Constantinides, G.A. (eds.) FPL 2003. LNCS, vol. 2778, pp. 61–70. Springer, Heidelberg (2003)
6. Mei, B., Vernalde, S., Verkest, D., De Man, H., Lauwereins, R.: DRESC: A Retargetable Compiler for Coarse-Grained Reconfigurable Architectures. In: International Conference on Field Programmable Technology, pp. 166–173 (2002)
7. Dimitroulakos, G., Galanis, M.D., Goutis, C.E.: Design space exploration of an optimized compiler approach for a generic reconfigurable array architecture. J. Supercomput. 40(2), 127–157 (2007)
8. Kim, Y., Lee, J., Lee, J., Mai, T.X., Heo, I., Paek, Y.: Exploiting both pipeling and data parallelism with SIMD reconfigurable architecture. In: Choy, O.C.S., Cheung, R.C.C., Athanas, P., Sano, K. (eds.) ARC 2012. LNCS, vol. 7199, pp. 40–52. Springer, Heidelberg (2012)
9. Ahn, M., Yoon, J.W., Paek, Y., Kim, Y., Kiemb, M., Choi, K.: A spatical mapping algorithm for heterogeneous coarse-grained reconfigurable architectures. In: Proceedings of the Conference on Design, Automation and Test in Europe, Munich, Germany, March 06-10 (2006)
10. Park, H., Fan, K., Mahlke, S.A., Oh, T., Kim, H., Kim, H.-S.: Edge-centric modulo scheduling for coarse-grained reconfigurable architectures. In: Proceedings of the 17th International Conference on Parallel Architectures and Compilation Techniques, Canada, October 25-29 (2008)
11. Rau, B.R.: Iterative modulo scheduling. Technical report, Hewlett-Packard Lab: HPL-94-115 (1995)
12. Yang, Z., Yan, M., Wang, D., Li, S.: Data Parallelism Optimization for CGRA Loop Pipelining Mapping. Chinese Journal of Computers 36(6) (2012) (in Chinese)
13. Zhou, L., Liu, D., Tang, M., Liu, H.: Mapping Loops onto Coarse-Grained Reconfigurable Array Using Genetic Algorithm. In: Yin, Z., Pan, L., Fang, X. (eds.) Proceedings of the Eighth International Conference on Bio-Inspired Computing: Theories and Application, BIC-TA. AISC, vol. 212, pp. 801–808. Springer, Heidelberg (2013)
14. Zhou, L., Liu, H., Liu, D.: A Novel CGRA Architecture and mapping algorithm for application acceleration. In: Xu, W., Xiao, L., Zhang, C., Li, J., Yu, L. (eds.) NCCET 2013. CCIS, vol. 396, pp. 218–227. Springer, Heidelberg (2013)
15. Synopsys Corp., http://www.synopsys.com (accessed January 10, 2014)
16. SMIC Corp., http://www.smics.com/ (accessed January 10, 2014)
17. Model Technology Corp., http://www.model.com (accessed January 10, 2014)
18. Livermore bench, http://www.netlib.org/benchmmark/livermorec (accessed January 10, 2014)
19. DSPstone, http://www.ert.rwth-aachen.de/Projekte/Tools/DSPSTONE (accessed January 10, 2014)
20. MiBench Version1.0, http://www.eecs.umich.edu/mibench (accessed January 10, 2014)

SRS: A Split-Range Shared Memory Consistency Model for Thousand-Core Processors

Hui Lyu, Fang Zheng, and Xianghui Xie

State Key Laboratory of Mathematical Engineering and Advanced Computing, Wuxi
{lyu.hui,zheng.fang,xie.xianghui}@meac-skl.cn

Abstract. A novel memory consistency model for thousand-core processors is presented. The model simplifies cache coherence for the full chip, and reduces cache design complexity. In addition, the model has the ability to describe the direct exchange of data on chip, thereby alleviating the off-chip memory bandwidth requirements. The paper gives a formal definition of the model, and proves that the model is sequentially consistent. All aspects of the definition are fully used in the process of proof, which means that there is no redundancy in the definition. Therefore, based on the split-range shared memory consistency model, a shared memory system can achieve high performance at low hardware cost. Meanwhile, the model is easy to be understood and used by programmers.

Keywords: many-core processor, memory system, memory consistency model, sequential consistency, formal description.

1   Introduction

As the technology of computer progresses, the number of processor-cores integrated onto a single die is constantly increasing, from tens to hundreds, even thousands[1, 2]. For processors with few cores (such as traditional single-core processors or multi-core processors), there have been some mature memory consistency models, including SC[3], TSO/X86[4], RMO[5], which can also be used for ten-core processors or hundred-core processors[6]. Meanwhile, for thousand-core processors, the traditional memory consistency models need to implement cache coherence at high hardware cost, whose performance is seriously degraded[7]. To solve this problem, several new memory consistency models(such as Acoherent Shared Memory[8], ASM) have been proposed. These models simplified cache coherence, and reduced cache design complexity.

Different from software-assisted caches[9], the ASM model avoids the complexities that arise from global cache coherence protocols, which simplifies hardware design and software programming. Different from message-passing programming models, the ASM model can localize cache coherence protocols and greatly simplify software programming and especially software migration.

However, the ASM model has no ability to describe the direct exchange of data on chip, and cannot make full use of the inherent data locality characteristics of programs for minimal additional demands on off-chip memory bandwidth. In addition, there is

J. Wu et al. (Eds.): ACA 2014, CCIS 451, pp. 31–42, 2014.

some redundancy in the formal definition of the ASM model, which could be optimized for better system performance.

In this paper, a split-range shared memory consistency model(SRS) is proposed. The SRS model avoids cache coherence between cores altogether, reduces hardware overhead and design complexity, owns the ability to describe the direct exchange of data on chip, and helps reduce the demand for off-chip memory bandwidth significantly; meanwhile, there is no redundancy in the definition of the model, based on which a system can obtain higher performance.

The remainder of this paper is organized as follows. Section 1 gives an overview of the split-range shared memory consistency model. Section 2 is dedicated to the formal description of the model. Next, it has been proved that the SRS model is sequentially consistent under the given constraints in Section 3. In Section 4, the model is extended for wider applied range. Finally, Section 5 concludes the paper and discusses future works.

2   Overview of the SRS Model

Data used for many-core software can be divided into four categories, including read-only data, private data, global data used for synchronization, and data exchanged between multiple cores[8, 10].

The demand for cache by the above four types of data is different from each other. Since read-only data(such as shared code) are not modified, they can be safely replicated without cache coherence enforcement mechanisms. Since private data are only accessed by the local processor core, they need not cache coherence enforcement mechanisms. Since global data used for synchronization are not frequently accessed, the system performance is not seriously affected without cache coherence enforcement mechanisms. It is only the data exchanged between cores that are frequently accessed by some processor cores and need to be supported by cache coherence.

Data exchanged between cores are shared by some processor cores. In most cases, however, cores cannot simultaneously access the data, but do the data by turns. With this feature, the paper presents the SRS model.

Shared memory system built on the SRS model can avoid cache coherence between many processor cores altogether, thereby reducing implementation costs. After having been extended, the SRS model can also be applied to process read-only data, private data, global data used for synchronization.

According to the proposed model, only after having right to cache some data can a processor core caches them. The right is named TOKEN. For a segment of data, at some point, there is only one core owning its TOKEN at most. The word split-range means that a TOKEN is passed between cores as a relay baton.

3   Formal Definition of the SRS Model

3.1   Basic Concept and Notation

For convenience of description, before describing the model formally, we need to introduce some concepts and notations.

Program Order: The term "program order" is used to describe the order of instructions as listed in the program being executed, which is the basis for achieving a deterministic result of running a program.

Memory Order: The term "memory order" is used to describe the order in which memory access instructions reach a certain section of a memory model.

A program order is a partial order. Instructions associated with the same processor are always ordered by a program order, while instructions from different processors are never ordered by a program order.

A memory order is a total order. All memory access instructions are ordered by a certain memory order, whether they are from same processor or not.

For the sake of simplicity, the notations used in the paper are shown in Table 1.

Table 1. Notation for Split-Range Shared Memory Consistency Model

Notation	Means
X	X means an instruction of Load(L) , Store(S) or Relay(RX)
L	L means an instruction of Load
S	S means an instruction of Store
$X_i^{Se}a$	$X_i^{Se}a$ means an instruction of Load or Store. The instruction is executed by the processor i, a is a memory address, Se is the data segment storing a. What $L_i^{Se}a$ or $S_i^{Se}a$ means is similar to $X_i^{Se}a$.
$\bar{X}$	$\bar{X}$ means another instruction which is not the same that X means. Similarly, $\bar{L}$ means another Load instruction which is not the same that L means, $\bar{S}$ means another Store instruction which is not the same that S means.
$\bar{X}_i^{Se}a$	$\bar{X}_i^{Se}a$ means another Load or Store instruction which is not the same that $X_i^{Se}a$ means. The instruction is executed by the processor i, a is a memory address, Se is the data segment storing a. What $\bar{L}_i^{Se}a$ or $\bar{S}_i^{Se}a$ means is similar to $\bar{X}_i^{Se}a$.
$<_p$	$<_p$, means the program order of memory access instructions. If $X <_p \bar{X}$, then X is prior to $\bar{X}$ in the program order. The program order is transitive; that is, for X , $\bar{X}$, $\bar{\bar{X}}$, if $X <_p \bar{X}$ and $\bar{X} <_p \bar{\bar{X}}$, then $X <_p \bar{\bar{X}}$.
$<_m$	$<_m$, means the memory order of memory access instructions. If $X <_m \bar{X}$, then X is prior to $\bar{X}$ in the memory order. The program order is transitive; that is, for X , $\bar{X}$, $\bar{\bar{X}}$, if $X <_m \bar{X}$ and $\bar{X} <_m \bar{\bar{X}}$, then $X <_m \bar{\bar{X}}$.
$value(L)$	$value(L)$ means the return value of a Load instruction.
$value(S)$	$value(S)$ means the value written by a Store instruction.

Table 1. (*continued*)

Notation	Means
$\max_{<_p}(X, X', X'', \ldots\ldots)$	$\max_{<_p}(X, X', X'', \ldots\ldots)$, means the last instruction in a sequence acquired by sorting X , X' , $X'' \ldots \ldots$in the program order.
$\max_{<_m}(X, X', X'', \ldots\ldots)$	$\max_{<_m}(X, X', X'', \ldots\ldots)$, means the last instruction in a sequence acquired by sorting X , X' , $X'' \ldots \ldots$in the memory order.
RX	RX means a Relay instruction(RelayFrom or RelayTo).
RT	RT means a RelayTo instruction.
RF	RF means a RelayFrom instruction.
RX_i^{Se}	RX_i^{Se} means a RT_i^{Se} or RF_i^{Se} instruction.
RT_i^{Se}	RT_i^{Se} means a $RT_i^{Se}j$ or $RT_i^{Se}m$ instruction.
RF_i^{Se}	RF_i^{Se} means a $RF_i^{Se}j$ or $RF_i^{Se}m$ instruction.
$RF_j(RT_i^{Se})$	If RT_i^{Se} means $RT_i^{Se}j$, then $RF_j(RT_i^{Se})$ means $RF_j^{Se}i$.
$RF_j(RT_i^{Se})$	If RT_i^{Se} means $RT_i^{Se}m$, then $RF_j(RT_i^{Se})$ means $RF_j^{Se}m$.
$RT_j(RF_i^{Se})$	If RF_i^{Se} means $RF_i^{Se}j$, then $RT_j(RF_i^{Se})$ means $RT_j^{Se}i$.
$RT_j(RF_i^{Se})$	If RF_i^{Se} means $RF_i^{Se}m$, then $RT_j(RF_i^{Se})$ means $RT_j^{Se}m$.
$RT_i^{Se}j$	$RT_i^{Se}j$ means a RelayTo instruction. The instruction is executed by the processor i. After executing the instruction, the processor i will complete preparations for sending (but not really obtain) the TOKEN of the data segment Se to the processor j.
$RF_i^{Se}j$	$RF_i^{Se}j$ means a RelayFrom instruction. The instruction is executed by the processor i. After executing the instruction, the processor i will complete preparations for receiving (but not really obtain) the TOKEN of the data segment Se from the processor j. $RT_j^{Se}i$ and $RF_i^{Se}j$ must be supplied as a pair when a TOKEN is passed from the processor i to the processor j. Before All paired RF/RT are finished, a processor cannot really send/receive a TOKEN, which is owned by the source processor.
$RT_i^{Se}m$	$RT_i^{Se}m$ means a RelayTo instruction. The instruction is executed by the processor i. After executing the instruction, the processor i will give the TOKEN of the data segment Se to the memory system.
$RF_i^{Se}m$	$RF_i^{Se}m$ means a RelayFrom instruction. The instruction is executed by the processor i. After executing the instruction, the processor i will get the TOKEN of the data segment Se from the memory system.
$\Rightarrow$	$\Rightarrow$, means that the expression on the left is a sufficient condition of that on the right.

3.2   Formal Definition of the Model

Based on the above notations, the SRS model is formally described as follows:

$$L_i^{Se}a <_p S_i^{Se}a \Rightarrow L_i^{Se}a <_m S_i^{Se}a \tag{1}$$

$$S_i^{Se}a <_p \bar{S}_i^{Se}a \Rightarrow S_i^{Se}a <_m \bar{S}_i^{Se}a \tag{2}$$

$$S_i^{Se}a <_p L_i^{Se}a \Rightarrow S_i^{Se}a <_m L_i^{Se}a \tag{3}$$

$$X_i^{Se}a <_p RT_i^{Se}m <_m RF_j^{Se}m <_p \bar{X}_j^{Se}a \Rightarrow X_i^{Se}a <_m \bar{X}_j^{Se}a \tag{4}$$

$$X_i^{Se}a <_p RT_i^{Se}j <_m RF_j^{Se}i <_p \bar{X}_j^{Se}a \Rightarrow X_i^{Se}a <_m \bar{X}_j^{Se}a \tag{5}$$

$$RX <_p \overline{RX} \Rightarrow RX <_m \overline{RX} \tag{6}$$

$$value(L_i^{Se}a) = value(\max_{<_m}(S^{Se}a \mid S^{Se}a <_m L_i^{Se}a)) \tag{7}$$

Where, not both $X_i^{Se}a$ and $\bar{X}_j^{Se}a$ are Load instructions in Formula 4 or in Formula 5.

4   Proof of Sequential Consistency

It is proved in the section that the SRS model is sequentially consistent by imposing some constraints.

4.1   Sequential Consistency

A multiprocessor system is sequentially consistent[3] if the result of any execution is the same as if the operation of all the processors were executed in some sequential order, and the operations of each individual processor appear in this sequence in the order specified by its program.

4.2   An Interleaving-Order Memory Model

An interleaving-order memory model is the simplest sequential consistency model. The model is formally described as follows:

$$X_i <_p \bar{X}_i \Rightarrow X_i <_m \bar{X}_i \tag{8}$$

$$value(L_i a) = value(\max_{<_m}(Sa \mid Sa <_m L_i a)) \tag{9}$$

4.3   Sequential Consistency of the SRS Model

It is proved in the section that the SRS model satisfying the ordered pair condition is sequentially consistent.

Theorem 1. If for every execution WITHOUT branch instructions there exists a execution producing the same results and satisfying the interleaving-order memory model, then for every execution WITH branch instructions there also exists a similar execution.

Proof. The theorem is proved by using mathematical induction.

According to conditions of the theorem, for all instructions before the first branch instruction, there exists an instruction sequence producing the same results and satisfying the interleaving-order memory model. Hence, the two outcomes of the above two sequences used for the branch condition of the same first branch instruction are equal, and the same is also true for the branch target. Accordingly, adding the first branch instruction to the tail of the above two sequences does not affect the results.

Let us now assume that the theorem is true for every execution with the first n-1 branch instructions. It can easily be shown that the two outcomes of the two sequences used for the branch condition of the same nth branch instruction are equal, and the same is also true for the branch target. Accordingly, adding the nth branch instruction to the tail of the above two sequences does not affect the results. Q.E.D.

According to Theorem 1, it follows that branch instructions does not need special consideration during the proof of sequential consistency. Therefore, in what follows, every instruction sequence does not include a branch instruction.

According to Formula 4, Formula 5 and the transitivity of the memory order, **if** " $X_i^{Se}a <_p RT_i^{Se}m <_m RF_j^{Se}m <_p \bar{X}_j^{Se}a$ " or " $X_i^{Se}a <_p RT_i^{Se}j <_m RF_j^{Se}i <_p \bar{X}_j^{Se}a$ " or " $X_i^{Se}a <_m \bar{\bar{X}}_j^{Se}a <_m \bar{X}_j^{Se}a$ ", then " $X_i^{Se}a <_m \bar{X}_j^{Se}a$ ". By enhancing the above constraint, that is, **if and only if** " $X_i^{Se}a <_p RT_i^{Se}m <_m RF_j^{Se}m <_p \bar{X}_j^{Se}a$ " or " $X_i^{Se}a <_p RT_i^{Se}j <_m RF_j^{Se}i <_p \bar{X}_j^{Se}a$ " or " $X_i^{Se}a <_m \bar{\bar{X}}_k^{Se}a <_m \bar{X}_j^{Se}a$ ", then " $X_i^{Se}a <_m \bar{X}_j^{Se}a$ ".

The above enhanced constraint is described as the following ordered pair condition.

Ordered Pair Condition

$$\forall X_i^{Se}a, \bar{X}_j^{Se}a; X_i^{Se}a <_m \bar{X}_j^{Se}a, i \neq j$$
$$\Rightarrow \exists PATH_{<_m}(RT_i^{Se}, RF_j^{Se}): X_i^{Se}a <_p PATH_{<_m}(RT_i^{Se}, RF_j^{Se}) <_p \bar{X}_j^{Se}a \quad (10)$$

Where, not both $X_i^{Se}a$ and $\bar{X}_j^{Se}a$ are Load instructions.

$PATH_{<_m}(RT_i^{Se}, RF_j^{Se})$ is defined as follows.

$$PATH_{<_m}(RT_i^{Se}, RF_j^{Se}) = \begin{cases} \varnothing, i = j; \\ RT_i^{Se} <_m RF_k(RT_i^{Se}) <_p PATH_{<_m}(RT_k^{Se}, RF_j^{Se}), i \neq j. \end{cases}$$

Theorem 2. If any memory order α determined by the a memory consistency model M corresponds to a memory order β determined by the interleaving-order memory model, where the result of β is the same with α, then the memory consistency model M is sequentially consistent.

Proof. According to the definition of the interleaving-order memory model, it follows that in a memory order determined by the interleaving-order memory model, the instructions from the same processor are ordered by the program order. Again, according to the definition of sequential consistency, the memory consistency model M is sequentially consistent. Q.E.D.

Theorem 3. Let α be any memory order determined by the SRS model, then there exists a memory order β determined by the interleaving-order memory model, where, all RX instructions satisfy the relation: $RX <_\alpha \overline{RX} <_\alpha \cdots <_\alpha \overline{\overline{RX}}$ in α, and they also satisfy the relation: $RX <_\beta \overline{RX} <_\beta \cdots <_\beta \overline{\overline{RX}}$ in β.

Proof. For convenience of description, we number all RX instructions in the memory order α, and abbreviate $RX <_\alpha \overline{RX} <_\alpha \cdots <_\alpha \overline{\overline{RX}}$ as $x_1 <_\alpha x_2 <_\alpha \cdots <_\alpha x_n$.

With RX as a delimiter, all instructions are split in the program order as follows: $Y_i = \{y \mid y <_p x_i \, and \, \neg \exists x_j : y <_p x_j <_p x_i\} \cup \{y \mid (x_i <_p y \, and \, \neg \exists x_j : x_i <_p x_j <_p y)$ $and \, \neg \exists x_j : y <_p x_j\}$, and all instructions in Y_i are ordered by the program order.

According to the definition of the SRS model(Formula 6), $x_1 <_\alpha x_2 <_\alpha \ldots <_\alpha x_n$ also satisfy the interleaving-order memory model. Hence, only for RX instructions, there exists a memory order determined β by the interleaving-order memory model, where $x_1 <_\beta x_2 <_\beta \ldots <_\beta x_n$. Again, since both x_i and Y_i are one to one, it follows that $Y_1 <_\beta Y_2 <_\beta \ldots <_\beta Y_n$. Again, since the instructions in Y_i are ordered by the program order, the instruction sequence produced by unfolding $Y_1 <_\beta Y_2 <_\beta \ldots <_\beta Y_n$ keep satisfying the interleaving-order memory model.

Thus, for all instructions, we find a memory order β determined by the interleaving-order memory model, where, all RX instructions satisfy the relation: $RX <_\alpha \overline{RX} <_\alpha \ldots <_\alpha \overline{\overline{RX}}$ in α, and they also satisfy the relation: $RX <_\beta \overline{RX} <_\beta \ldots <_\beta \overline{\overline{RX}}$ in β. Q.E.D.

For convenience of description, we refer $\hat{L}^{Se}a$ or $\tilde{L}^{Se}a$ to a specific $L^{Se}a$ instruction, and refer $\hat{S}^{Se}a$ or $\tilde{S}^{Se}a$ to a specific $S^{Se}a$ instruction.

Theorem 4. Let α be any memory order determined by the SRS model which satisfies the ordered pair condition. If in α, $\forall \hat{L}_i^{Se}a$, $\hat{S}_j^{Se}a : value(\hat{L}_i^{Se}a) = value(\hat{S}_j^{Se}a)$, then $\hat{S}_j^{Se}a <_\alpha \hat{L}_i^{Se}a$ and $\neg \exists \tilde{S}_k^{Se}a : \hat{S}_j^{Se}a <_\alpha \tilde{S}_k^{Se}a <_\alpha \hat{L}_i^{Se}a$.

Proof. In the memory order α, $value(\hat{L}_i^{Se}a) = value(\hat{S}_j^{Se}a)$. Again, according to Formula 7, $value(\hat{S}_j^{Se}a) = value(\hat{L}_i^{Se}a) = value(\max_{<_\alpha}(S^{Se}a \mid S^{Se}a <_\alpha \hat{L}_i^{Se}a))$. Thus, $\hat{S}_j^{Se}a <_\alpha \hat{L}_i^{Se}a$ and $\neg \exists \tilde{S}_k^{Se}a : \hat{S}_j^{Se}a <_\alpha \tilde{S}_k^{Se}a <_\alpha \hat{L}_i^{Se}a$. Q.E.D.

Theorem 5. Let α be any memory order determined by the SRS model which satisfies the ordered pair condition. If in α, $\forall \hat{L}_i^{Se}a$, $\hat{S}_j^{Se}a : value(\hat{L}_i^{Se}a) = value(\hat{S}_j^{Se}a)$, then $\hat{S}_j^{Se}a <_p \hat{L}_i^{Se}a$, where $i = j$.

Proof. If the theorem were false, then $\hat{L}_i^{Se}a <_p \hat{S}_j^{Se}a$. Again, according to Formula 1, it follows that $\hat{L}_i^{Se}a <_\alpha \hat{S}_j^{Se}a$. This is contrary to Theorem 4. Hence, $\hat{L}_i^{Se}a <_p \hat{S}_j^{Se}a$ is not true. Q.E.D.

Theorem 6. Let α be any memory order determined by the SRS model which satisfies the ordered pair condition. If in α, $\forall \hat{L}_i^{Se}a$, $\hat{S}_j^{Se}a : value(\hat{L}_i^{Se}a) = value(\hat{S}_j^{Se}a)$, then $\neg \exists \tilde{S}_j^{Se}a : \hat{S}_j^{Se}a <_p \tilde{S}_j^{Se}a <_p \hat{L}_i^{Se}a$, where $i = j$.

Proof. If the theorem were false, then $\exists \tilde{S}_j^{Se} a: \hat{S}_j^{Se} a <_p \tilde{S}_j^{Se} a <_p \hat{L}_i^{Se} a$. Again, according to Formula 2, it follows that $\hat{S}_j^{Se} a <_\alpha \tilde{S}_j^{Se} a$. According to Formula 3, it follows that $\tilde{S}_j^{Se} a <_\alpha \hat{L}_i^{Se} a$. That is, $\hat{S}_j^{Se} a <_\alpha \tilde{S}_j^{Se} a <_\alpha \hat{L}_i^{Se} a$. This is contrary to Theorem 4. Hence, $\exists \tilde{S}_j^{Se} a: \hat{S}_j^{Se} a <_p \tilde{S}_j^{Se} a <_p \hat{L}_i^{Se} a$ is not true, where $i = j$. Q.E.D.

Theorem 7. If β be a memory order determined by the interleaving-order memory model, then $X_i <_\beta \bar{X}_i \Rightarrow X_i <_p \bar{X}_i$.

Proof. Proof by contradiction. Suppose that $\bar{X}_i <_p X_i$. According to the definition of the interleaving-order memory model (Formula 8), it follows that $\bar{X}_i <_\beta X_i$. This contradicts the fact that $X_i <_\beta \bar{X}_i$. Thus, $X_i <_\beta \bar{X}_i \Rightarrow X_i <_p \bar{X}_i$. Q.E.D.

Theorem 8. Let α be any memory order determined by the SRS model which satisfies the ordered pair condition, and let β be a memory order determined by the interleaving-order memory model which satisfies Theorem 3. If in α, $\forall \hat{L}_i^{Se} a$, $\hat{S}_j^{Se} a$: $value(\hat{L}_i^{Se} a) = value(\hat{S}_j^{Se} a)$, where $i = j$, then in β, $value(\hat{L}_i^{Se} a) = value(\hat{S}_j^{Se} a)$.

Proof. According to Theorem 5, it follows that $\hat{S}_j^{Se} a <_p \hat{L}_i^{Se} a$. Again, according to the formal definition of the interleaving-order memory model (Formula 8), it follows that $\hat{S}_j^{Se} a <_\beta \hat{L}_i^{Se} a$.

Then, we prove that if $i = j$, then $\neg \exists \tilde{S}_k^{Se} a: \hat{S}_j^{Se} a <_\beta \tilde{S}_k^{Se} a <_\beta \hat{L}_i^{Se} a$, where k is any natural number. Therefore, the proof is divided into two cases: (a) $k = i$; (b) $k \neq i$.

Firstly, we prove the theorem is true in the case (a): $k = i$. If the theorem would not hold, then $\exists \tilde{S}_k^{Se} a: \hat{S}_j^{Se} a <_\beta \tilde{S}_k^{Se} a <_\beta \hat{L}_i^{Se} a$, where $k = i$, $i = j$. Again, According to Theorem 7, it follows that $\exists \tilde{S}_k^{Se} a: \hat{S}_j^{Se} a <_p \tilde{S}_k^{Se} a <_p \hat{L}_i^{Se} a$, where $k = i$, $i = j$. This is contrary to Theorem 6. Hence, $\neg \exists \tilde{S}_j^{Se} a: \hat{S}_j^{Se} a <_\beta \tilde{S}_k^{Se} a <_\beta \hat{L}_i^{Se} a$, where $k = i$, $i = j$.

Secondly, we prove the theorem is true in the case (b): $k \neq i$. $\forall \tilde{S}_k^{Se} a$, since the memory order α is a total order, there must exist sequence relation in α between $\tilde{S}_k^{Se} a$ and $\hat{S}_j^{Se} a$, and there also must exist sequence relation in α between $\tilde{S}_k^{Se} a$ and $\hat{L}_i^{Se} a$. Again, according to Theorem 4, it follows that $\tilde{S}_k^{Se} a <_\alpha \hat{S}_j^{Se} a$ or $\hat{L}_i^{Se} a <_\alpha \tilde{S}_k^{Se} a$.

If $\tilde{S}_k^{Se} a <_\alpha \hat{S}_j^{Se} a$, then according to the ordered pair condition, it follows that $\exists \; PATH_{<_\alpha}(RT_k^{Se}, RF_j^{Se}): \tilde{S}_k^{Se} a <_p PATH_{<_\alpha}(RT_k^{Se}, RF_j^{Se}) <_p \hat{S}_j^{Se} a$. Again, since β is a memory order determined by the interleaving-order memory model and β satisfies Theorem 3, it follows that $\tilde{S}_k^{Se} a <_\beta PATH_{<_\beta}(RT_k^{Se}, RF_j^{Se}) <_\beta \hat{S}_j^{Se} a$. That is $\tilde{S}_k^{Se} a <_\beta \hat{S}_j^{Se} a$.

Similarly, since $\hat{L}_i^{Se} a <_\alpha \tilde{S}_k^{Se} a$, it follows that $\hat{L}_i^{Se} a <_\beta \tilde{S}_k^{Se} a$. Hence, $\neg \exists \tilde{S}_k^{Se} a: \hat{S}_j^{Se} a <_\beta \tilde{S}_k^{Se} a <_\beta \hat{L}_i^{Se} a$, where $k \neq i$, $i = j$.

Considering the two cases discussed above, it can easily be seen that if $i = j$, then $\neg \exists \tilde{S}_k^{Se} a: \hat{S}_j^{Se} a <_\beta \tilde{S}_k^{Se} a <_\beta \hat{L}_i^{Se} a$, where k is any natural number.

We have thus proved that $\neg\exists \tilde{S}_k^{Se}a : \hat{S}_j^{Se}a <_\beta \tilde{S}_k^{Se}a <_\beta \hat{L}_i^{Se}a$, where $i = j$, k is any natural number. Finally, according to the definition of the interleaving-order memory model (Formula 9), it follows that $value(\hat{L}_i^{Se}a) = value(\hat{S}_j^{Se}a)$. Q.E.D.

Theorem 9. Let α be any memory order determined by the SRS model which satisfies the ordered pair condition, and let β be a memory order determined by the interleaving-order memory model which satisfies Theorem 3. If in α, $\forall \hat{L}_i^{Se}a$, $\hat{S}_j^{Se}a$: $value(\hat{L}_i^{Se}a) = value(\hat{S}_j^{Se}a)$, where $i \neq j$, then in β, $\hat{S}_j^{Se}a <_\beta \hat{L}_i^{Se}a$.

Proof. According to Theorem 4, it follows that $\hat{S}_j^{Se}a <_\alpha \hat{L}_i^{Se}a$. Again, according to the ordered pair condition, it follows that $\exists \ PATH_{<_\alpha}(RT_j^{Se},RF_i^{Se})$: $\hat{S}_j^{Se}a <_p PATH_{<_\alpha}(RT_j^{Se},RF_i^{Se}) <_p \hat{L}_i^{Se}a$. Finally, according to Theorem 3 and Formula 8, it follows that $\hat{S}_j^{Se}a <_\beta PATH_{<_\beta}(RT_j^{Se},RF_i^{Se}) <_\beta \hat{L}_i^{Se}a$. That is, $\hat{S}_j^{Se}a <_\beta \hat{L}_i^{Se}a$. The proof of the theorem is now completed. Q.E.D.

Theorem 10. Let α be any memory order determined by the SRS model which satisfies the ordered pair condition, and let β be a memory order determined by the interleaving-order memory model which satisfies Theorem 3. If in α, $\forall \hat{L}_i^{Se}a$, $\hat{S}_j^{Se}a$: $value(\hat{L}_i^{Se}a) = value(\hat{S}_j^{Se}a)$, where $i \neq j$, then in β, $\neg\exists \tilde{S}_k^{Se}a : \hat{S}_j^{Se}a <_\beta \tilde{S}_k^{Se}a <_\beta \hat{L}_i^{Se}a$, where k is any natural number.

Proof. Since $i \neq j$, the proof is divided into three cases: (a) $k = j$ and $k \neq i$; (b) $k \neq j$ and $k = i$; (c) $k \neq j$ and $k \neq i$.

Firstly, we prove the theorem is true in the case (a): $k = j$ and $k \neq i$. If the theorem would not hold, then $\exists \tilde{S}_k^{Se}a : \hat{S}_j^{Se}a <_\beta \tilde{S}_k^{Se}a <_\beta \hat{L}_i^{Se}a$. According to Theorem 7, it follows that $\hat{S}_j^{Se}a <_p \tilde{S}_k^{Se}a$. Again, according to Formula 2, it follows that $\hat{S}_j^{Se}a <_\alpha \tilde{S}_k^{Se}a$.

Since the memory order α is a total order, there must exist sequence relation in α between $\tilde{S}_k^{Se}a$ and $\hat{L}_i^{Se}a$. That is, $\tilde{S}_k^{Se}a <_\alpha \hat{L}_i^{Se}a$ or $\hat{L}_i^{Se}a <_\alpha \tilde{S}_k^{Se}a$.

If $\tilde{S}_k^{Se}a <_\alpha \hat{L}_i^{Se}a$, then $\hat{S}_j^{Se}a <_\alpha \tilde{S}_k^{Se}a <_\alpha \hat{L}_i^{Se}a$. This is contrary to Theorem 4.

If $\hat{L}_i^{Se}a <_\alpha \tilde{S}_k^{Se}a$, then according to the ordered pair condition, it follows that $\exists \ PATH_{<_\alpha}(RT_i^{Se},RF_k^{Se})$: $\hat{L}_i^{Se}a <_p PATH_{<_\alpha}(RT_i^{Se},RF_k^{Se}) <_p \tilde{S}_k^{Se}a$. Again, according to Theorem 3 and Formula 8, it follows that $\hat{L}_i^{Se}a <_\beta PATH_{<_\beta}(RT_i^{Se},RF_k^{Se}) <_\beta \tilde{S}_k^{Se}a$. That is, $\hat{L}_i^{Se}a <_\beta \tilde{S}_k^{Se}a$. This is contrary to the assumption that $\exists \tilde{S}_k^{Se}a : \hat{S}_j^{Se}a <_\beta \tilde{S}_k^{Se}a <_\beta \hat{L}_i^{Se}a$.

Hence, if $k = j$ and $k \neq i$, then $\neg\exists \tilde{S}_k^{Se}a : \hat{S}_j^{Se}a <_\beta \tilde{S}_k^{Se}a <_\beta \hat{L}_i^{Se}a$.

Secondly, we prove the theorem is true in the case (b): $k \neq j$ and $k = i$. If the theorem would not hold, then $\exists \tilde{S}_k^{Se}a : \hat{S}_j^{Se}a <_\beta \tilde{S}_k^{Se}a <_\beta \hat{L}_i^{Se}a$. According to Theorem 7, it follows that $\tilde{S}_k^{Se}a <_p \hat{L}_i^{Se}a$. Again, according to Formula 2, it follows that $\tilde{S}_k^{Se}a <_\alpha \hat{L}_i^{Se}a$.

Since the memory order α is a total order, there must exist sequence relation in α between $\tilde{S}_k^{Se}a$ and $\hat{S}_j^{Se}a$. That is $\tilde{S}_k^{Se}a <_\alpha \hat{S}_j^{Se}a$ or $\hat{S}_j^{Se}a <_\alpha \tilde{S}_k^{Se}a$.

If $\hat{S}_j^{Se}a <_\alpha \tilde{S}_k^{Se}a$, then $\hat{S}_j^{Se}a <_\alpha \tilde{S}_k^{Se}a <_\alpha \hat{L}_i^{Se}a$. This is contrary to Theorem 4.

If $\tilde{S}_k^{Se}a <_\alpha \hat{S}_j^{Se}a$, then according to the ordered pair condition, it follows that $\exists\ PATH_{<_\alpha}(RT_k^{Se}, RF_j^{Se}):\ \tilde{S}_k^{Se}a <_p PATH_{<_\alpha}(RT_k^{Se}, RF_j^{Se}) <_p \hat{S}_j^{Se}a$. Again, according to Theorem 3 and Formula 8, it follows that $\tilde{S}_k^{Se}a <_\beta PATH_{<_\alpha}(RT_k^{Se}, RF_i^{Se}) <_\beta \hat{S}_j^{Se}a$. That is, $\tilde{S}_k^{Se}a <_\beta \hat{S}_j^{Se}a$. This is contrary to the assumption that $\exists\tilde{S}_k^{Se}a:$ $\hat{S}_j^{Se}a <_\beta \tilde{S}_k^{Se}a <_\beta \hat{L}_i^{Se}a$.

Hence, if $k \neq j$ and $k = i$, then $\neg\exists\tilde{S}_k^{Se}a:\ \hat{S}_j^{Se}a <_\beta \tilde{S}_k^{Se}a <_\beta \hat{L}_i^{Se}a$.

Thirdly, we prove the theorem is true in the case (c): $k \neq j$ and $k \neq i$. $\forall\tilde{S}_k^{Se}a$, since the memory order α is a total order, there must exist sequence relation in α between $\tilde{S}_k^{Se}a$ and $\hat{S}_j^{Se}a$, and there also must exist sequence relation in α between $\tilde{S}_k^{Se}a$ and $\hat{L}_i^{Se}a$. Again, according to Theorem 4, it follows that $\tilde{S}_k^{Se}a <_\alpha \hat{S}_j^{Se}a$ or $\hat{L}_i^{Se}a <_\alpha \tilde{S}_k^{Se}a$.

If $\tilde{S}_k^{Se}a <_\alpha \hat{S}_j^{Se}a$, then according to the ordered pair condition, it follows that $\exists\ PATH_{<_\alpha}(RT_k^{Se}, RF_j^{Se}):\ \tilde{S}_k^{Se}a <_p PATH_{<_\alpha}(RT_k^{Se}, RF_j^{Se}) <_p \hat{S}_j^{Se}a$. Again, according to Theorem 3 and Formula 8, it follows that $\tilde{S}_k^{Se}a <_\beta PATH_{<_\alpha}(RT_k^{Se}, RF_j^{Se}) <_\beta \hat{S}_j^{Se}a$. That is, $\tilde{S}_k^{Se}a <_\beta \hat{S}_j^{Se}a$.

Similarly, if $\hat{L}_i^{Se}a <_\alpha \tilde{S}_k^{Se}a$, then $\hat{L}_i^{Se}a <_\beta \tilde{S}_k^{Se}a$.

Hence, if $k \neq j$ and $k \neq i$, then $\neg\exists\tilde{S}_k^{Se}a:\ \hat{S}_j^{Se}a <_\beta \tilde{S}_k^{Se}a <_\beta \hat{L}_i^{Se}a$.

Considering the three cases discussed above, it can easily be seen that if $i \neq j$, then $\neg\exists\tilde{S}_k^{Se}a:\ \hat{S}_j^{Se}a <_\beta \tilde{S}_k^{Se}a <_\beta \hat{L}_i^{Se}a$, where k is any natural number. Q.E.D.

Theorem 11. Let α be any memory order determined by the SRS model which satisfies the ordered pair condition, and let β be a memory order determined by the interleaving-order memory model which satisfies Theorem 3. If in α, $\forall\ \hat{L}_i^{Se}a$, $\hat{S}_j^{Se}a:$ $value(\hat{L}_i^{Se}a) = value(\hat{S}_j^{Se}a)$, where $i \neq j$, then in β, $value(\hat{L}_i^{Se}a) = value(\hat{S}_j^{Se}a)$.

Proof. According to Theorem 9 , Theorem 10, and Formula 9, it follows that if $i \neq j$, then $value(\hat{L}_i^{Se}a) = value(\hat{S}_j^{Se}a)$. Q.E.D.

Theorem 12. If α is any memory order determined by the SRS model which satisfies the ordered pair condition, then there must exist a memory order β determined by the interleaving-order memory model. The relationship between α and β as follows: if in α, $\forall\ \hat{L}_i^{Se}a$, $\hat{S}_j^{Se}a:$ $value(\hat{L}_i^{Se}a) = value(\hat{S}_j^{Se}a)$, then in β, the equation that $value(\hat{L}_i^{Se}a) = value(\hat{S}_j^{Se}a)$ still holds.

Proof. According to Theorem 3, Theorem 8, and Theorem 11, it is evident to see that the theorem to be proved holds. Q.E.D.

Theorem 13. The SRS model satisfying the ordered pair condition is sequentially consistent.

Proof. Let α be any memory order determined by the SRS model which satisfies the ordered pair condition. According to Theorem 12, it follows that there must exist a memory order β determined by the interleaving-order memory model, where the result of β is the same with α. Again, according to 2, it is evident to see that the above SRS model is sequentially consistent. Q.E.D.

5   Extending the SRS Model

Data used for many-core software can be divided into four categories, including read-only data, private data, global data used for synchronization, and data exchanged between cores. For the above four categories of data, the original SRS model is only applied to the data exchanged between multiple cores. Therefore, the original SRS model needs to be extended for the remaining three categories of data.

5.1   Extending for Read-Only Data

The original SRS model is extended for read-only data as follows:

1. A STORE instruction in the original SRS model is treated as a null instruction
2. The TOKEN of any read-only data segment is owned by all processor cores at the same time. Therefore, RF/RT instructions may not be needed.
3. The initial placement of read-only data is completed by a specific processor core. From the perspective of the processor core, the data are not read-only data, but data exchanged between cores.

Since no STORE instruction is used for read-only data, the SRS model is still sequentially consistent after being extended for read-only data.

5.2   Extending for Private Data

The original SRS model is extended for private data as follow: The TOKEN of any private data segment is only owned by a specific processor core, and the TOKEN needn't be passing to other processor core. Therefore, RF/RT instructions may not be needed.

Since any private data segment is accessed by only one processor core, not shared by multiple processor cores, the SRS model is still sequentially consistent after being extended for private data.

5.3   Extending for Global Data

The original SRS model is extended for global data used for synchronization by building a transactional load and a transactional store.

1. A transactional load(notation: $TML_i^{Se}a$) is a sequence of " $RF_i^{Se}m$, $L_i^{Se}a$, $RT_i^{Se}m$ ", which is an atomic operation.
2. A transactional store(notation: $TMS_i^{Se}a$) is a sequence of " $RF_i^{Se}m$, $S_i^{Se}a$, $RT_i^{Se}m$ " , which is an atomic operation.

Since both $TML_i^{Se}a$ and $TMS_i^{Se}a$ are atomic operations, it follows that the SRS model extended for global data still satisfies the ordered pair condition. Therefore, the SRS model is still sequentially consistent after being extended for global data.

6   Conclusion

The paper completes the formal description of the SRS model and the proof of sequential consistency. The above proof shows that the model is complete, correct and usable.

Different from traditional memory consistency models(such as SC, TSO/X86, RMO), the SRS model simplifies cache coherence for the full chip, and reduces design complexity, which is suitable for thousand-core processors.

Different from existing memory consistency models(such as ASM) for thousand-core processors, the SRS model has no redundancy, and has the ability to describe the direct exchange of data on chip, which reduces the demand for off-chip memory bandwidth.

In future work, we plan to build the appropriate hardware and software infrastructures based on the SRS model, and then to migrate some typical applications to the infrastructures. In this way, we can accurately analyze the hardware cost, the performance and the usability of the system based on the SRS model.

References

1. Tile-gx100 manycore processor: acceleration interfaces and architecture,
    http://www.hotchips.org/wp-content/uploads/hc_archives/hc23/
    HC23.18.2-security/HC23.18.220-TILE-GX100-Ramey-Tilera-e.pdf
    (accessed May 15, 2014)
2. Johnson, D.R., Johnson, M.R., Kelm, J.H.: Rigel: A 1,024-core single-chip accelerator architecture. IEEE Micro 31, 30–41 (2011)
3. Lamport, L.: How to make a multiprocessor computer that correctly executes multiprocess programs. IEEE Transactions on Computers 28, 690–691(1979)
4. Owens, S., Sarkar, S., Sewell, P.: A better x86 memory model: x86-TSO. In: Berghofer, S., Nipkow, T., Urban, C., Wenzel, M. (eds.) TPHOLs 2009. LNCS, vol. 5674, pp. 391–407. Springer, Heidelberg (2009)
5. Weaver, D.L., Germond, T.: The SPARC architecture manual (Version 9). PTR Prentice Hall, Englewood Cliffs (1994)
6. Hechtman, B.A., Sorin, D.J.: Exploring memory consistency for massively-threaded throughput-oriented processors. In: Proc. of the 40th Annual International Symposium on Computer Architecture, pp. 201–212. ACM, New York (2013)
7. Kelm, J.H., Johnson, M.R., Lumettta, S.S.: Waypoint: Scaling coherence to thousand-core architectures. In: Proc. of the 19th International Conference on Parallel Architectures and Compilation Techniques, pp. 99–110. ACM, New York (2010)
8. Hower, D.: Acoherent shared memory. University of Wisconsin-Madison, Madison (2012)
9. Kelm, J.H., Johnson, D.R., Tuohy, W.: Cohesion: An adaptive hybrid memory model for accelerators. IEEE Micro 31, 42–55 (2011)
10. Kelm, J.H., Johnson, D.R., Lumetta, S.S.: A Task-Centric Memory Model for Scalable Accelerator Architectures. IEEE Micro 30, 29–39 (2010)

A Partition Method of SoC Design Serving the Multi-FPGA Verification Platform

Shenglai Yang, Kuanjiu Zhou[*], Jie Wang, Bin Liu, and Ting Li

Dalian University of Technology (DUT), School of Software, Dalian, China
zhoukj@dlut.edu.cn

Abstract. FPGA (Field-Programmable Gate Array) technology can provide excellent accuracy and efficiency for Chip verification, which has become the key bottleneck of SoC design. Due to the resource constraints of single FPGA chip, Multi-FPGA architecture was applied to the verification of the large scale SoC design. In recent years, a variety of Multi-FPGA verification platforms have been developed, but most of them indirectly part the SoC design on the Netlist level after the synthesis procedure. A partition method is proposed in this paper, which works directly on the RTL (Register Transfer Level) code. It presents a universal partition methodology with realistic and detailed implementation, applying a linear partition algorithm. The experiment simulation of leon3, a SoC design based on SPARC processor, runs at a speed of 8 MHz correctly, over 100,000 times faster than software simulation, 1-2 times of the BEE4 FPGA based recognizable platforms.

Keywords: verification, Multi-FPGA, partition algorithm, leon3.

1 Introduction

With the vast growth of the SoC (System on Chip) design size and system complexity, chip verification has become the key bottleneck of SoC design. Reconfigurable prototyping technology based on hardware comes to be a good method to accelerate chip verification. Several logic emulators with reconfigurable FPGA chips have been developed with excellent accuracy and efficiency for the verification of the SoC design [1]. The simulation of the SoC design can run at a speed close to actual chip environment in these logic emulators, which provide a functionally equivalent hardware prototype for the SoC design. However, the FPGA-based method also faces many challenges, such as timing closure and signal integrity. But the most serious challenge is that due to the constraints of logic size and I/O capacity, the contemporary FPGA chip is not enough to hold the complete SoC design. Multi-FPGA platform is an efficient way to overcome such constraints.

Related Works. In recent years, a variety of state-of-the-art Multi-FPGA verification platforms have been developed. Intel has reported a Multi-FPGA [2] platform consist-

---

[*] This work is supported by "the Fundamental Research Funds for the Central Universities" (DUT14QY32).

J. Wu et al. (Eds.): ACA 2014, CCIS 451, pp. 43–57, 2014.

ing of Xilinx Virtex-4 and Virtex-5 FPGA chips to speed up the verification for x86 architecture. In the Bluegene project, IBM developed a cycle-accurate, cycle-reproducible Multi-FPGA system to accelerate the simulation of multi-core processor [3]. An FPGA based recognizable platforms named BEEcube, was proposed by the University of California, Berkeley, where founders conducted decades of leading research on the FPGA-based Berkeley Emulation Engine (BEE) platforms and development environments[4]. But most of them indirectly part the SoC design on the Netlist level after synthesis procedure. Such method firstly converts the source code of the SoC design to Netlist files using synthesis tools and then parts the design on Netlist level. During the indirect and sightless partition of Netlist, some key modules may be split into pieces, leading to unsatisfactory of the verification demands. This paper researches on a RTL code partition method of the SoC design with the hierarchy of the digital design. In our method, module is the basic partition unit, which is named MODULE in Verilog or ENTITY in VHDL. The SoC design is divided into pieces under the guidance of the module hierarchy tree directly and explicitly. Through optimization of the partition algorithm and procedure flow, our method minimizes the time consuming of synthesis. It also provides a universal partition methodology with realistic and detailed implementation, applying a linear partition algorithm.

This paper organizes as follows. It introduces the partition methodology and related works in Section 1. The flow of partition methodology will be proposed in Section 2. Then, the preparatory work for the SoC partition is described in Section 3. The core partition algorithm is shown in Section 4. In Section 5, a specific Multi-FPGA verification platform is introduced to conduct the experiment simulation and provides the experiment result of leon3, a SoC design based on SPARC processor. Section 6 is for the summary.

2   Partition Flow

This paper proposes a partition method of the SoC design serving the Multi-FPGA verification platform. It divides the SoC design into several parts, and then properly maps them into corresponding FPGA chips on the platform.

A given SoC design consists of a number of modules and sub-modules described by Verilog or VHDL, which are organized in a hierarchical way. Our method parts the HDL code of the SoC on RTL source code and regards module as the basic partition unit. The partition flow is described in Fig. 1. In RTL source code, module is the basic hardware unit, represented by circles in Fig. 1. In order to part the SoC design logically, we firstly obtain the top-down module hierarchy tree of the SoC, which contains the module basic information represented by rhombuses in Fig. 1. Secondly synthesize and analyze each module for their resource demands which are the key factors of the partition algorithm. Thirdly divide the module hierarchy tree into sub-trees through the partition procedure in O(n) time. Fourthly, modify the RTL code using syntax matching tools and package the sub-trees with communication signals according to the partition result. Finally, program the bit files synthesized from sub-trees into the corresponding FPGA chips.

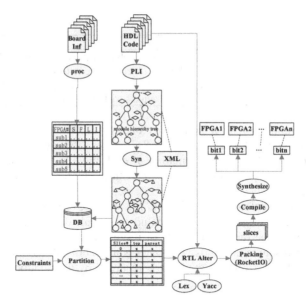

Fig. 1. Partition Flow

3   Preparations

To divide the SoC design logically, the partition algorithm needs some preparatory work. We obtain the top-down module hierarchy tree of the SoC design, and then synthesize and analyze each module for their resource demands. In this process, the input is RTL code and the output is a top-down module hierarchy tree which conveys the basic information and resource demands of each module.

3.1   Extraction and Storage of the Module Tree

A complete HDL model of a complex digital system is constituted by many modules named MODULE in Verilog or ENTITY in VHDL. A module can contain many sub-modules called instantiations, through which the top-module organizes sub-modules to define its own function. A typical SoC design follows the Top-Down design methodology. According to the instantiation relationship, all the modules constitute a module hierarchy tree rooted by a top module. The ultimate goal of the partitioning algorithm is to divide the module hierarchy tree into several sub-trees mapping to the corresponding FPGA chips. Before the partition, we should obtain the module hierarchy tree. There is a C language procedural interface standard known as the Programming Language Interface (PLI) named VPI in Verilog or VHPI in VHDL, which provides a means for HDL users to access and modify data in an instantiated HDL data structure dynamically. Table 1. shows VPI routines for module utilities, whose specific usage refers on IEEE-1326 standard [5].

Table 1. Vpi Routines for Module Utilities

Utilities	Function
vpi_handle()	Obtain a handle for an object with a one-to-one relationship
vpi_iterate();vpi_scan()	Obtain handles for objects in a one-to-many relationship
vpi_handle_multi()	Obtain a handle for an object in a many-to-one relationship
vpi_get()	Get the value of objects with types of int or bool

Generally, a digital system contains only one top-module rooting of the module hierarchy tree. Through BFS (Breadth First Search), use these routines to extract the module tree and store the basic information of each module. This paper uses XML (Extensible Markup Language) files to record both the hierarchy and basic information of modules.

Fig. 2 shows the label structure of XML file where every module node has two fields. One is to record basic information including module definition name, instantiation name, and the name of definition file or instantiation file, which is essential for obtaining module resource demands. The other is to record sub-modules instanced in current module. The hierarchy of modules is recorded by the relationship of module nodes in XML file.

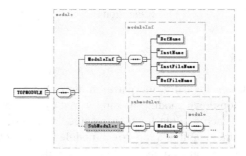

Fig. 2. Structure of XML File

The partition method is mainly based on the resource demands of the SoC design, including the amount of Slices, LUTs, IOBs and Flip-flops. We should obtain the resource demands data in advance to avoid the blindness of partition and improve success rate.

Existing mainstream EDA tools can achieve an efficient and accurate calculation of resource demands for digital systems. Since the experimental platform employs Xilinx FPGA chip, the partition method selects Xilinx ISE XST for synthesize procedure. A fragment of the Synthesis Report (Final Report) is shown in Fig. 3.

```
--------------------------
Device utilization summary:
--------------------------
Selected Device : 2s15cs144-6
Number of Slices:           101  out of   192   52%
Number of Slice Flip Flops:   95  out of   384   24%
Number of 4 input LUTs:      184  out of   384   47%
Number of bonded IOBs:        31  out of    90   34%
--------------------------
```

Fig. 3. Fragment of Synthesis Report

To formalize the resource demands of module, quintuple vector (S, F, L, I) is proposed, S denotes Slices, F denotes Flips Flops, L denotes LUTs, I denotes IOBs. With basic information recorded in XML file, XST can synthesize resources demands of any module, and then fill the quintuple vector (S, F, L, I). The partition method of this paper makes two optimizations to avoid frequent calls of the time consuming synthesis tool.

- The analysis depth of the resource demands synthesis procedure is only accurate to modules which affect the partition algorithm. Say in other words, during module synthesizing, if a module resource demands (S, F, L, I) don't exceeded the given constraints, we just synthesis itself rather than all its sub-modules.
- In the SoC design, the same modules would be instantiated several times. To avoid repetitive synthesis, our partition method will record any synthesized module and compare the modules to be synthesized with previous records.

After resource demands analysis, a module hierarchy tree with the basic information and resource demands data is obtained.

4   Partition

In this section, with the preparatory work above, the partition problem of the SoC design is formalized into a weighted tree waiting for partition. Nodes of the tree denote modules of the SoC design, while the multidimensional weight of each node denotes the multiple resource demands of the module. Our goal is to partition the tree design into sub-trees, ensuring the resource demands of any sub-tree meets the given constraints. This section consists of two parts. Firstly introduce a partition algorithm whose time complexity is $O(n)$. Secondly modify the source code of the SoC design with the result partition algorithm.

4.1   Partition Algorithm

Problem. With preparation work above, the partition problem has been converted into a K-partition [6] problem of a multidimensional weighted tree. In the context of the paper, the weight represents the resource demands of a module.

Problem Formalization. Let T_n denote a tree rooted by node n, $S(n)$ is the set of sons of node n. Node q represent a module in SoC design. $w(q)$ is the weight of node p ,while $W(q)$ is the sum of node weights in T_q. A feasible K-partition of T_n is C_f, a set of edges cut from the tree. Through cutting edges, it partitions the tree into sub-trees and each of them has a total node weight (sum resource demands of every module) at most K. Our goal is to find a minimal feasible K-partition C_{opt} named optimal K-partition satisfying $|C_{opt}| \leq |C_f|$. A $O(n)$ partition algorithm will be presented to find an optimal k-partition, where n is the number of nodes in the tree.

One-dimensional Situation. To describe the partition algorithm clearly, the one-dimensional K-partition problem is handled firstly, in which the weight of tree is just a positive integer. The solution of Sukhmay and Jayadev [6] is referred to interpret the K-partition algorithm of one-dimensional situation, which is the foundation of multi-dimensional algorithm. Firstly two basic lemmas should be proved.

Lemma1. Let p such node that $W(p) > K$ and for any son node r of p $W(r) \leq K$. Then there must be a optimal k-partition C that contains (p, r_0), $W(r_0) = \max_{r \in S(p)}\{W(r)\}$.

Briefly Proof. Since $W(p) > K$, an optimal partition C at least has one edge from Tp. Let (u, v) be such edge in C from Tp. If $u \neq p$, then (u, v) is in the sub tree T_r, $r \in S(p)$.

Assume $C_1 = C - \{(u, v)\} + \{(p, r)\}$ is another feasible partition. $ly |C_1| = |C|, W(r) \leq K$, $W_1(q) \leq W(q) + w(r) < W(q) \leq K$ in C_1 partition, so C_1 is also an optimal partition. Assume $C_2 = C_1 - \{(p, r)\} + \{(p, r_0)\}$ is another feasible partition, r_0 is called the heaviest son of p. Obviously $W(r_0) \leq K$, $W_2(q) = W_1(q) - W_1(r_0) + W(r)$, $|C_1| = |C_2|$, $W(r_0) = W_1(r_0) = \max_{r \in S(p)}\{W(r)\} \geq W(r)$, so $W_2(q) \leq W_1(q) \leq K$, means that C_2 is also an optimal partition .

Lemma2. Let (p, r) be a edge in an optimal partition of T, while C_1 is an optimal partition of $T - T_r$, C_2 is an optimal partition of T_r, then $C = C_1 + C_2 + \{(p, r)\}$ is an optimal partition of T.

Briefly Proof. Obviously, C is a feasible partition. Let C3 an optimal partition including edge (p,r).let C4 be the edges from $T - T_r$ of C3 and C4 be the edges from T_r of C3. Obviously, $|C_1| <= |C_4|$ $|C_2| <= |C_5|$ then $|C_1| + |C_2| <= |C_4| + |C_5|$,so $|C| <= |C_3|$. Hence $C = C_1 + C_2 + \{(p, r)\}$ is an optimal partition of T.

According to lemma 2, we can partition a tree through looking for the optimal partitions of its sub-trees level by level from leaf nodes to root. According to Lemma 1, we can partition basic sub-tree through looking for the special node p that meets the conditions of Lemma 1 and cut the heaviest sons of p one by one until $W(p) \leq K$. A simple algorithm is shown as Fig. 4.

```
Algorithm K-partition
Input: T (The tree with positive weight to node)
Output: C ( Set of edge for partition)
    Let C=Ø
    Let W(q)=w(q) for all the leaf of T
    foreach I variable from deepest level of T to 1
    While there is p node satisfies lemma 1
    {
        Remove the heaviest son r of p one by one
        Until W(q)=W(q)-W(r)<=K
        Add (q,r) into C
    }
```

Fig. 4. Algorithm K-partition

It is clear that most of time is cost on looking for the weightiest sons. Since the upper bound of the time complexity of comparison-based sorting algorithm is $O(n \ln n)$, the best time complexity of the simple K-partition algorithm is $O(n \ln n)$.

Next, this paper briefly introduces an improved algorithm. Through an anonymous referee method, the time complexity of node p handling drops to $O(S(p))$. Its main idea is to split the sons of p into two parts SL(p) and SH(p) to meet three conditions:

(1) if $q \in SL(p)$ and $r \in SH(p)$ then $W(q) \leq W(r)$,

(2) $\sum_{q \in SL(p)} W(q) + w(p) \leq K$,

(3) $\sum_{q \in SL(p)} W(q) + w(p) + W(r) > K, \forall r \epsilon SH(p)$.

Split procedures run as follows. Firstly apply a linear median finding algorithm [7] to split the S(p) into SH(p) and SL(p) satisfy $|SH(p)| \leq |SL(p)| \leq |SH(p)| + 1$, and condition (1). Secondly, check condition (2)(3) to shift the boundary of SH(p) and SL(p). Once (2) satisfied while (3) unsatisfied, apply the linear median finding algorithm to split SH(p) iteratively. Once (3) satisfied while (2) unsatisfied, apply the linear median finding algorithm to split SL(p) iteratively. Until (2) and (3) are satisfied simultaneously, end the splitting to get the dividing line in S(p). The optimal Algorithm is presented as Fig.5.

Algorithm **optimal K-partition**

Input: T (The tree with positive weight to node)

Output: C (Set of edge for partition)

    Let C=∅

    Let W(q)=w(q) for all the leaf of T

    foreach I variable from deepest level of T to 1

    while there is p node satisfies lemma 1

    {

        Split S(p) into SL(p) and SH(p)

        Remove the sons r from SH(p) one by one

        Until W(q)=W(q)-W(r)<=K

        Add (q,r) into C

    }

Fig. 5. Algorithm Optimal K-partition

The linear median finding algorithm time complexity is $O(n)$, so the time complexity of p handling is $O\left(|S(p)| + \frac{|S(p)|}{2} + \frac{|S(p)|}{4} + \cdots + \frac{|S(p)|}{2^n}\right) = O(|S(p)|)$. Hence the time complexity of this algorithm is $O(n)$, n is the total node number of Tree.

Algorithm Analysis. Through the observation of algorithm above, the general steps of the K-partition problem can be concluded. Firstly, look for the special node p described in lemma 1 from down to top of the tree. Secondly, handle the specific node p. Thirdly, follow divide and conquer methodology to handle the partition of the whole tree from bottom to top according to lemma 2. To lower the time complexity of node p handling, anonymous referee methodology is applied in the linear median finding algorithm to split SL(p) into SH(p) and SL(p). The son nodes of SH(p) will be separated out from T_p.

Multi-dimensional Situation. When the weight is two-dimensional, X weight and Y weight, it needs to make some redefinitions.

$K = (X_k, Y_k), W(q) = (W_x(q), W_y(q))$,

$W(q) \leq K$ means $(W_x(q) \leq X_k, W_y(q) \leq Y_k)$,

$W(q) > K$ means $(W_x(q) > X_k, W_y(q) > Y_k)$.

Referring to the K-partition algorithm in one-dimensional case, our goal is to find node p of lemma1 that $W(p) > K$ and for any son node r of p $W(r) \leq K$. There are three cases for node p handling:

Case 1. When $W_x(p) > X_k$ and $W_y(p) \leq Y_k$, X resource of T_p overflows. This paper just considers the resource X during the splitting of $S(p)$ into $SH(p)$ and $SL(p)$. Processing method is similar to the one-dimensional case.

Case 2. When $W_x(p) \leq X_k$ and $W_y(p) > Y_k$, Y resource of T_p overflows. It just considers the resource Y during the splitting of $S(p)$ into $SH(p)$ and $SL(p)$. Processing method is similar to case 1.

Case 3. When $W_x(p) > X_k$ and $W_y(p) > Y_k$, that case is much more complex. During the handling of p, it cannot just simply consider any weigh of X or Y. Our object is to split $S(p)$ into $SH(p)$ and $SL(p)$, satisfying $\sum_{q \in SL(p)} W(q) + w(p) \leq K$ and $W(r) < K, \forall r \epsilon SH(p)$. Due to $SH(p)$ is the set of nodes waiting to be partitioned. Due to $|SH(p)| = |S(p)| + |SL(p)|$, it tries to reduce $|SL(p)|$. How to split $SL(p)$ and $SH(p)$is a Multi-objective Optimization Problem (MOP). Unilaterally scrupling X or Y will cause division resources on the negative results. According to MOP solutions, this paper set a priority vector $Prio(p) = \left(P_x(p), P_y(p)\right)^T$ and a standard value for every son node r of p $Value(r) = Prio(p) * \left(W_x(r), W_y(r)\right)$. The Setting of $P_x(p)$ and $P_y(p)$ is dynamic to measure the overflow of X and Y. $P_x(p) = W_x(p) - X_k$ and $P_y(p) = W_y(p) - Y_k$. $Value(r)$ denotes severity of resource overflow. The linear median finding algorithm is based on $Value(r)$ to split $S(p)$ into $SH(p)$ and $SL(p)$.

Summing up the above three cases, it describes node p handling. It uses $Prio(p)$ to denote priority of each kind of resource and $Value(r)$ to calculate severity of resource overflow. $Prio(p)$ equals

$$\begin{cases} \left(\quad 0 \quad , W_y(p) - Y_k\right)^T if\ W_x(p) \leq X_k, W_y(p) > Y_k \\ \left(W_x(p) - X_k, \quad 0 \quad \right)^T if\ W_x(p) \leq X_k, W_y(p) > Y_k \\ \left(W_x(p) - X_k, W_y(p) - Y_k\right)^T if\ W_x(p) > X_k\ W_y(p) > Y_k \end{cases}$$

$$Value(r) = Prio(p) * \left(W_x(r), W_y(r)\right)$$

In the context of this paper, the weight (S, F, L, I) is four-dimensional. $Prio(p) = \left(P_s(p), P_f(p), P_l(p), P_i(p)\right)^T$.

Define $f(x) = \begin{cases} x; if\ x > 0 \\ 0; if\ x \leq 0 \end{cases}$, then $Prio(p) = (f(W\_s\,(p) - S\_k), f(W\_f\,(p) - S\_f), f(W\_l\,(p) - S\_l), f(W\_i\,(p) - S\_i))\wedge T$, $Value(r) = Prio(p) * (W\_s\,(r), W\_f\,(r), W\_l\,(r), W\_i\,(r))$

To split $S(p)$ into $SH(p)$ and $SL(p)$ and satisfy three conditions.

(1) if $q \in SL(p)$ and $r \in SH(p)$ then $Value(q) \leq Value(r)$,

(2) $\sum_{q \in SL(p)} W(q) + w(p) \leq K$,

(3) $\sum_{q \in SL(p)} W(q) + w(p) + W(r) > K, \forall r \epsilon SH(p)$.

Detailed process is similar to the one-dimensional case. To apply the linear median finding algorithm [7] to split the $S(p)$ into $SH(p)$ and $SL(p)$ satisfy $|SH(p)| \leq |SL(p)| \leq |SH(p)| + 1$, and condition (1). Secondly, check condition (2)(3) to shift the boundary of $SH(p)$ and $SL(p)$. Once (2) satisfied while (3) unsatisfied, apply the linear median finding algorithm to split $SH(p)$ iteratively. Once (3) satisfied while (2) unsatisfied, apply the linear median finding algorithm to split $SL(p)$ iteratively. Until (2) and (3) are satisfied simultaneously, end the splitting to get the dividing line in $S(p)$. The Multi- Dimensional Algorithm is presented as follows Fig. 6.

The linear median finding algorithm time complexity is $O(n)$, so the time complexity of p handling is $O\left(|S(p)| + \frac{|S(p)|}{2} + \frac{|S(p)|}{4} + \cdots + \frac{|S(p)|}{2^n}\right) = O(|S(p)|)$. Hence the time complexity of that algorithm is $O(n)$, n is the total node number of Tree.

Algorithm **Multi-Dimensional K-partition**

Input: T (The tree with positive weight to node)

Output: C (Set of edge for partition)

Let C= Ø

Let W(q)=w(q) for all the leaf of T

foreach I variable from deepest level of T to 1

while there is p node satisfies lemma 1

{

    Calculate Prio(p) and Value(r) of the nodes of S(p)

    Split S(p) into SL(p) and SH(p)

    Remove the sons r from SH(p) one by one

    Until W(q)=W(q)-W(r)<=K

    Add (q,r) into C

}

Fig. 6. Algorithm Multi-Dimensional K-partition

4.2　RTL Code Modification

After the partition of the module tree, we get a set of edge C, whose number is $|C| + 1$. Each edge denotes one cut. For any edge of C (A, B), A is the parent module and B is the son node cute from A. The partition result is a table II shown as follows.

Table 2. The Partition result

Slice#	Top module	Parent module
0	x	x
1	SUB	ModuleA
···	x	x
n	x	x

Next, what should be done is to modify the RTL code to achieve the concrete division of the SoC design. This paper uses an example to describe the RTL code modification of the partition method, parting SUB module from ModuleA, shown as Fig.7.

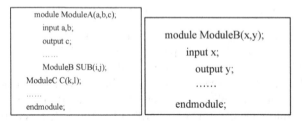

Fig. 7. Example of Source Code

According to the result of partition algorithm C, it needs to divide module SUB from ModuleA. The partition steps shown as follows:

- Find the ports from definition file of sub module and record their names and directions. E.g. SUB is defined in ModuleA and there are two ports, x for inport, y for outport.
- According to the port list of sub module, add port signal in the parent module. The type and size of the ports remain the same as definition in sub-module definition file. But the direction of ports invert. E.g. the port of ModuleB x need to be added to the ModuleA as outport x. While the port of ModuleB y need to be added to the ModuleA as outport y.
- To remove sub-module instantiation statement from definition file of parent module and add some assign statement to connect such two modules.

The code result of partition SUB from ModuleA show as follows.

```
module ModuleA(a,b,c,x,y);
    input a,b;
    output c;
    output x;
    input y;
    ......
    assign x=i;
    assign j=y;
endmodule;
```

Fig. 8. Partition SUB From ModuleA

After the partition, sub module and parent module are allocated into different FPGA chips. The communication between such modules will be handled by specific control module. This paper chooses RocketIO to take over it, the modification of module code need to add the RocketIO module and to assign related signals. The relationship of FPGA chips is shown as follows.

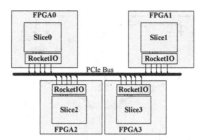

Fig. 9. Packing of Slices

5   Experiment

Although the proposed partition method is generic, we used a specific hardware platform for experiments. The VHDL code of leon3, a SoC design based on SPARC processor [8], is used as the DUT (Device under Test) design and a free, commercially
representative embedded benchmark suite [9] is used to check the speed and accuracy
of the DUT design. During the experiments, a same leon3 is instantiated in the BEE4
FPGA based recognizable platforms acting as a reference.

5.1   Platform

The overview of our Multi-FPGA verification platform is described as Fig. 10. The
verification platform consists of a host computer and a Multi-FPGA platform.

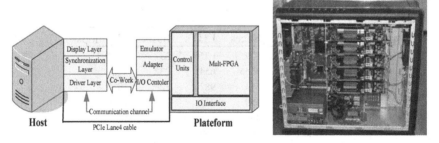

Fig. 10. Structure and photograph of Verification Platform

As a control and display terminal, the host computer is connected with the Multi-
FPGA platform through Molex 74546-040x Series PCIe Lane4 cable that supports
PCIe 2.0 Protocol. EDA software tools such as ISE of Xilinx, ModelSim of Mentor
Graphics and the implementation tool of our partition algorithm are installed on host
computer to assist the verification of DUT.

The Multi-FPGA Platform consists of a backplane and sub-boards. Fig. 11 shows a
photograph of the Multi-FPGA Platform. The relationship between FPGAs is shown
as Fig. 12. The backplane provides a PCIe bus to support the sub-boards. It also in-
stantiates peripheral circuit controller providing with file configuration, operational
control, global clock generation, communication and monitoring functions. Each sub-
board utilizes a Xilinx Virtex5-F1738 LXT serial high-capacity FPGA.

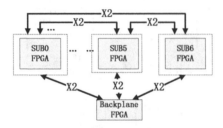

Fig. 11. Commucation Architecure

5.2   Results

To conduct better experiments, it has to choose a DUT design carefully. The leon3 system is a state-of-the-art SoC design based on SPARC V8 architecture. It is complex and large enough to be parted, while its RTL code is open source. The same leon3 system instantiated in the BEE4 FPGA based recognizable platforms runs as a reference.

Due to the capacity of any chip from the experiment platform is enough to hold the DUT design, we manually lower the resource constrains to get more significant effect on the partition. During the system configuration, K is set as (1792,4032,112,3584) that equals to the size of Xilinx Spartan-3A XC2S200A/AN chip. The partial hierarchy and resource demands of the leon3 SoC design are shown in Table 3, and the partition results under configuration above are shown in Table 4.

Table 3. Partial Hierarchy and Resource Demands

Module	Parent	Slices	LUTs	IOBs	Flip-flops
leon3mp	null	5395	9256	337	11478
leon3s	leon3mp	3656	6541	232	8024
ahbctrl	leon3mp	554	982	32	1023
apbctrl	leon3mp	459	812	33	1578
mctrl	leon3mp	432	654	29	546
proc3	leon3s	1647	3495	72	3470
cachemem	leon3s	764	1082	53	1853
fpu0	leon3s	851	962	25	1641
regfile_3p	leon3s	362	902	57	960
...	...	...	...	...	...

To test the speed and accuracy of partitioned leon3, we boots linux-2.6.21.1 on the different environment. Table 5 shows the time consuming results of Linux booting. Simulation on the ModelSim is so slow that we can just guess the theoretical estimation results. The leon3 instantiated in BEE4 platform and UltraSPARC T1, a kind of SPARC V8 ASIC, act as the experiment reference. The experiment of partitioned leon3 runs at a speed of 8 MHz, over 100,000 times faster than software simulation, 1-2 times of the BEE4 platform.

Table 4. Partition Result

FPGA#	Top_module	Paent_module	Slices	LUTs	IOBs	Flip-flops
0	leon3mp	null	1739	2715	105	3454
1	leon3s	leon3mp	1245	1964	107	2701
2	proc3	leon3s	1647	3495	72	3470
3	cachemem	leon3s	764	1082	53	1853
4	null	null	-	-	-	-
5	null	null	-	-	-	-

Table 5. Time to Boot Linux

Platform	Frequency	Time to boot Linux
Software Simulation	10Hz	5.7years
ASIC(UltraSPARC T1)	1000-1400MHz	1second
Our Multi-FPGA	8MHz	360 second
Bee Multi-FPGA	5.4MHz	560second

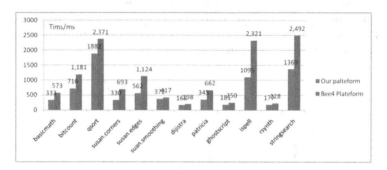

Fig. 12. Structure of Verification Platform

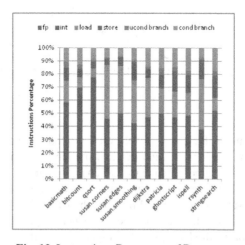

Fig. 13. Instructions Percentage of Programs

For further verification of the effectiveness of this partition method, the free and commercially representative embedded benchmark suite [9] is used to check the speed and accuracy of the leon3. Our experiments pick twelve programs from the packages of Mibench suit.

The twelve programs run both on the Multi-FPGA platform and the BEE4 platform of which the cross-reference results demonstrate the accuracy of the partitioned leon3 on the Multi-FPGA platform. The run time data shown on Fig. 12 demonstrated its speed. It is discovered that different programs have different time rate values between the Multi-FPGA platform and the BEE4 platform. To find the root cause of that phenomenon, this paper tries to analyze the instruction percentage of these programs. We use BCC (Bare-C Cross-Compiler) [10] to compile C/C++ code into instructions and categorize them into five classes: floating point, integer, load, store, unconditional branch and conditional branch. Their statistics percentage is presented in Fig. 13.

At the same time, we calculate the IO instruction (load and store instructions) percentage shown as the IS rate in Fig. 14. Through comparison of instruction rate and time rate, it can figure out certain regularity clearly--higher IO instruction percentage causes higher time rate between the Multi-FPGA platform and the BEE4 platform. It coincides with some previous studies [11], which confirm our partitioning algorithm correctness and effectiveness from another aspect.

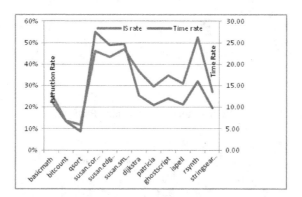

Fig. 14. Comparison Between Instruction Rate and Time Rate

6   Conclusion

In this paper, we focus on RTL code level partition method and provide a universal partition methodology with realistic and detailed implementation. It presents the core partition algorithm whose time complexity is O(n). The simulation of leon3, a SoC design based on SPRC processor, runs at a speed of 8 MHz correctly, over 100,000 times faster than software simulation, 1-2 times of the BEE4 FPGA based recognizable platforms. Experimental results on a number of benchmarks from Mibench demonstrate that this partition method works well on practical application with excellent accuracy and efficiency. The partition method proposed in this paper is generic and can be well applied to large scale IC design verification.

References

1. Krupnova, H., Saucier, G.: FPGA-based emulation: Industrial and custom prototyping solutions. In: Grünbacher, H., Hartenstein, R.W. (eds.) FPL 2000. LNCS, vol. 1896, pp. 68–77. Springer, Heidelberg (2000)
2. Huang, C.Y., Yin, Y.F., Hsu, C.J., Chang, T.M.: SoC HW/SW verification and validation. In: 2011 16th Asia and South Pacific Design Automation Conference (ASP-DAC), pp. 297–300. IEEE (2011)
3. Asaad, S., Bellofatto, R., Brezzo, B., Haymes, C., Kapur, M., Parker, B., ... Tierno, J.: A cycle-accurate, cycle-reproducible multi-FPGA system for accelerating multi-core processor simulation. In: Proceedings of the ACM/SIGDA International Symposium on Field Programmable Gate Arrays, pp. 153–162. ACM (2012)
4. Rothman, J., Chang, C.: BEE technology overview. In: 2012 International Conference on Embedded Computer Systems (SAMOS), p. 277. IEEE (2012)
5. IEEE Std p1364-2001, IEEE Standard Hardware Description Language Based on the Verilog® Hardware Description Language. The Institute of Electrical and Electronics Engineers (2001)
6. Kundu, S., Misra, J.: A linear tree partitioning algorithm. SIAM Journal on Computing 6(1), 151–154 (1977)
7. Blum, M., Floyd, R.W., Pratt, V., Rivest, R.L., Tarjan, R.E.: Time bounds for selection. Journal of Computer and System Sciences 7(4), 448–461 (1973)
8. Gaisler, J.: The LEON processor user's manual. Gaisler Research (2001)
9. Guthaus, M.R., Ringenberg, J.S., Ernst, D., Austin, T.M., Mudge, T., Brown, R.B.: MiBench: A free, commercially representative embedded benchmark suite. In: 2001 IEEE International Workshop on Workload Characterization, WWC-4, pp. 3–14. IEEE (2001)
10. Gaisler, J., Eisele, K.: BCC-Bare-C Cross-Compiler User's Manual. Aeroflex Gaisler AB. Junio (2012)
11. Kring, C., Newton, A.R.: A Cell-Replicating Approach to Minicut-Based Circuit Partitioning. In: ICCAD, pp. 2–5 (1991)

A Novel Node-to-Set Node-Disjoint Fault-Tolerant Routing Strategy in Hypercube

Endong Wang[1,2], Hongwei Wang[1,2], Jicheng Chen[1,2], Weifeng Gong[1,2], and Fan Ni[1,2]

[1] State Key Laboratory of High-end Server& Storage Technology, Beijing, China, 100085
[2] Inspur Group Co., Ltd. Beijing, China, 100085
{wangend,wanghongwei,chenjch,gongwf,nifan}@inspur.com

Abstract. This paper proposes a node-to-set node-disjoint routing algorithm based on a path storage model for the hypercube networks with faulty nodes. Two properties of the storage model are listed in the paper on condition that the n-dimension hypercube has no more than n-1 faulty nodes. The first is that its path length is no more than hamming distance plus 2, and the second is that its sub-cube model can be partitioned from the global model. Based on the model, a novel routing algorithm is brought up to generate node-to-set node-disjoint fault-tolerant path. It adopts divide-and-conquer strategy to take full advantage of the regularity of hypercube. The routing algorithm can reduce the path length to $n + f + 2$ at most and decrease the time complexity to $O(mn)$ in a faulty-node hypercube system(where n is the number of dimensions, m is the number of destination nodes and f is number of faulty nodes). Experiment results show that the average path length is shorten by 9~10% compared with existing algorithms in a ten-dimension hypercube with no more than nine faulty nodes.

Keywords: Interconnection networks, Hypercube networks, disjoint path, Fault tolerance.

1 Introduction

Hypercube topology for parallel computing has received many attentions in recent years due to its recursive structure, efficient routing, and built-in robustness [1-3]. It is widely used in large scale parallel computer systems. For example, Fujitsu K computer has ever ranked first in the TOP500 [4], which includes 548,352 cores with an extending hypercube topology.

A hypercube H_n has 2^n nodes and $n*2^{n-1}$ links. As the system become large, the node or links fault occurs more frequently. Many fault tolerant routing strategies [5, 6, 7] are proposed to reach balance between transmission performance and fault tolerant capability. Attempts to resolve this dilemma have resulted in the development of node-disjoint routing strategy with fault tolerant function such as node-to-node [8, 9], node-to-set[10-13] and set-to-set routing. The node-to-node node-disjoint path routing can be used to avoid congestion, accelerate transmission, and provide alternative paths and the node-to-set node-disjoint path routing has strong fault tolerant ability for multicasting communication. To raise efficiency in networks, the related

J. Wu et al. (Eds.): ACA 2014, CCIS 451, pp. 58–67, 2014.

researches focus on generating paths which have reduced maximal length and minor average length.

Gu [13] described a node-to-node fault-tolerant routing algorithm in hypercube H_n, which returns paths length at most $n+1$ with $O(n)$ time complexity. In ref[14] they proposed a fault-tolerant node-to-set routing algorithm in H_n, which returns paths length at most $n+2$ with $O(|F|n)$ time complexity(requires d(|F|) ≤1, where F is the faulty node set, d operation is to obtain the network diameter of the node set). Bossard [15] proposed a fault-tolerant node-to-set node-disjoint path routing algorithm with $O(n^2)$ time complexity, which adopts the partitioning and mapping operation. Nevertheless, the paper does not consider the average length of paths.

Sinanoglu[9] proposed a method providing node-disjoint paths for node-to-node in fault-free hypercube, Lai[10] proposed an algorithm that optimizes node-disjoint node-to-set routing paths in fault-free hypercube, but they do not refer the hypercube with faulty nodes. Although the paths generated by above two algorithms are relatively short, the paths are fixed and the methods have insufficient flexibility to avoid congestion. Another disadvantage is that the communication would be crashed in the case of that a node in the path fails.

The algorithms stated above are either based on fault-free hypercube, or not optimized sufficiently for reducing paths length. This paper introduces a node-to-set node-disjoint fault-tolerant path routing algorithm based on a novel storage strategy in hypercube. The rest of the paper is organized as follows: In section 2, fault tolerance optimized path length matrix is stated, and the fault tolerant node-disjoint path routing algorithms are presented. In section 3, the analysis of the novel algorithm is showed. The final section is the conclusion.

2   Storage Model and Routing Strategy

The storage model for fault tolerant optimized path is illustrated and two properties follow at first. Subsequently, according to recursive structure of hypercube, a divide-and-conquer routing strategy is stated. Finally, an example is shown.

2.1   A Optimized Path Storage Model

The novel storage model is based on optimized path length, which is defined as follow:

Definition (Optimized path length, OPL) OPL is the number of hops required by the optimized path between two nodes in n-dimensional hypercube H_n having failure nodes. It is formalized as:

$$OPL(u,v) = \begin{cases} 1 & \text{if } u \text{ is neighbor of } v \text{ AND } v \text{ is working} \\ min\{OPL(u\text{'s neighbor, v})\} + 1 & \text{if } \exists\, OPL(u\text{'neighbor of } u, v) < 2^k \\ 2^k & \text{others} \end{cases} \tag{1}$$

Since the formula is based on recursive structure and the health status of each node can be acquired by information exchange method, the OPL can be calculated iteratively. Based on OPL, the optimized path length matrix is listed as following.

$$OPL_{\text{Matrix}}(H_n) = \begin{pmatrix} 2^n & OPL(v_1, v_2) & \cdots & OPL(v_1, v_n) \\ OPL(v_2, v_1) & 2^n & \cdots & OPL(v_2, v_n) \\ \cdots & \cdots & \cdots & \cdots \\ OPL(v_n, v_1) & OPL(v_n, v_2) & \cdots & 2^n \end{pmatrix} \tag{2}$$

For each node pair (u, v), $OPL(u, v)$ and $OPL(v, u)$ are always equal, so the matrix is symmetrical. Based on OPL_{Matrix}, the unicast routing algorithm can be a distributed strategy listed as following steps with $O(n)$ time complexity.

Step 1: Find the node w in node u's neighbors, which meets $OPL(w, u) = 1$ and $OPL(w, v) = OPL(u, v)$-1. (When the number of satisfied nodes is more than one, make an arbitrary choice).

Step 2: Route the message to the node w.

Due to the characteristic of hypercube, the sub matrix of OPL_{Matrix} is derived as:

$$OPL_{\text{sub-Matrix}}(H_k) = \begin{pmatrix} 2^k & OPL(v_1, v_2) & \cdots & OPL(v_1, v_k) \\ OPL(v_2, v_1) & 2^k & \cdots & OPL(v_2, v_k) \\ \cdots & \cdots & \cdots & \cdots \\ OPL(v_k, v_1) & OPL(v_k, v_2) & \cdots & 2^k \end{pmatrix} \tag{3}$$

For H_n with no more than n-1 faulty nodes, OPL_{Matrix} has two properties.

Property 1. In n-dimensions hypercube H_n with no more than n-1 faulty node, the $OPL(u, v)$ in OPL_{Matrix} is no more than $dist(u, v) + 2$, where $dist(u, v)$ is the hamming distance between two nodes.

Proof: in an n-dimensional hypercube H_n, let F be the set of its faulty components. If $|F| < n$, then for any two nodes s and d, there lies a path $P(s, d)$ with Length($P(s, d)$) $\leq$ Hamming $(s, d) + 2$ [14]. It can be concluded from above achievement that the length of the fault free path between nodes (s, d) is at most Hamming$(s, d) + 2$. From optimized path length definition, it is an inherent nature that the OPL_{Matrix} stores the length of the optimized paths between all node pairs. Hence, the elements in OPL_{Matrix} are no more than Hamming $(u, v) + 2$.

Property 2. Hypercube H_k is a sub-cube of H_n, which has f_k ($f_k < k$) faulty nodes, $OPL_{\text{Matrix}}(H_k)$ can be obtained by selecting corresponding rows and columns from $OPL_{\text{Matrix}}(H_n)$.

Proof: It is assumed that H_k' is opposite sub-cube of H_k without faulty node. The length of path from node s via H_k' to node d of H_k is:

$$LP(s,d)_{\text{via } Hk'} = \text{Hamming}(s', d') + \text{Hamming}(s, s') + \text{Hamming}(d, d')$$

$$= \text{Hamming}(s, d) + 2 \tag{4}$$

And by property 1, the maximal length of path in H_k contained by $OPL_{\text{Matrix}}(H_k)$ is:

$$LP(s, d)_{\text{via } Hk} = \text{Hamming}(s, d) + 2. \tag{5}$$

It means that the stored path from s to d in H_k is no longer than LP(s, d) via H_k'. Therefore, sub-matrix OPL$_{Matrix}$(H_k) can be constructed by selecting corresponding rows and columns of OPL$_{Matrix}$(H_n).

In order to further illustrate above properties, two cases of H_5 are shown in figure 1 and figure 2. The bold lines shows one of the optimized paths from node s to the node d in sub-cube H_4, and the dashed lines show a path from node s via H_4' to node d. In figure 1, H_4 and H_4' are two opposite sub-cubes of hypercube H_5 (3 faulty nodes in H_4, and no faulty node in H_4'). The length of optimized path in H_4 from node s to node d is 2 and the length of path via H_4' is 4. Therefore, the OPL(s, d) in the sub matrix OPL$_{Matrix}$(H_4) can be obtained from OPL$_{Matrix}$(H_5). In figure 2, the length of optimized path in H_k from node s to node d is 4 and the optimized path length via H_k' is also 4. It is obvious that the path in H_k is the one of the optimized paths in H_5. That means the values in sub matrix OPL$_{Matrix}$(H_k) can be obtained directly by OPL$_{Matrix}$(H_5).

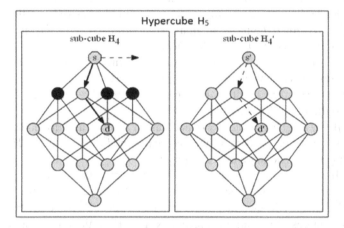

Fig. 1. An example with OPL(s, d) = Hamming(s, d) in sub-cube H_4

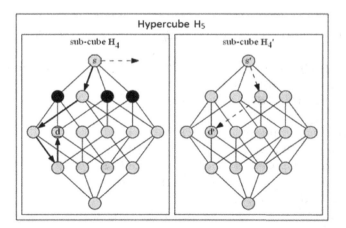

Fig. 2. An example with OPL(s, d) = Hamming(s, d)+2 in sub-cube H_4

2.2 Node-to-Set Routing Algorithm

Based on the storage model, a novel node-to-set node-disjoint fault-tolerant routing algorithm (NNFR for abbreviated) is proposed to reduce the paths length. NNFR is a divide-and-conquer strategy to take full advantage of the regularity of hypercube. The $OPL_{Matirx}(H_n)$ contains all the optimized path information after the initialization. Should the hypercube H_n be divided into sub-cube H_k with f_k ($f_k < k$) faulty nodes, the $OPL_{Sub-Matirx}(H_k)$ could be derived directly. Besides this, $OPL_{Matirx}(H_k)$ is not necessary to be stored independently.

The process of NNFR includes two major steps: hypercube dividing and path making. At first, the hypercube is divided by a dimension i ($0 \le i \le n-1$) into two sub-cubes with lower dimension. One of sub-cubes is called H^0_{n-1} (H^0 for abbreviated) containing the source node s and the other is called H^1_{n-1} (H^1 for abbreviated). Suppose the set of faulty nodes in H_j ($j = 0$ or 1) is called F_j, and the set of destination nodes in H_j is called D_j. Node-disjoint path routing procedure could be derived as following steps.

Step 1: If $|D|=1$, route the message along with optimized path generated by unicast algorithm on $OPL_{Matrix}(H_n)$. NNFR is finished.

Step 2: If $|F| \ge 1$, chooses a dimension to divide H_n into H^0 / H^1 and ensure $|F^1| < n-1$. If $|F|=0$, chooses any dimension to divide H_n into H^0 / H^1.

Step 3: If $D^1=\emptyset$, then partition H^0 repeatedly until $D^1 \ne \emptyset$. When $D^1 \ne \emptyset$, two cases are classified as followings.

Case 1 - If the neighbor node of s (named as s') in H^1 is a faulty node, performs a back-mapping operation to route all the destination nodes of H^1 to H^0. The length of back-mapping paths is no more than 2 in this case.

Case 2 - If s' is a working node, choose a destination node v with minimal OPL (s', v) in D^1, deliver the message from s to s' directly, and unicast it to the node v based on $OPL_{sub-Matrix}(H^1)$, then map the remained nodes in D^1 back into H^0.

After case 1 or case 2 operation, repeat NNFR in H^0 until all the destination nodes are routed. The NNFR could also be expressed by mathematics as follows.

```
Algorithm NNFR(Hₙ, s, D={d₁,…dₖ}, F = {…}, P={Ø})
If |D|=1
   P(d) = P(d)∪{(s,s')} for s' ∈H' s.t. OPL(s, s')=1
       &OPL(s',d)=OPL(s,d)-1
   NNFR (H', s', {d}, F')
End if
Split Hₙ to H⁰ and H¹ s.t. |F¹|<n-1
If ∃ s' s.t. OPL(s',s)=1 & s' ∈ H¹
   select d s.t. OPL(s', d) = min{OPL(s',dᵢ)}
   P(d) = P(d)∪{(s, s')}, D¹ = D¹ - {d}
   NNFR (H¹, s', {d}, F¹)
   For ∀ dᵢ∈ D¹ s.t. OPL (dᵢ,dᵢ')≤2 & dᵢ' ∈ D⁰
      D⁰ = D⁰∪{dᵢ'}
      P(dᵢ) = P(dᵢ)∪{(dᵢ', dᵢ)}
```

```
   NNFR (H⁰, s', D⁰, F⁰)
Else
    For ∀ dᵢ∈ D¹ s.t. OPL (dᵢ, dᵢ')≤2 & dᵢ'∈ D⁰
       D⁰ = D⁰∪{dᵢ'}
       P(dᵢ) = P(dᵢ)∪{(dᵢ',dᵢ)}
    NNFR (H⁰, s', D⁰, F⁰)
End if
```

2.3   An Example

This example shows the procedure of NNFR algorithm in a 5-dimension hypercube H_5. The source node s, the destinations and the faulty nodes are set as following.

$s = 00000$, $D = \{d_1 = 01011, d_2 = 10111, d_3 = 10100\}$

$F = \{f_1 = 10010, f_2 = 10101\}$

Firstly, H_5 is partitioned by dimension 2 (00010) into sub-cube H^0 containing $\{d_3\}$ and sub-cube H^1 containing $\{d_1, d_2\}$. Since s' (Neighbor node of s in H^1, address 00010) is a working node, a routing path is built from s via s' to d_1, and the d_2 (10111) is mapped to d_2' (10100) in H^0 via 00111, then the new $D_0 = \{10100, 00101\}$. The procedure is shown in figure 3.

Secondly, H_4 is partitioned by dimension 1 (00001) into sub-cube H^0 containing $\{10100\}$ and sub-cube H^1 containing $\{00101\}$. Since s' (00001) is a working node, a routing path is built from s via s' to node 00101 in H^1, then the new $D^0 = \{10100\}$. Finally, H^0 is a fault free hypercube, and the destination node 10100 is the last one. A routing path is built from s to node 10100. The second and the final procedures are shown in figure 4.

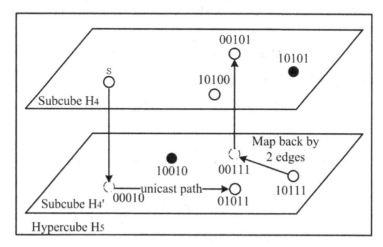

Fig. 3. The first procedure in the example

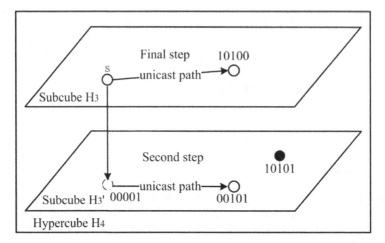

Fig. 4. The second and final procedures in the example

3   Performance Evaluation

In an n-dimensional hypercube H_n with f ($f \leq n$ - 1) faulty nodes, it can be found there lies k ($k \leq n$ - f) fault-free node-disjoint paths connecting k nodes in H^1_{n-1} to H^0_{n-1}, of which the length is no more than 2[15]. The reduction operation will be implemented no more than f times in NNFR. Based on above conclusions, a destination node can be mapped back f times with 2*f length at most.

If the sub-cube H_k of H_n has only one destination node, a unicast path with length no more than k ($k = n$ - f) can be obtained. If the sub-cube H_k of H_n has only more than one destination node, the paths with length n - f + 2 at most can be obtained. Therefore, the maximal path length on H_n with f faulty nodes and m destinations can be represented as:

$$L_{Max}(P) = \text{Max} \ \{2f + (n\text{-}f),\ 2f + (n\text{-}f)+2\}= n + f + 2 \tag{6}$$

For average path length, the upper bound result meets:

$$L\ (P_m) \leq \text{Hamming}(s,\ d_m) + 2 + 2*m \tag{7}$$

And the average length of m paths can be obtained by:

$$L_{Average}(P) = \ \frac{1}{m}\sum_{i=1}^{m}L(P_i) \leq \frac{1}{m}(\sum_{i=1}^{m}\text{hamming}(s,d_i)) + 2 + (1+m)$$

$$= \frac{1}{m}(\sum_{i=1}^{m}\text{hamming}(s,d_i)) + m + 3 \tag{8}$$

As we know, a time complexity of $O(n)$ is required for each cube reduction listed in chapter 2.1, so a time complexity of $O(mn)$ is required for NNFR, where m is the number of destination nodes in H_n.

A H_{10} is created by OPNET tools to give some performance comparisons among Lai's strategy [10], Bossard's algorithm [15] and the novel NNFR method presented in the paper. The experiment contains three steps. Firstly, select d ($d<10$) destinations in the working nodes randomly in H_{10}, and set f ($f = 0$ or $f = 10 - d$) nodes as fault randomly. Secondly, invoke the algorithms to get paths. Finally, analyze the collected data in the network. The collected data is the average paths length from 1000 times experiment.

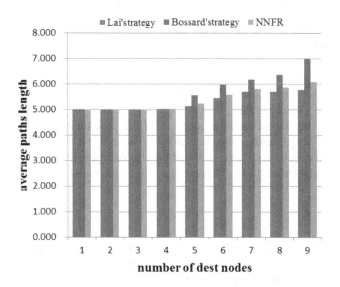

Fig. 5. Average path length comparison with no faulty node on H_{10}

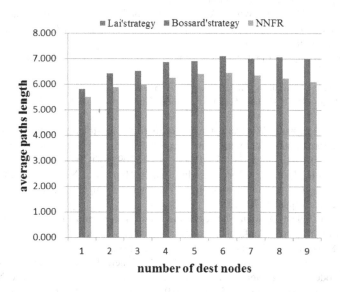

Fig. 6. Average path length comparison with faulty nodes on H_{10}

The node-to-set routing results with no faulty node case (i.e. $f = 0$) are shown in figure 5. It can be seen that the path length of NNFR has about 6% better than Bossard's method and about 4% worse than Lai's strategy.

The node-to-set routing results with faulty nodes case ($f = 10 - d$) are shown in figure 6. It can be seen that the path length of NNFR has about 10% better than Bossard's method while Lai's strategy cannot work in this case. So NNFR can work effectively both in no faulty node and faulty nodes modes.

4   Conclusions

A fault-tolerant node-to-set node-disjoint fault tolerant path routing algorithm is introduced based on an optimized path storage model in hypercube networks. The optimized storage model contains two properties on condition that H_n has no more than n-1 faulty nodes. Based on the model, a NNFR algorithm can effectively reduce the average path length and time complexity of node-to-set node-disjoint system. Experiment results show that there is about 9~10% path length reduction compared with the existing algorithms in H_{10} with no more than nine faulty nodes.

References

1. Lu, S., Yang, X.D.: A Multicast Path Algorithm on Hypercube Interconnection Networks. In: Proceedings of IEEE International Conference on High Performance Computing and Communications, Dalian, China, pp. 641–646 (2008)
2. Duoto, J., Yalamanchili, S., Ni, L.: Interconnection Networks: an Engineering Approach, pp. 149–160. Morgan Kaufmann Publishers (2002)
3. Gao, F., Li, Z.C., Min, Y.H., Wu, J.: A fault-tolerant routing strategy based on extended safety vectors in hypercube multicomputers. Chinese Journal of Computers 23(3), 248–254 (2000) (in Chinese with English abstract)
4. Home TOP500 Supercomputer Sites, http://www.top500.org/ (accessed October 12, 2013)
5. Dasgupta, M., Choudhury, S., Chaki, N.: A Secure Hypercube based Team Multicast Routing Protocols (S-HTMRP). In: Advance Computing Conference, pp. 1265–1269 (2009)
6. Liu, Y., Liu, H., Zhang, Y.: The connectivity of edge-fault-tolerant enhanced hypercube. In: 2011 International Conference on Electric Information and Control Engineering (ICEICE), April 15-17, pp. 805–807 (2011), doi:10.1109/ICEICE.2011.5777262
7. Lu, S., Fan, B.H., Dou, Y.: Clustering Multicast on Hypercube Network. In: Proceedings of IEEE International Conference on High Performance Computing and Communications, Munich, Germany, pp. 61–70 (2006)
8. Qiu, K.: An Efficient Disjoint Shortest Paths Routing Algorithm for the Hypercube. In: 14th IEEE International Conference on Parallel and Distributed Systems, ICPADS 2008, December 8-10, pp. 43–47 (2008), doi:10.1109/ICPADS.2008.119
9. Sinanoglu, O., Karaata, M.H., AlBdaiwi, B.: An Inherently Stabilizing Algorithm for Node-To-Node Routing over All Shortest Node-Disjoint Paths in Hypercube Networks. IEEE Transactions on Computers 59(7), 995–999 (2010), doi:10.1109/TC.2010.76

10. Lai, C.-N.: Optimal Construction of All Shortest Node-Disjoint Paths in Hypercubes with Applications. IEEE Transactions on Parallel and Distributed Systems 23(6), 1129–1134 (2012), doi:10.1109/TPDS.2011.261
11. Zhang, Y., Liu, H.: The Disjoint Paths in Enhanced Hypercube. In: 2010 International Conference of Information Science and Management Engineering (ISME), August 7-8, vol. 1, pp. 54–56 (2010), doi:10.1109/ISME.2010.82
12. Cheng, E., Gao, S., Qiu, K., Shen, Z.: On Disjoint Shortest Paths Routing on the Hypercube. In: Du, D.-Z., Hu, X., Pardalos, P.M. (eds.) COCOA 2009. LNCS, vol. 5573, pp. 375–383. Springer, Heidelberg (2009)
13. Gu, Q., Peng, S.: An Efficient Algorithm for Node-to-node Routing in Hypercubes with Faulty Clusters. The Computer Journal 39(1), 14–19 (1996)
14. Gu, Q., Peng, S.: Node-to-set and Set-to-set Cluster Fault Tolerant Routing in Hypercubes. Parallel Computing 24(8), 1245–1261 (1998)
15. Bossard, A., Kaneko, K., Peng, S.: Fault-Tolerant Node-to-Set Disjoint-Path Routing in Hypercubes. In: Hsu, C.-H., Yang, L.T., Park, J.H., Yeo, S.-S. (eds.) ICA3PP 2010, Part I. LNCS, vol. 6081, pp. 511–519. Springer, Heidelberg (2010)

Filtering and Matching of Data Blocks to Avoid Disk Bottleneck in De-duplication File System

Jiajia Zhang⋆, Xingjun Zhang, Runting Zhao, and Xiaoshe Dong

Department of Computer Science and Technology
Xi'an Jiaotong University, Xi'an 710049, China
xjzhang@mail.xjtu.edu.cn

Abstract. Since the growing scale of data has generated huge redundancy, de-duplication which can eliminate redundancy and improve space utilization of storage device has been widely adopted. De-duplication filesystem can provide a unified interface to the upper application and implement inline de-duplication. In this paper, we design and implement FmdFS, a kernel-space de-duplication filesystem. Due to memory limitation, metadata of FmdFS is stored on disk group. Meanwhile a scale-adaptive binary tree filter is constructed in memory, which not only avoids access to the metadata on disk for searching fingerprints of most new data, but also records the groups where duplicate data is stored. In addition, FmdFS uses LRU hash cache, which holds the metadata group that has been recently accessed, to exploit locality to match the duplicate data to avoid access to the metadata on disk. In comparison with traditional de-duplication filesystems, FmdFS has the higher write performance.

Keywords: De-duplication Filesystem, Scale-adaptive Binary Tree Filter, LRU Hash Cache.

1 Introduction

According to the prediction of IDC [1], the global scale of data will reach 40ZB till 2020. Data redundancy increases progressively as the scale of data grows. De-duplication is a technology that eliminates redundancy among data and improves space utilization of storage device. File system is the most commonly used tool to organize and operate data on the storage, so adding de-duplication technology into the file system is a more general way. In comparison with the traditional de-duplication storage software, de-duplication file system provides a unified interface to the upper application, and eliminates duplicate data in the process of data writing.

⋆ This work was supported by the project of the National Key Technology R&D Program (Grant No.2011BAH04B03), the project of the State 863 Program (Grant No.2012AA01A306), the NSFC project (Grant No.61173039) and the project DE-TERMINE funded under the Marie Curie IRSES Actions of the European Union Seventh Framework Program (EU-FP7 contract nr.318906).

J. Wu et al. (Eds.): ACA 2014, CCIS 451, pp. 68–82, 2014.

Although de-duplication helps improve storage space utilization, it brings performance overhead and scalability issue, which are both research focus. If metadata is stored in memory, de-duplication file system only supports the limited non-duplicate scale of data. In order to support a larger amount of data, many de-duplication system store metadata on disk. As the access speed of disk is much slower than memory, how to manage metadata, and how to try to avoid disk access, are both primary issues to solve performance bottleneck.

In addition, most traditional de-duplication file systems (e.g. SDFS [2],LessFS [3], ZFS [4],) are implemented as user-space file system, thus each I/O operation requires multiple system calls. However, frequent switching between user state and kernel state will affect the performance of the file system.

In this paper, we design and implement FmdFS, a kernel-space file system which supports inline de-duplication. FmdFS can avoid the drawbacks of user-space file system. FmdFS has two features:

Filter of data blocks: A scale-adaptive binary tree filter is constructed in the memory, and each node of scale-adaptive binary tree filter is a Bloom Filter. They and can avoids access to the metadata on disk for searching fingerprints of most new data blocks.

Match of data block: In order to reduce seek time, data block and its metadata are stored in the same group. Disk group where duplicate data blocks are stored can be located through scale-adaptive binary tree filter, which records the group paths of duplicate data blocks. LRU hash cache exploits data locality, thus if there is duplicate data in a disk group, fingerprint table of the group will be mapped into LRU hash cache. If the LRU hash cache is full, the fingerprint of the group which has not been hit for the longest time will be covered.

The remainder of the paper proceeds as follows. In section 2, we present the design of FmdFS as a de-duplication file system. Section 3 introduces the filter and match of data blocks in FmdFS. In section 4, the implementation and test results of FmdFS is presented. Section 5 is the related work. In section 6, we conclude this paper.

2   FmdFS Design

FmdFS is a kernel-space file system which supports inline de-duplication, and is an improvement and extension of traditional Ext2 file system. Data block is the basic unit of data transmission of Linux. The principle of FmdFS implementing de-duplication is as follow. First calculate a MD5 [13] fingerprint(unique identification of data block) for every data block in the kernel-space memory, and then determine whether the data block is duplicate on the basis of the fingerprint. Modify references of blocks which are detected as duplicate and point their block pointers to existing duplicate blocks on disk, then abandon the duplicate data block in the memory. If the data block is not duplicate one, FmdFS allocates disk block space for the data block, then updates metadata and stores the data block on the disk.

The MD5 fingerprint consists of 128 bits, assuming random fingerprint with a uniform distribution, a collection of n different data blocks, the probability p that there will be one or more collisions:

$$P \leq \frac{n(n-1)}{2} * 2^{-128}. \tag{1}$$

FmdFS designed by this paper supports for 2TB. If the block size is 4KB, 2^{29} different data blocks will be stored, so the probability of a collision is less than 2^{-71}. Because of the extra-low probability, we ignore it and use the MD5 fingerprint as a unique identification for a block.

Due to memory limitation, the metadata (fingerprint and reference count of a duplicate data block) for de-duplication is stored on disk by group. Reference count represents times which the block is pointed by data block pointer. In order to reduce seek time, data block and its metadata are stored in the same group.Fig.1 shows disk structure of FmdFS, and the fingerprint table and reference count table is proprietary of FmdFS. The N-th entry in fingerprint table is the fingerprint of the N-th data block of the group. The structure of reference count table is similar to the fingerprint table. And if a data block is deleted, and only when the reference count is 0, the data block is really deleted. When a data block is stored on disk, FmdFS updates fingerprint and reference count on disk.

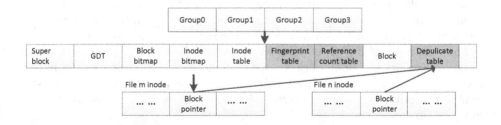

Fig. 1. Disk structure of FmdFS

Fig.2 shows the flow chart of write data block of FmdFS. In this figure, the fingerprint calculation module is used to calculate the fingerprints of data blocks. FmdFS block allocation strategy is used to map the duplicate data blocks. File metadata manager module is similar to that of Ext2. FmdFS metadata manager module is used to store and operate metadata of data blocks in FmdFS. Status manager of page and block buffer module is used to control the status of page and block buffer in kernel.

The main challenge of FmdFS is looking up address of the duplicate data block. After the fingerprint of a data block is calculated, we use scale-adaptive binary tree filter to reducing accessing to the fingerprint table on disk and locate group of duplicate data block. Then LRU hash cache holds fingerprints and

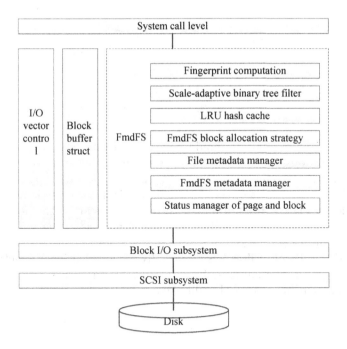

Fig. 2. Framework of FmdFS

addresses of data blocks which have been accessed or will be accessed. If a data block is found in LRU hash cache, we will read corresponding fingerprint table into fingerprint hash table to find the data block. Scale-adaptive binary tree filter, LRU hash cache and fingerprint hash table will be explained in detail in section 3.

3   Data Block Filtering and Matching

Each node of Scale-adaptive binary tree filter is a Bloom Filter. Scale-adaptive binary tree filter has two main functions. Firstly, it can avoid fingerprints of most new data blocks accessing to metadata on disk; Secondly, disk group where duplicate data blocks are stored can be located through scale-adaptive binary tree filter, duplicate data blocks can be accurately matched in LRU hash cache.

3.1   Bloom Filter

Data structure of Bloom Filter is a bit array of m bits, which represents a set. There are k mutually independent hash functions, each of which maps to one of the m array positions. When Bloom Filter contains 0 element, all bits are set to 0. As shown in Fig.3, it represents set x, y, z. In this figure, $m = 17, k = 3$.

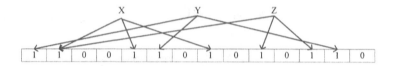

Fig. 3. Bloom Filter

When adding an element, it should be fed to each of the k hash functions to get k array positions, and set the bits at these positions to 1. When query for an element, fed it to each of the k hash functions to get k array positions. If any of bits at these positions is 0, the determination is negative and the element is definitely not in the set. If all of bits at these positions are 1, the determination is positive and there is a probability that the element is in the set. However if the element isnt actually in the set, the determination is false positive.

Assume that a Bloom Filter has k mutually independent hash functions, and value of every hash function is uniform distribution in m bits array. When the set contains n elements, the probability that a certain bit is 1:

$$1 - (1 - \frac{1}{m})^{kn}. \tag{2}$$

Adding the next element, the false positive rate:

$$(1 - [1 - \frac{1}{m}]^{kn})^k. \tag{3}$$

When n is sufficiently large, formula (3) is approximately given as:

$$(1 - e^{-\frac{nk}{m}})^k. \tag{4}$$

Via formula (4) we can determine the number of hash functions in every of Bloom Filter of scale-adaptive binary tree filter.

3.2   Binary Tree Filter

Each leaf node of scale-adaptive binary tree filter corresponds to disk group. The N-th leaf node corresponds to the N-th group. If FmdFS supports N groups, the height of binary tree filter is $logN$, shown in Fig.4. Assume that the number of levels of binary tree filter is h, then:

$$h = \lceil logN \rceil + 1. \tag{5}$$

When fingerprint of a data block is coming, FmdFS needs to determine whether the data block is a duplicate one on the basis of the fingerprint. Feed fingerprint of the data block to root filter, if the determination is positive, then feed the fingerprint to the child node filter. If the determination is negative, no

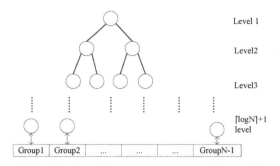

Fig. 4. Binary tree filter

longer feed the fingerprint its left and right child node filterand so forth, till complete the depth-first traversal of the binary tree filter.

If a data block is new, the probability of traversing out a path from root to leaf is very low. When a new data block is written on disk, fingerprint of the data block should be inserted in the corresponding filter. Firstly, insert the fingerprint in the leaf node filter corresponding to this group of the data block, then insert the fingerprint in parent node filter of this leafand so forth till the fingerprint is inserted in the root node. Fig.5 shows that a new data block A, which is stored in 4th group, is inserted in a four-level binary tree filter.

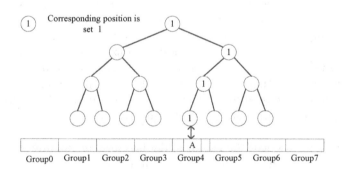

Fig. 5. Insert a new data block A

If there is a path from root to leaf, the block is very likely to be stored in the group corresponding to this leaf. Fig.6 shows a process of looking up a duplicated data block B in four-level binary tree filter, and that block B has been stored in the 3th group.

Because the number of elements contained in each level filter, from the root to the leaf nodes, progressively reduces, so length of each level filter progressively shortens to save memory. In order to accurately locate the disk group where

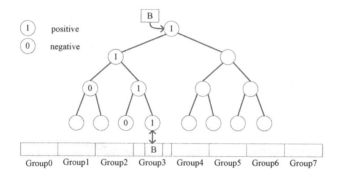

Fig. 6. Look up duplicate data block B

the duplicate data blocks are stored, and to avoid unnecessary disk access, false positive rate in the last level of binary tree filter shouldnt be too low, and so the length of the last level of the filter should be large enough.

3.3   Number of Hash Functions

To reduce the false positive rate, number of hash functions of every level filter should be appropriate. Formula (4) expresses the false positive rate. Next, find the minimum value of formula (4).

Assume that $(1 - e^{-\frac{nx}{m}})^x$ and $y = \frac{nx}{m}$, then find the minimum value of the function $f(y) = (1 - e^{-y})^y$. Fig.7 shows graph of function $f(y)$. when $y = -ln\frac{1}{2}$, that is to say, $x = -\frac{m}{n}ln\frac{1}{2}$, function $f(y)$ gets the minimum value.

Due to memory limitation, the length of Bloom filter m is not enough large, Fig.7 shows that when $k=1$ the false positive rate gets the minimum value. Namely, every filter has only one hash function. Every level of binary tree filter uses the same hash function. Since the MD5 algorithm has good randomness, a MD5 fingerprint can be used for four level filters. If one MD5 fingerprint is not enough, compute fingerprint of the fingerprint, until the number of fingerprints is enough.

As previously mentioned, the length of the last level of the filter shouldnt be too short, so the number of hash functions will also change.

3.4   Scale-adaptive Binary Tree Filter

Because the scale of FmdFS expands progressively, some node filters of binary tree filter only work until the system reaches a certain scale. According to this feature, binary tree filter can be constructed adaptively.

When a new data group is created, FmdFS allocates the leaf node filter corresponding to this group, and then determine whether parent node filter of this leaf exists. If it does not exist, FmdFS allocates the node filter. Then determine whether parent node filter of this node existsand so forth till the

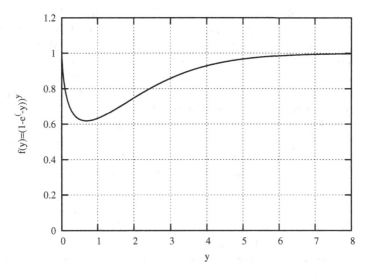

Fig. 7. Graph of function $f(y) = (1 - e^{-y})^y$

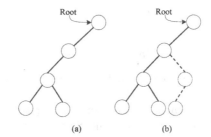

Fig. 8. Construction of the binary tree filter

parent node filter exists. Assume that binary tree filter has four levels; the third group will be created. Fig.8(a) shows the state of adaptive binary tree filter before the third group is created, and Fig.8(b) shows the state after the third group is created, the dotted circle represents binary node filter which is just allocated. Figure 8 shows the construction of the binary tree filter. Figure (a) is the state of self-adaptive binary tree filter before the third group is created, and figure (b) is the state of self-adaptive binary tree filter after the third group is created. Scale-adaptive binary tree filter saves memory usage to a great extent.

3.5 LRU Hash Cache

LRU hash cache is designed based on the locality of duplicate data stream. Locality means that if there is duplicate data in a disk group, other data within this group is also likely duplicate. If there is duplicate data in a disk group, insert fingerprint table of the group into LRU hash cache. Before looking up fingerprint table on disk to find a fingerprint, the fingerprint first looks up LRU hash cache to find it. If the cache is hit, the disk access is avoided.

If a block obtains a path from root to leaf by traversing binary tree filter, looks up LRU hash cache to find its fingerprint. If the cache is hit, LRU list of hash cache should be updated. If the cache is not hit, fingerprint table of the group corresponding to the leaf should be inserted into fingerprint hash table. If fingerprint of the data block is not found in in the fingerprint hash table, it means that the false positive happens in the last level filter. Afterwards, the fingerprint returns to binary tree filter, and seeks for the second path from root to leafand so forth. When obtaining three paths, the maximum false positive rate is:

$$P_{h-1}P_h^3(h = \lceil logN \rceil + 1). \tag{6}$$

In the formula (6), P_i is the false positive rate of the i-level node filter.

Each entry of fingerprint hash table consists of the fingerprint and disk address of data block. Fingerprint hash table uses quadratic probing. $h_1(k)$ is the first hash function, and k represents the fingerprint of data block. $h_2(k,i)$ is the second hash function, and m represents the number of entries of fingerprint hash table, $i = 1, 2, m - 1$.

$$h_1 = k\%m. \tag{7}$$

$$h_2 = (h_1(k) + i^2)\%m. \tag{8}$$

If a fingerprint is found in a certain fingerprint hash table, the fingerprint hash table should be inserted into LRU hash cache.

Each entry of LRU hash cache consists of the fingerprint, disk address and the group number of data block. When the fingerprint hash table is inserted into LRU hash cache, LRU hash cache uses quadratic probing similar to the above. There are two cases. If LRU hash cache is not full, the group number of the fingerprint hash table should be added to head of LRU list. If LRU hash cache is full, the tail of LRU list should be deleted, and the group number of the fingerprint hash table is added to head of LRU list.

4   Implementation and Experiments

FmdFS designed by this paper supports for 2TB of non-duplicate data. When the block size is 4KB, FmdFS consists of 2^{14} groups. The number of binary tree filter levels is 15 under formula (5). m_i represents the array length in i-th level of the filter, and k_i represents the number of hash functions in i-th level of the filter. Under the section 3.2 and section 3.3, their values are as follow:$m_1 = 2^{30}, k_1 = 1, m_2 = 2^{29}, k_2 = 1, m_3 = 2^{28}, k_3 = 1, m_4 = 2^{27}, k_4 = 1, m_5 = 2^{26}, k_5 = 1, m_6 = 2^{25}, k_6 = 1, m_7 = 2^{24}, k_7 = 1, m_8 = 2^{23}, k_8 = 1, m_9 = 2^{22}, k_9 = 1, m_{10} = 2^{21}, k_{10} = 1, m_{11} = 2^{20}, k_{11} = 1, m_{12} = 2^{19}, k_{12} = 1, m_{13} = 2^{18}, k_{13} = 1, m_{14} = 2^{17}, k_{14} = 1, m_{15} = 2^{17}, k_{15} = 3.$

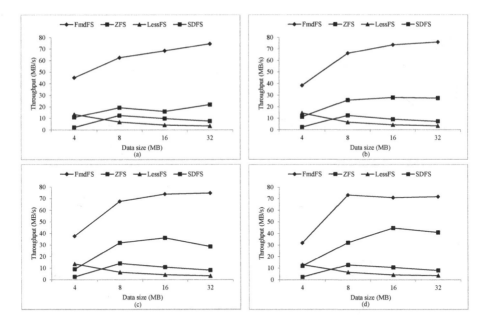

Fig. 9. Write non-duplicate data performances of each file system

When the scale of non-duplicate data reaches 2TB, 2048MB of memory is occupied by the scale-adaptive binary tree filter.

FmdFS is loaded as a module into the kernel, when writing data to the file system, the kernel enters into FmdFS through function defined by file operations table.

Implementation environment of FmdFS is as follow, operating system Ubuntu11.10, kernel version Linux 2.6.34, CPU Intel Pentium dual-core E5800 @3.20GHz, memory 3GB, disk 7200 revolutions per minute.

The following experiment tests write throughputs of each file system. Test program firstly generates b MB data, and then calls the write function to write the data into files. It costs t seconds from the beginning of writing till that all data is written to disk. Then the write throughput is:

$$T = b/t. \tag{9}$$

Fig.9 shows write throughputs of each file system when data stream doesnt consist of duplicate data. In Fig.9, the abscissa indicates the size (MB) of data written in file system, and the ordinate indicates the throughputs(MB/s) of each file system. Figure a, b, c, d respectively represents the results when the writing data unit is 4kb, 8kb, 16kb, 32kb. In this experiment LessFS uses Berkeley DB. Fig.9 shows that performance of FmdFS is vastly superior to ZFS, LessFS, and SDFS. The cause of this result is that when judging whether a fingerprint is one of a new data block, FmdFS avoids accessing metadata from disk, and the times of switching between user state and kernel state are less in the FmdFS.

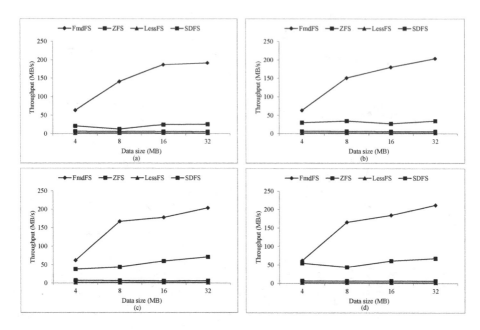

Fig. 10. Write duplicate and localized data performances of each file system

Fig.10 shows write throughputs of each file system when writing duplicate data stream. In Fig.10, the abscissa indicates the size (MB) of data written in file system, and the ordinate indicates the throughputs (MB/s) of each file system. Figure a, b, c, d respectively represents the results when the writing data unit is 4kb, 8kb, 16kb, 32kb. In this experiment LessFS uses Berkeley DB. Fig.10 shows that when writing duplicate data stream, the performance of FmdFS is vastly superior to ZFS, LessFS, and SDFS. The cause of this result is that LRU hash cache of FmdFS holds fingerprints and addresses of data blocks to avoid disk access of duplicate data blocks, and the times of switching between user state and kernel state are less in the FmdFS.

As the scale of data of the system grows, false positive rate of binary tree filter increases. In the case, some duplicate data blocks cannot be detected, and searching fingerprints of new data blocks will lead to disk access of fingerprint table. The following experiment test shows the false positive rate changes with growth of the system scale.

Fig.11 shows the test of false positive rate of non-duplicate data blocks with the increasing the scale of data. Experiment method: write new data blocks to FmdFS with a disk group containing 32000 data blocks. We record the false positive rate of data blocks when the scale of data increases. Data set: Each data block will be numbered sequentially from the No.0 upward. The serial number is stored in the first byte of the data block, and the remaining bytes are set to 0.

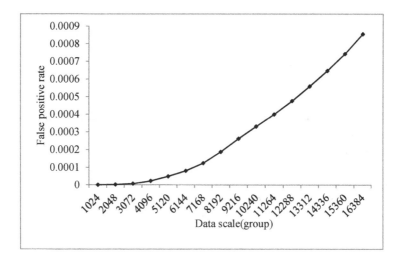

Fig. 11. Overall false positive rate of non-duplicate data blocks

In Fig.11, the abscissa indicates the different scale of data in file system, and the ordinate indicates the overall false positive rate in FmdFS. This figure shows the overall false positive rate of non-duplicate data blocks in the different scale of data. This figure indicates that although the overall false positive rate increases with the increasing scale of data, but when the scale of data reaches the maximum, the overall false positive rate is still less than 0.001. Less false positive rate leads to less disk access times. Thus, when writing non-duplicate data into FmdFS, there is little chance of accessing the metadata on disk. Even with the increase scale of data, FmdFS can still have a high performance when writing non-duplicate data.

Fig.12 shows the test of false positive number of duplicate data blocks with the increasing scale of data. Experiment method: rewrite the data of last group into FmdFS in the different scale of data, and then test the false positive number when writing duplicate data blocks.

In Fig.12, the abscissa indicates the different scale of data in file system, and the ordinate indicates the false positive number of duplicate data blocks in a group. The figure shows the false positive number of duplicate data blocks in the last group of the different scale of data. Because LRU hash cache pre-reads the metadata of the group which contains the duplicate data, if the group which contains duplicate data is hit then the remaining duplicate data blocks in the group can be hit. In the figure, before hitting the group of duplicate data, there are few (one or two in the figure, it depends on the data used) duplicate data blocks misjudged as new blocks. On the basis of this figure, we can calculate that overall false positive rate of duplicate data blocks is about 0.00003. Less false positive rate leads to less disk access times. Even with the increase scale of data, FmdFS can still have a high performance when writing duplicate data.

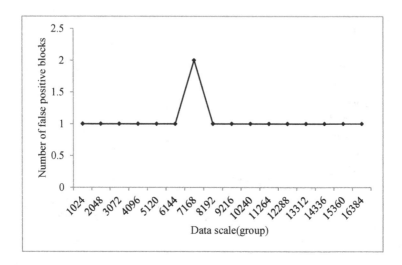

Fig. 12. False positive number of duplicate data blocks

5 Related Work

SDFS [1] is an open source de-duplication file system on the basis of FUSE. The metadata of de-duplication is stored in memory to obtain higher performance. SDFS provides flexible storage strategy, and data through de-duplication is stored n the local node, the remote node, or cloud. In addition, SDFS provides a snapshot function of file or folder.

LessFS [1] is a high performance inline data de-duplication file system for Linux. Meanwhile, LessFS is an open source file system on the basis of FUSE. LessFS supports de-duplication of fixed block, and uses database to store the metadata of de-duplication.

ZFS [1] is an open source file system designed by Sun Microsystems. The features of ZFS include protection against data corruption, support for high storage capacities, efficient data compression and so on. Meanwhile, ZFS supports de-duplication.

Some systems have been implemented to solve the issues of data scalability and performance overhead, including file systems and backup systems. The major systems are listed as follows.

Venti [5] is the first archival storage system which introduces the technology of data de-duplication. Because of the memory limitation, the index of data blocks is implemented using a disk-resident hash table. When search the fingerprint of a data block, the system firstly needs to go through the index cache; and if the index cache is not hit, disk accesses are needed. Though the striping technique is used, such disk accesses still degrade performance of the system. FmdFS uses binary tree filter and LRU cache to avoid most disk accesses of duplicate data blocks and non-duplicate data blocks.

Data Domain [6]is a backup product which supports inline de-duplication from EMC, it uses Bloom Filter algorithm to reduce disk accesses when look up the fingerprints of new data blocks. BloomStore [7] propose efficient key-value store on flash with a Bloom Filter based index structure so that a small RAM space can support a large number of key-value pairs. But because there is only one Bloom Filter in Data Domain and Bloom Filter, the false positive rate of Bloom Filter will be higher with the increase of data. FmdFS uses binary tree filter, including multi Bloom Filter, even when the amount of data reaches a certain size, it can still reduce most of the disk access to look up fingerprints of new data blocks.

Sparse indexing [1] is also a backup system; it first breaks up an incoming stream into relatively large segments. When a data stream is written, only the fingerprints of large segments which is similar to this data stream are kept in RAM. Extreme Binning [9] stores the fingerprints of every data block stored on the disk. When a new file is backed up, the system first select the representative data block, then find out whether the fingerprint of the representative data block exists. If it exits, the system only de-duplicate within the file which contains this block. Sparse indexing and Extreme Binning both de-duplicate according to the similarity of sampling; and if the sampling is not accurate, the de-duplication rate and the performance of system will be affected. FmdFS de-duplicates within the global scope, and it will make global judgment for every data block through binary tree filter, which acquires higher de-duplication rate than Sparse indexing and Extreme Binning.

Flash memory does not have latencies of hard drives and perform well in random access, thus it has become a choice used for improving de-duplication performance. SAR [11] [12] effectively exploits the high random-read performance properties of SSDs and the unique data-sharing characteristic of deduplication-based storage systems by storing in SSDs the unique data chunks with high reference count, small size, and non-sequential characteristics. In BloomStore [7], index structure and key-value pairs are stored compactly on flash memory to improve its performance. Chunkstash [12] builds up an index table in memory, so only one flash memory access is required for each query. But query for fingerprints in flash still requires flash memory access, which doesnt advantage over the operations performed in memory. Besides, flash memory is high in cost.

6   Conclusions

In this paper, we have designed and implemented FmdFS, a kernel-space de-duplication file system. First we illustrate the difference between FmdFS and the traditional file system. Then we propose a scale-adaptive binary tree filter, which not only avoids fingerprints of most new data blocks accessing to metadata on disk, but also records the group where duplicate data blocks are stored. And then analyze the false positive rate of scale-adaptive binary tree filter. Whats more, we exploit data locality to propose LRU hash cache. Via these methods, FmdFS reduces tremendously the frequency of disk accesses. Experimental results show that FmdFS has a high write performance, particularly when the data stream is duplicate. When the scale of data of the system reaches the maximum, the overall false positive rate of non-duplicate data blocks is less than 0.001,and that of duplicate data blocks about 0.00003. Less false positive rate leads to less disk access times. Even with the increase scale of data, FmdFS can still have a high performance when writing duplicate or non-duplicate data.

In the future, in order to improve the comprehensive performance of FmdFS, the read performance will be investigated.

References

1. Gantz, J., Reinsel, D.: The digital universe in 2020: Big data, bigger digital shadows, and biggest growth in the far east. IDC iView: IDC Analyze the Future (2012)
2. Opendedup (2013), http://www.opendedup.org
3. LessFS (2013), http://www.lessfs.com
4. Rodeh, O., Teperman, A.: zFS-a scalable distributed file system using object disks. In: Proceedings of the 20th IEEE/11th NASA Goddard Conference on Mass Storage Systems and Technologies (MSST 2003), pp. 207–218. IEEE (2003)
5. Quinlan, S., Dorward, S.: Venti: A New Approach to Archival Storage. In: FAST, vol. 2, pp. 89–101 (2002)
6. Zhu, B., Li, K., Patterson, R.H.: Avoiding the Disk Bottleneck in the Data Domain Deduplication File System. In: Fast, vol. 8, pp. 1–14 (2008)
7. Lu, G., Nam, Y.J., Du, D.H.: BloomStore: Bloom-filter based memory-efficient key-value store for indexing of data deduplication on flash. In: 2012 IEEE 28th Symposium on Mass Storage Systems and Technologies (MSST), pp. 1–11. IEEE (2012)
8. Lillibridge, M., Eshghi, K., Bhagwat, D., Deolalikar, V., Trezis, G., Camble, P.: Sparse Indexing: Large Scale, Inline Deduplication Using Sampling and Locality. In: Fast, vol. 9, pp. 111–123 (2009)
9. Bhagwat, D., Eshghi, K., Long, D.D., Lillibridge, M.: Extreme binning: Scalable, parallel deduplication for chunk-based file backup. In: IEEE International Symposium on Modeling, Analysis & Simulation of Computer and Telecommunication Systems, MASCOTS 2009, pp. 1–9. IEEE (2009)
10. Mao, B., Jiang, H., Wu, S., Fu, Y., Tian, L.: Read-performance optimization for deduplication-based storage systems in the cloud. ACM Transactions on Storage (TOS) 10(2), 6 (2014)
11. Mao, B., Jiang, H., Wu, S., Fu, Y., Tian, L.: SAR: SSD Assisted Restore Optimization for Deduplication-Based Storage Systems in the Cloud. In: 2012 IEEE 7th International Conference on Networking, Architecture and Storage (NAS), pp. 328–337. IEEE (2012)
12. Debnath, B., Sengupta, S., Li, J.: ChunkStash: speeding up inline storage deduplication using flash memory. In: Proceedings of the 2010 USENIX Conference on USENIX Annual Technical Conference, p. 16. USENIX Association (2010)
13. Rivest, R.: The MD5 message-digest algorithm (1992)

Performance Optimization of a CFD Application on Intel Multicore and Manycore Architectures

Yonggang Che*, Lilun Zhang, Yongxian Wang, Chuanfu Xu,
Wei Liu, and Xinghua Cheng

Science and Technology on Parallel and Distributed Processing Laboratory
National University of Defense Technology, Changsha, China
ygche@nudt.edu.cn

Abstract. This paper reports our experience optimizing the performance of a high-order and high accurate Computational Fluid Dynamics (CFD) application (HOSTA) on the state of art multicore processor and the emerging Intel Many Integrated Core (MIC) coprocessor. We focus on effective loop vectorization and memory access optimization. A series techniques, including data structure transformations, procedure inlining, compiler SIMDization, OpenMP loop collapsing, and the use of Huge Pages, are explored. Detailed execution time and event counts from Performance Monitoring Units are measured. The results show that our optimizations have improved the performance of HOSTA by 1.61× on a two Intel Sandy Bridge processors based computer node and 1.97× on a Intel Knights Corner coprocessor, the public MIC product. The microarchitecture level effects of these optimizations are also discussed.

Keywords: Computational Fluid Dynamics, multicore, manycore, performance optimization, performance analysis.

1 Introduction

Computational Fluid Dynamics (CFD) is a technology that uses complex mathematics to create computer simulations, with the goal of better understanding fluid related problems. It is one of the grand challenge application areas of High Performance Computing (HPC). As HPC hardware is progressing rapidly, there is a consensus that significantly new CFD algorithms and software are required to exploit emerging hardware capabilities [1].

Current processor designs continue to grow towards ever-increasing numbers of cores. Almost all general purpose processors have multiple cores on a chip now. As a key strategy toward Exascale Computing (10^{18} calculations per second), Intel proposed the Many Integrated Core (MIC) architecture and released the product, the Knights Corner (KNC) coprocessor [2]. By integrating 50+ cores on one chip and the usage of 512-bit Vector Processing Unit (VPU), a KNC coprocessor provides a peak floating-point performance of over 1 Tflop/s in double precision (DP). The advancement of the hardware also increases the difficulties of efficient HPC application development, since the applications must be carefully

---

* Corresponding author.

J. Wu et al. (Eds.): ACA 2014, CCIS 451, pp. 83–97, 2014.
© Springer-Verlag Berlin Heidelberg 2014

optimized to exploit the plenty of architecture features. HOSTA [3,4] is a CFD application with high-order and high accurate feature that has been successfully applied to a wide range of flow simulations. We address the techniques to optimize the performance of HOSTA for Intel multicore and manycore architectures in this paper. Based on the characteristics of the application code, a series of optimization techniques are applied. We perform detailed performance evaluation and show up a speedup of 1.61× on a Intel Xeon E5 Sandy Bridge processor based computer node and a speedup of 1.97× on an Intel KNC coprocessor over the previously optimized version. Our major contributions are:

- We apply a series transformation techniques to the HOSTA code based on the analysis of its data structures and computations patterns. These techniques effectively improved HOSTA's performance, both on Intel multicore processor and Intel MIC coprocessor. They can also be extended to other applications on Intel multicore and manycore architectures.
- With the microarchitectural level data from the hardware counters, we are able to uncover the architectural effects of the optimization transformations used. This helps to identify the performance bottlenecks and opportunities of future optimization.

The rest of this paper is organized as follows: Section 2 introduces the background of Intel multicore architecture, Intel MIC architecture and the HOSTA application. Section 3 introduces our performance optimization techniques applied to HOSTA code. Section 4 describes the performance evaluation methods and the results. Section 5 presents a short conclusion.

2 Background

2.1 Intel Multicore and Manycore Architectures

Currently, all HPC systems are using general-purpose multicore processors, mostly from Intel, AMD and IBM. In the top500 supercomputers list [5] published on October 2013, 94 percent of the systems use general purpose processors with six or more cores. More than half (307) systems from the list are using the Intel Xeon E5 Sandy Bridge processors [6]. Sandy Bridge is a general-purpose processor microarchitecture that offers many features for high performance computing and was first released in 2011. Each Sandy Bridge chip contains 2 to 8 cores. Each core has a separate 32 KB L1 instruction cache and a separate 32 KB L1 data cache, and also a unified 256 KB L2 cache. A bi-directional 32-byte ring connects the cores, the LLC (Last Level Cache), the QPI (Quick Path Interconnect) agent and the integrated memory controller.

Meanwhile, as a strategy toward Exascale Computing, Intel announced the MIC architecture at the 2010 International Supercomputing Conference. On December 2012, Intel released the first MIC product, the Knights Corner coprocessor, under the Intel Xeon Phi brand [2]. KNC combines 57 to 61 Intel CPU cores on a single chip. Each core is a modified P54C-design in-order execution core. Each core can execute two instructions per clock cycle. Each core is capable of supporting 4 hardware threads, resulting in 200+ hardware threads per coprocessor. Each core has a private L2 cache that is kept fully coherent by a globally-distributed tag directory. The memory controllers and the PCIe client logic provide a direct interface to the GDDR5 memory and the PCIe bus, respectively. All these components are connected together by a bidirectional ring. An important component of the KNC core is its Vector Processing Unit (VPU), which features a 512-bit SIMD instruction set. The VPU supports Fused Multiply-Add (FMA) instructions and can execute 32 SP or 16 DP floating point operations per cycle. A KNC coprocessor provides over 1 Tflop/s floating-point DP performance on a single card, with a power consumption within 300 watts.

The MIC architecture provides general-purpose programming environments similar to that of the Intel Xeon processor[7,8]. Currently, a MIC coprocessor is used as an accelerator connected to a general-purpose processor based node through the PCIe bus. It is able to run a full service Linux OS and application codes written in standard programming languages like FORTRAN, C/C++. The parallel programming of the MIC can be made by using industry-standard parallel programming techniques like OpenMP, POSIX threads, or MPI. As a result, application performance optimization on MIC coprocessors will also benefit the application performance when runs on Intel Xeon processors. Intel also provides middleware to manage data transfers between the processor and coprocessor. The high performance, power-efficiency and easy to programming features have made MIC attractive for the HPC community. Vendors are releasing MIC based servers and large scale computers. In the top500 supercomputers list [5] published on November 2013, the Tianhe-2 (No. 1) and the Stampede (No. 7) are equipped with MIC coprocessors. While the peak performance of the MIC architecture is attractive, the performance achieved by real applications are more desirable. Intel has demonstrated the high performance that can be obtained on MIC architecture with some math kernels and the Linpack. However, few works have been done to demonstrate the effectiveness of using MIC coprocessors to accelerate large scale applications. Performance engineering of real world applications on the MIC architecture makes sense to the HPC community.

2.2 The HOSTA Application

HOSTA is a high-order and high accurate CFD application initially developed by the State Key Laboratory of Aerodynamics of China. It solves the time-dependent and time-independent Navier-Stokes equations on multi-block structured grids based on the Weighted Compact Nonlinear Schemes (WCNS) [3,4] proposed by Xiaogang Deng et al. The governing equations are discretized by using the finite difference methods (FDM). The unique feature of HOSTA is its ability to solve flow problems with complex grids. It has been successfully applied to a wide range of flow simulations. HOSTA is parallelized in hybrid MPI/OpenMP programming model with about 25000 lines of Fortran-90 code. At the MPI level, each process is assigned one or more distinct grid blocks. For the calculations within each block, OpenMP parallelism is utilized.

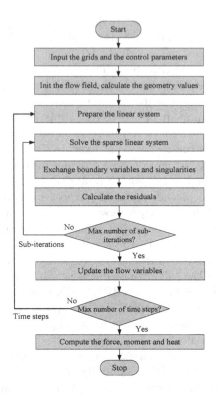

Fig. 1. The high-level flow chart of HOSTA. The figure shows the case for steady state flow computation. In case of unsteady state flow computation, the linear system preparation and flow variables updating will be enclosed in the sub-iteration loop.

Fig. 1 shows the high-level flow chart of HOSTA. HOSTA spends most of its runtime in the time step loop. Each time step includes the following phases: 1) Preparing the linear system. This phase includes operations to set the boundary conditions, to exchange the boundary variables and singular variables, to fill corners and to calculate the inviscid and viscid flux. A large fraction of runtime is spent on the inviscid and viscid flux calculations. 2) Solving the sparse linear system. This phase also takes a large fraction of runtime. 3) Exchanging of boundary variables and singular variables. This involves communication among processes that have neighboring grid blocks and common singular points. 4) Calculating the residuals, which involves global reduction operations. We have applied several techniques to optimize HOSTA's performance in our previous work [9]. These optimizations include defining critical arguments into constant parameters to enable specific compiler optimizations, multi-level data buffering to enable better memory access, and loop transformations to optimize the memory access performance. Performance evaluation showed a uniprocessor performance improvement of 22.2% to 28.9% over the original version on a Intel Xeon X5670 processor. The optimized version of HOSTA is the baseline in this paper.

3   Optimizing HOSTA

A series of performance optimizations techniques are applied to the HOSTA code. We detail these techniques in this section.

3.1   Data Structure Transformations

HOSTA is a multi-block structured grids based CFD application. Its main data structures are hierarchically defined as user defined structures. In the baseline HOSTA code, the main data structures are defined as the follows. At the lowest level, a fld_array structure is defined as:

```
type fld_array
  integer(kind_int) :: fldtype
  real(kind_real),pointer :: r3d(:,:,:)
end type fld_array
```

where the three dimensions of r3d determine the indices of the three axes. Based on fld_array, a structure var_block is defined as:

```
type var_block
  character(len=len_char_name) :: varname
  type(fld_array), pointer :: fld(:)
end type var_block
```

Then the actual data structures are defined as follows, where different elements of the arrays point to different blocks:

```
type(var_block), pointer :: mb_qc(:)     ! conservation variables
type(var_block), pointer :: mb_pv(:)     ! primitive variables
type(var_block), pointer :: mb_vol(:)    ! grid jacobian
type(var_block), pointer :: mb_sxyz(:)   ! grid derivatives
type(var_block), pointer :: mb_dpv(:)    ! speed and temperature gradient
...
```

Such data structures correspond naturally to the variables stored on multi-block structured grids. For example, mb_pv(NB)%fld(1)%r3d(I,J,K) stores the first primitive variable at the coordinate point (I,J,K) of the NB-th block. We take as example the subroutine that calculate the viscid flux to show the access patterns of these data structures, as shown in Fig. 2. We omit a lot of other lines of code and focus the access patterns of the data structures of mb_pv and mb_dpv. We use several ";" separated states in a single line to save space.

As can be seen from Fig. 2, for the upper data structures, the data accesses of the two inner most loops encounter large stride. Further, the three-tier data structures require more instructions to resolve in the execution. So we transform the thee-tier data structure into two-tier data structure. First, we change the two tiers data structures fld_array and var_block into a one tier structure by defining a new var_block as follows:

```
type var_block
  character(len=len_char_name) :: varname
  integer(kind_int) :: fldtype
  real(kind_real), dimension(:,:,:,:), pointer :: r4d
end type var_block
```

```
real, pointer:: vn(:,:),ve(:,:); real :: kx,ky,kz,ex,ey,ez,cx,cy,cz
type(fld_array), pointer :: dpv(:),pv(:)
dpv => mb_dpv(nb)%fld; pv => mb_pv(nb)%fld
! I-direction
!$OMP parallel private(vn,ve,...)
....
!$OMP do
  do k=kMIN,kMAX; do j=jMIN,jMAX
    do i=iMIN,iMAX
      do m=4,15
        vn(i,m) = dpv(m-3)%r3d(i,j,k)
      end do
      vn(i,16) = vis; vn(i,17) = kcp; vn(i,18) = pv(2)%r3d(i,j,k)
      vn(i,19) = pv(3)%r3d(i,j,k); vn(i,20) = pv(4)%r3d(i,j,k)
    end do
    call sub_intplt(vn,ve,...)
    do i=iMIN,iMAX
      kx = ve(i,1); ky = ve(i,2); kz = ve(i,3)
      call flux_vis(kx,ky,kz,...)
    end do
  end do; end do
!$OMP end do nowait
!$OMP end parallel


! J-direction
!OMP parallel private(vn,ve,...)
...
!$OMP do
  do k=kMIN,kMAX; do i=iMIN,iMAX
    do j=jMIN,jMAX
      do m=4,15
        vn(j,m) = dpv(m-3)%r3d(i,j,k)
      end do
      vn(j,16) = vis; vn(j,17) = kcp; vn(j,18) = pv(2)%r3d(i,j,k)
      vn(j,19) = pv(3)%r3d(i,j,k);  vn(j,20) = pv(4)%r3d(i,j,k)
    end do
    call sub_intplt(vn,ve,...)
    do j=jMIN,jMAX
      ex = ve(i,1); ey = ve(i,2); ez = ve(i,3)
      call flux_vis(ex,ey,ez,...)
    end do
  end do; end do
!$OMP end do nowait
!$OMP end parallel


! K-direction
!$OMP parallel private(vn,ve,...)
...
!$OMP do
  do j= jMIN,jMAX; do i= iMIN,iMAX
    do k=kMIN,kMAX
      do m=4,15
        vn(k,m) = dpv(m-3)%r3d(i,j,k)
      end do
      vn(k,16) = vis; vn(k,17) = kcp; vn(k,18) = pv(2)%r3d(i,j,k)
      vn(k,19) = pv(3)%r3d(i,j,k); vn(k,20) = pv(4)%r3d(i,j,k)
    end do
    call sub_intplt(vn,ve,...)
    do k=kMIN,kMAX
      cx = ve(k,1); cy = ve(k,2); cz = ve(k,3)
      call flux_vis(cx,cy,cz,...)
    end do
  end do; end do
!$OMP end do nowait
!$OMP end parallel
```

Fig. 2. Code extracted from the baseline viscid flux calculating subroutine

where the left most three dimensions of r4d determine the indices of the three
axes, and the right most dimension of r4d determines the variable. Then the
actual data structures are defined as follows, where different elements of the
arrays point to different blocks:

```
type(var_block), pointer :: mb_qc(:)     ! conservation variables
type(var_block), pointer :: mb_pv(:)     ! primitive variables
type(var_block), pointer :: mb_vol(:)    ! grid jacobian
type(var_block), pointer :: mb_dpv(:)    ! speed and temperature gradient
...
```

The form of the actual data structures seems not changed but the structure that they point to has changed. These new data structures will facilitate our later optimizations. As most parts of HOSTA uses these data, data structure transformations involve a large amount of work. After data structure transformations, the previous code changes into the following form shown in Fig. 3 (to save space, only the code for I-direction is shown):

```
real, pointer:: vn(:,:),ve(:,:); real ::kx,ky,kz,ex,ey,ez,cx,cy,cz
type(fld_array), pointer :: dpv(:),pv(:)
dpv  => mb_dpv(nb)%fld; pv   => mb_pv(nb)%fld
!I-direction
!$OMP parallel private(vn,...)
...
!$OMP do
do k=kMIN,kMAX; do j=jMIN,jMAX
    do i=iMIN,iMAX
      do m=4,15
        vn(i,m) = dpv(i,j,k,m-3)
      end do
      vn(i,16) = vis; vn(i,17) = kcp; vn(i,18) = pv(i,j,k,2)
      vn(i,19) = pv(i,j,k,3); vn(i,20) = pv(i,j,k,4)
    end do
    call sub_intplt(vn,ve,...)
    do i=iMIN,iMAX
      kx = ve(i,1); ky = ve(i,2); kz = ve(i,3)
      call flux_vis(kx,ky,kz,...)
    end do
end do; end do
!$OMP end do nowait
...
!$OMP end parallel
```

Fig. 3. The code from the viscid flux calculating subroutine after data structure transformation (only code for I-direction is shown)

3.2 Code Transformation to Enable Better Vectorization

Effective utilization of vector instructions is crucial on both Intel multicore and manycore architecture. Using the low level programming methods (e.g. the compiler Intrinsics) is not practical since HOSTA is programmed in Fortran and the code size is large. We are intended to enable the compiler to identify vectorization opportunities and generate vector instructions automatically. In the code shown in Fig. 3, simply vectorize the inner most loop (the do m loop) is less optimal since only a small fraction of computations is vectorized. It is better to vectorize the second inner most loop. Since the vectorization is better to be applied to the innermost loop of a nest [10], we fully unrolled these "do m" loops.

Vectorization of loop also requires that there are no function or subroutine calls except intrinsic math functions in the loop. The Intel Fortran compiler supports using "DIR$ ATTRIBUTES FORCEINLINE" directive to enable compiler automatic inline. However, when we tried to use this directive for the subroutines (e.g. flux_vis in Fig. 3) in the innermost loops, the Intel Fortran compiler fails to vectorize these innermost loops, even when the !dir$ SIMD directive is

placed before these loops to enforce automatic vectorization. So we have manually inlined the subroutine in the innermost loops. Fig. 4 shows the transformed
code of Fig. 3 as an example of our vectorization optimizations.

```
real,pointer:: vn(:,:),ve(:,:); real :: kx,ky,kz,ex,ey,ez,cx,cy,cz
type(fld_array), pointer :: dpv(:),pv(:)
   dpv => mb_dpv(nb)%fld; pv  => mb_pv(nb)%fld
! I-direction
...
!$OMP parallel private(vn,)
...
!$OMP do
      do k=kMIN,kMAX; do j=jMIN,jMAX
!DIR$ SIMD LINEAR(i:1)
        do i=iMIN,iMAX
            vn(i,4 ) =dpv(i,j,k,1 )
            vn(i,5 ) =dpv(i,j,k,2 )
            ...
            vn(i,15) =dpv(i,j,k,12)
            vn(i,16) = vis
            vn(i,17) = kcp
            vn(i,18) = pv(i,j,k,2)
            vn(i,19) = pv(i,j,k,3)
            vn(i,20) = pv(i,j,k,4)
        end do
        call sub_intplt(vn,ve,)
!DIR$ SIMD LINEAR(i:1)
        do i=iMIN,iMAX
            kx = ve(i,1)
            ky = ve(i,2)
            kz = ve(i,3)
            {code for the inlined subroutine flux_vis}
        end do
      ...
      end do;  end do
!$OMP end do nowait ... !$OMP end parallel
```

Fig. 4. The code after transformations to enable vectorization

While the code for J-direction and K-direction are vectorized in much the
same way as for I-direction, there are some differences. In the vectorized loops in
code for I-direction, the access strides to array dpv and array pv are 1. However,
in the vectorized loops in code for J-direction and K-direction, the access strides
to array dpv and array pv are much larger, as J and K are not the left most
dimensions of these arrays. This may negatively affect the vectorization performance. Based our test, vectorizing the code for J-direction and K-direction also
improves the performance despite such effects.

In some circumstances, we have to permute some adjacent loops to enable
better vectorization. Fig. 5 shows an example. The code shown in Fig. 5 (a) is
extracted from the subroutine that calculates the viscid flux (after data structure
transformation). We permute loop m and loop i, and fully unroll the loop m, as
shown in Fig. 5 (b). While the access strides to array rhs and array dn increase
from 1 to large numbers, the code in Fig. 5 (b) performs better than the code
in Fig. 5 (a).

3.3   Using Collapse Clause to Optimize OpenMP Parallelism

The OpenMP 3.0 specification provides the collapse clause to combine multiple closely nested loops into one. If more than one loop is associated with the
loop construct, then the iterations of all associated loops are collapsed into one
larger iteration space which is then divided according to the schedule clause.

```
do m=1,neqn
do i=1,ni
  rhs(i,j,k,m)=rhs(i,j,k,m)+re*dn(i,m)
end do
end do
```
(a)The original loop nest

```
!dir$ SIMD LINEAR(i:1)
do i=1,ni
  rhs(i,j,k,1)=rhs(i,j,k,1)+re*dn(i,1)
  rhs(i,j,k,2)=rhs(i,j,k,2)+re*dn(i,2)
  rhs(i,j,k,3)=rhs(i,j,k,3)+re*dn(i,3)
  rhs(i,j,k,4)=rhs(i,j,k,4)+re*dn(i,4)
  rhs(i,j,k,5)=rhs(i,j,k,5)+re*dn(i,5)
end do
```
(b)permuted and fully unrolled loop

Fig. 5. Loop permutation to enable better vectorization

Collapsing increases the iteration space and is considered to be more efficient than nested parallel regions. We have tried to use the collapse clause for HOSTA's OpenMP loops wherever is applicable. We find that in HOSTA, all key loop nests in the linear system preparation, the inviscid and viscid flux calculations, and the residual calculations can be collapsed. However, the collapse clause cannot be applied to any of the OpenMP loops in the subroutines for the sparse linear system solution due to data dependencies.

3.4 Using Huge Pages

On modern processors, access to the memory must be mapped from virtual to physical address, and reading the page table every time can be costly. Translation Look aside Buffer (TLB) is used to cache the virtual to physical address mappings. When a TLB miss occurs, the page tables must be searched for the correct mapping. Larger page size means that a TLB cache of the same size can keep track of larger amounts of memory, hence reduces the costly TLB misses and memory allocation overhead. The KNC coprocessor has a two-level TLB and two page sizes (4KB and 2MB). By default programs use 4K pages, in which the L2 TLB acts as a page table cache and reduces the L1 TLB miss penalty to around 25 clock cycles. It also support large (2 MB) pages, in which the L2 TLB acts as a standard TLB, and the L1 miss penalty is only around 8 cycles. To enable HOSTA to use the Huge Pages on KNC, the libhugetlbfs [11] is used. From our test, this evidently improves the performance.

The SNB processor also supports the default page size (4KB) and larger page size (2MB). However, it seems that enabling Huge Paging on SNB will not improve the performance of HOSTA. So Huge Pages is not enabled when we test the performance of HOSTA on SNB.

4 Performance Evaluation

4.1 Experimental Platforms

The performance evaluation is done on a computer node based on two eight-core Intel Xeon E5-2670 processors, with one KNC coprocessor attached to the node through the PCIe bus. The setup of the two platforms is shown in Table 1.

Table 1. The hardware and software setup of the experimental platforms

Items	KNC	SNB
Code name	Intel Xeon Phi 3110P	Intel Xeon E5-2670
Cores	57	8
Clock rate	1.1 GHz	2.60 GHz
DP Peak	1003.2 GFlop/s	332.8 GFlop/s
L1 cache	32/32 KB per core	32/32 KB per core
L2 cache	512 KB per core	256 KB per core
L3 cache	none	20 MB
Vector width	512Bit	256Bit (AVX)
Memory	6GB GDDR5 (ECC on)	48GB DDR3 (ECC on)
Memory bandwidth	240 GB/s	102.4 GB/s
OS	Intel MSPP release 2.1	RedHat Linux Server 6.1
Compiler	Intel composer XE 2013.0.079	
Compiler switches	-mmic -O3 -ipo -no-prec-div -fno-alias -align array64byte	-O3 -AVX -ipo -no-prec-div -fno-alias -align array32byte

For the performance measurement on SNB, the target application runs exclusively on the host node. The Hyper-Threading (HT) feature of SNB is disabled through the BIOS, as HOSTA is a CPU-intensive HPC application that does not benefit from HT technology. For the performance measurement on KNC, all applications run exclusively in native model on the single KNC card. Huge Pages is enabled with the libhugetlbfs when test of the performance of the optimized version of HOSTA. We have disabled most of the KNC's power and frequency settings by setting the "PowerManagement" field to "cpufreq_off; corec6_off; pc3_off; pc6_off" in the configure file. This will reduce the performance fluctuation across different runs for the same application configuration.

4.2   Application Configuration

The baseline version and the optimized version of the HOSTA are used in the experiment. In the test, the floating-point data type used in HOSTA is double precision. The test case is the viscous flow around the naca0012 airfoil. The velocity and the pressure of the whole flow field are calculated. The original mesh of the naca0012 airfoil has a single block with 940576 grid cells, 1000100 grid points. For this mesh, HOSTA consumes about 1.7 GB memory when runs with 1 process. For MPI parallelization, an off-line repartition tool is used to partition the mesh into multiple blocks before the test. Load balance can be achieved by near evenly partitioning the grid points to each MPI process. We should note that after the partition, the total number of the cells of the mesh remains the same, but the total number of the grid points of the mesh will increase slightly with the number of processes. When 64 MPI processes are used, the total number of grid points of the mesh is 1064000, 6.4% more than the original one. As HOSTA is discretized by using the FDM, the increase in the number of grid points will also increase the number of calculations proportionally.

4.3   Runtime Comparison

In real-world simulation, HOSTA will converge after tens of thousands time steps and most of the runtime is spent on the time step loops. The performance of the time step loops is of primary concern. So the runtime of 10 "pure" time steps instead of the whole application is reported here. The number of sub-steps in each time step is 12. As for the OpenMP thread affinity, the OpenMP affinity variable is not set on SNB and is set as "KMP_AFFINITY=compact,1" on KNC, based our performance test.

Fig. 6 shows the runtime in seconds of 10 time steps of the two versions of HOSTA codes for different MPI / OpenMP configurations on SNB, where the horizontal axis is the number of OpenMP threads per MPI rank. The legend "1P" represents 1 process, "2P" presents 2 processes, and so forth. Since the HT feature of SNB processor is turned off, there are only 16 physical threads on a SNB node. So the maximum number of threads per process is set to 16. As shown in Fig. 6 (a), the baseline version spends a runtime of 536.10 seconds when it runs with a single thread (1 process / 1 thread) on SNB. The shortest runtime is achieved when the application runs with 4 processes and each process has 4 threads, where the runtime is 38.30 seconds. The maximum parallel speedup obtained on a SNB node over a single thread is 14.00. As shown in Fig. 6 (b), the optimized version spends a runtime of 305.83 seconds when it runs with a single thread on SNB. The shortest runtime is also achieved when the application runs with 4 processes and each process has 4 threads, where the runtime is 23.77 seconds. The maximum parallel speedup obtained on a SNB node over a single thread is 12.87.

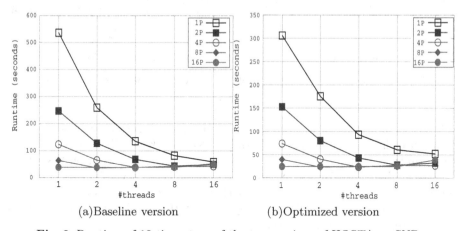

(a)Baseline version   (b)Optimized version

Fig. 6. Runtime of 10 time steps of the two versions of HOSTA on SNB

Fig. 7 shows the runtime in seconds of 10 time steps of two versions of HOSTA codes for different MPI / OpenMP configurations on KNC. While there are 57 cores on the KNC coprocessor used in this experiment, using only 56 cores may achieve better performance because one core is reserved for the OS and services. So the numbers of OpenMP threads per MPI rank used in the test not only include 1, 2, 4, ..., 128, but also include 7, 14, 28, 56 and 112. As shown in Fig. 7 (a), the baseline version of HOSTA spends a runtime of 7759.72 seconds when it runs with a single thread on KNC. The shortest runtime is achieved when the application runs with 32 processes and each process has 7 threads, where the runtime is 171.38 seconds. The maximum parallel speedup obtained on a coprocessor over a single thread is 45.28. As shown in Fig. 7 (b),the optimized version of HOSTA spends a runtime of 4054.47 seconds when it runs with a single thread on KNC. This compares sharply with the single thread runtime on SNB. The shortest runtime is achieved when the application runs with 32 processes and each process has 8 threads, where the runtime is 86.87 seconds. The maximum parallel speedup obtained on a coprocessor over a single thread is 46.67.

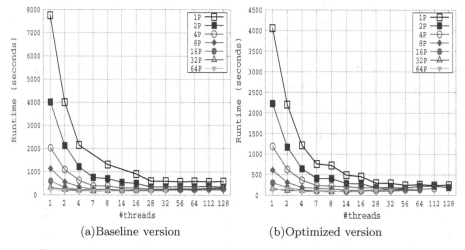

(a)Baseline version   (b)Optimized version

Fig. 7. Runtime of 10 time steps of the two versions of HOSTA on KNC

From the above data, we see that the performance improvement of our optimization techniques is significant both on SNB and KNC. For a single thread, the optimized version runs 1.75× faster on SNB and 1.91× faster on KNC than the baseline version. For the maximum performance on a whole SNB node, the optimized version is about 1.61× faster than the baseline version. For the maximum performance on a whole KNC coprocessor, the optimized version is about 1.97× faster than the baseline version.

4.4   Microarchitecture Performance Analysis

To further investigate the interaction of the application and the underlying architectures, and to reveal the reasons of the performance improvement of our performance optimization techniques, we go into the microarchitecture level. Both SNB and KNC have on chip Performance Monitoring Units (PMUs) to facilitate collecting microarchitecture level performance data. A series of PMU events on the KNC and SNB are measured with the Intel Vtune [12], a powerful profiling tool that can collect hardware performance data through the on chip PMUs. To facility the performance analysis and to avoid the effect of parallel scalability difference, we only measure the microarchitecture level performance of the serial (single thread) code.

Table 2 shows the number of event counts of the baseline code and the optimized code on SNB. The description of the PMU events on SNB can be found in Intel 64 and IA-32 Architectures Software Developer's Manual [13]. The ratios of the event counts of the optimized code divided by the event counts of the baseline code are also provided. The data in table 2 clearly show the effects of the optimization techniques to the microarchitecture. The number of 256-bit AVX instructions increases for more than 2.0× and most of the floating-point operations are performed by AVX instructions in the optimized code. The number of packed SSE instructions also increases for more than 4.6×. This verifies that the optimized code makes much better use of the vector instructions. The number of loads and the number of stores are also significantly reduced as a result of the data structure transformation. The number of instructions is reduced by more than one half, whose reasons include that less number of floating instructions are executed because the more efficient usage of the AVX instructions and packed SSE instructions, accessing the two-tier data structures requires less instructions, and the reduced instructions as a result of loop unrolling and subroutine inline. The number of branches and the number of mispredicted branches are reduced owing to the loop unrolling and subroutine inlining optimizations. However, the number of LLC misses increases in the optimized code. The reason is that the loop permutations applied (see 3.2) have increased the memory access strides of some arrays. The cost of DTLB misses and also increases for the same reason. The number of LLC misses is much smaller as compared with the number of loads and stores. The cost of DTLB misses is also much smaller as compared with the total number of CPU clocks. So their negative effects to the performance are limited.

Table 2. Number of event counts in K for the two versions of codes on SNB

Events	Baseline	Optimized	Ratio
INST_RETIRED.ANY	1936208000	873492000	0.4511
CPU_CLK_UNHALTED.THREAD	1378612000	809870000	0.5875
MEM_UOPS_RETIRED.ALL_LOADS	697216000	318528000	0.4569
MEM_UOPS_RETIRED.ALL_STORES	197840000	100760000	0.5093
MEM_LOAD_UOPS_RETIRED.LLC_MISS	1436800	2280600	1.5873
MEM_LOAD_UOPS_RETIRED.LLC_HIT	2993200	2175600	0.7268
FP_COMP_OPS_EXE.X87	2600000	2704000	1.0400
FP_COMP_OPS_EXE.SSE_PACKED_DOUBLE	2216000	10232000	4.6173
FP_COMP_OPS_EXE.SSE_SCALAR_DOUBLE	346072000	61896000	0.1789
SIMD_FP_256.PACKED_DOUBLE	53816000	118536000	2.2026
BR_INST_EXEC.ALL_BRANCHES	77627200	45203200	0.5823
BR_MISP_EXEC.ALL_BRANCHES	122400	69600	0.5686
DTLB_STORE_MISSES.WALK_DURATION	6272000	7520000	1.1990
DTLB_LOAD_MISSES.WALK_DURATION	51976000	108408000	2.0857

Table 3. Number of event counts in K for the two versions of codes on KNC

Events	Baseline	Optimized	Ratio
INSTRUCTIONS_EXECUTED	3205984809	1163881746	0.3630
CPU_CLK_UNHALTED	8465052698	4818967228	0.5693
BRANCHES	155070465	112860339	0.7278
BRANCHES_MISPREDICTED	43020129	28710086	0.6674
DATA_PAGE_WALK	28080084	27540083	0.9808
LONG_DATA_PAGE_WALK	3060009	4410013	1.4412
DATA_READ	833762501	331740995	0.3979
DATA_READ_MISS	17550053	17910054	1.0205
DATA_WRITE	237600713	95310286	0.4011
DATA_WRITE_MISS	6030018	7200022	1.1940
L2_DATA_READ_MISS_MEM_FILL	5580017	6750020	1.2097
L2_DATA_WRITE_MISS_MEM_FILL	2790008	1800005	0.6452
VPU_ELEMENTS_ACTIVE	7687373062	3293109879	0.4284
VPU_INSTRUCTIONS_EXECUTED	1493104479	570601712	0.3822

Table 3 shows the number of event counts of the baseline code and the optimized code on KNC. The description of these PMU events can be found in the Intel Xeon Phi Coprocessor PMU document [14]. The ratios of the event counts of the optimized code divided by the event counts of the baseline code are provided, too. We see that the number of memory data reads committed by L1 cache, the number of memory data writes committed by L1 cache are significantly reduced. This is the result of the data structure transformations. The number of branches and the number of branch miss-predictions are significantly reduced owing to the loop unrolling and subroutine inline transformations. The number of instructions is also significantly reduced. Contrary to the circumstance on SNB, it seems that the number of VPU instructions and the cumulative number of elements active for VPU instructions issued are also significantly reduced. The reason is that about half instructions on KNC are executed by the VPU. As the number of instructions is greatly reduced, the number of VPU instructions is also reduced. The number of memory read accesses that miss the internal data cache and the number of memory write accesses that miss the internal data cache increase slightly, the reason is the loop permutations applied (see 3.2) have increased the memory access strides of some arrays. The number of "long" data page walks, the data read accesses that missed the L2 cache and were satisfied by main memory increases slightly. However, the number of data write accesses that missed the L2 cache and were satisfied by main memory is reduced. Overall, the optimized code costs much less CPU clocks.

5   Conclusion

This paper reports our experience optimizing HOSTA, a high-order and high accurate CFD application, for Intel multicore processors and the MIC coprocessors. The focused subject is the effective usage of the vector instructions, memory access optimizations and the improvement of the parallelism. A series of techniques are explored based on the characteristics of the application code. Detailed performance evaluation is performed on a two Intel Xeon E5 Sandy

Bridge processors based computer node and an Intel Knights Corner coprocessor. The results show that our optimization techniques have improved the performance of HOSTA by 1.61X on the computer node and by 1.97X on the coprocessor. The microarchitectural level performance data are measured and analyzed, which shows the interaction of the application and the underlying architectures, reveals the reasons of the performance improvement of our performance optimization techniques. The less hoped for is that the performance on a KNC coprocessor is not comparable to that on a SNB node, both before and after the optimization. This indicates that the MIC architecture should be improved to provide a better performance for such real-world CFD applications.

Acknowledgments. The authors would like to thank Huayong Liu from the State Key Laboratory of Aerodynamics of China for his help. This work was partially supported by the National Natural Science Foundation of China under Grant No. 60603055 and 11272352.

References

1. Slotnick, J., Khodadoust, A., Alonso, J., et al.: CFD Vision 2030 Study: A Path to Revolutionary Computational Aerosciences. Prepared for NASA Langley Research Center, Hampton, Virginia (2013)
2. Intel Corporation: Many Integrated Core (MIC) Architecture (2012)
3. Deng, X., Jiang, Y., Mao, M., et al.: Developing hybrid celledge and cell-node dissipative compact scheme for complex geometry flows. In: The Ninth Asian Computational Fluid Dynamics Conference (2012)
4. Deng, X., Jiang, Y., Mao, M., et al.: High-order and high accurate CFD methods and their applications for complex grid problems. Commun. Comput. Phys. 11, 1081–1102 (2012)
5. Top500 Supercomputers sites, http://www.top500.org (accessed December 19, 2013)
6. David, K.: Intel's Sandy Bridge Microarchitecture (2010)
7. Jim, J., James, R.: Intel Xeon Phi Coprocessor High Performance Programming. Morgan Kaufmann Press (2013)
8. Intel Corporation: An Overview of Programming for Intel Xeon rocessors and Intel Xeon Phi coprocessors. Technical report (2012)
9. Che, Y., Zhang, L., Wang, Y., et al.: Uniprocessor Performance Tuning of a tructured Grid based Parallel CFD Application. In: Annual Conference on High Performance Computing of China, Zhangjiajie, China, pp. 39–46 (2012) (in Chinese)
10. Intel Corporation: A Guide to Vectorization with Intel C++ Compilers (2012)
11. Nikolay, S.: Enabling Huge Paging on MIC with libhugetlbfs library. Technical report, Intel Corporation (2012)
12. Intel Vtune Amplifier 2013 XE, http://www.intel.com/software/products/vtune (accessed September 12, 2013)
13. Intel Corporation: Intel 64 and IA-32 Architectures Software Developer's Manual Combined Volumes (2013)
14. Intel Corporation: Intel Xeon Phi Coprocessor (codename: Knights Corner) Performance Monitoring Units. Revision 1.01 (2012)

A Throughput-Aware Analytical Performance Model for GPU Applications

Zhidan Hu, Guangming Liu, and Wenrui Dong

College of Computer, National University of Defense Technology Hunan, China
{Huzd,liugm,dongwr}@nscc-tj.gov.cn .

Abstract. Graphics processing units (GPUs) have shown increased popularity in general-purpose parallel processing. This massively parallel architecture allows GPUs to execute tens of thousands of threads in parallel to solve heavily data-parallel problems efficiently. However, despite the tremendous computing power, optimizing GPU kernels to achieve high performance is still a challenge due to the sea change from CPU to GPU and lacking of tools for programming and performance analysis.

In this paper, we propose a throughput-aware analytical model to estimate the performance of GPU kernels and optimizations. We construct a pipeline for global memory access servicing and redefine the compute throughput and memory throughput as the speed of memory requests arriving and leaving the pipeline. Based on concluding the kernel throughput limiting factor, GPU programs are classified into compute-bound and memory-bound categories and then we predict performance for each category. Besides, our model can provide useful information on the direction of optimization and predict the potential performance benefits. We demonstrate our model on a manually written benchmark as well as the matrix-multiply kernel and show that the geometric mean of absolute error of our model is less than 6.5%.

Keywords: GPU, compute-bound, memory-bound, performance prediction, performance bottleneck.

1 Introduction

In recent years, the ceiling of high performance computing has been updated multiple times by the GPU-based heterogeneous systems [1]. The GPU architecture has garnered wide popularity since the increasing programmability and the ever friendly programming model. Even though hardware is providing high performance computing, implementing and optimizing parallel programs to take full advantage of the potential computing power still remains a big challenge.

Several programming languages have been proposed to reduce programmer's burden in porting parallel applications to GPUs such as Brook++ [2], CUDA [3], and OpenCL [4]. However, even with these newly developed programming languages, programming and optimizing programs to achieve better performance is still time-consuming and error prone.

J. Wu et al. (Eds.): ACA 2014, CCIS 451, pp. 98–112, 2014.
© Springer-Verlag Berlin Heidelberg 2014

To provide insight into performance bottlenecks in massively parallel architectures, especially GPU architectures, we propose a simple analytical model. The model can be used statically without executing a GPU application. The basic intuition of our analytical model is that the ability to hide long latency memory operations with interleaving executions of computation from different thread warps can be obtained based on the warp level parallelism of both computations and memory operations. By constructing the memory pipeline model and extending the concept of compute throughput, we classify GPU applications into compute-bound and memory-bound categories, and then we estimate the execution time for each category.

We evaluate our analytical model based on the CUDA programming model, which is specific for the CUDA-enabled NVIDIA GPUs. We compare the results of our analytical model with the actual execution time collected on the NVIDIA GPUs. Our results show that the geometric mean of absolute error of our model is less than 6.5%.

The contributions of our work can be concluded as follows:

- We construct the memory pipeline model and extract the memory throughput based on capturing the performance factor of uncoalesced memory access
- We redefine the concept of compute throughput to be the frequency of global memory requests leaving the SMs and reaching the memory pipeline
- We classify GPU applications into two categories as memory-bound and compute-bound based on values of redefined compute throughput and memory throughput
- An analytical performance prediction model is proposed to estimate the performance of both compute-bound and memory-bound GPU kernels.

2   Background

We provide a brief background on the GPU architecture and the programming model that we have modeled. In this work, although we focus on a CUDA-enabled NVIDIA GPU, we believe our performance model is also applicable to any GPU architecture and GPU programming API.

2.1   Overview of GPU Architecture and CUDA Programming Model

Graphics Processing Units (GPUs) have emerged as a promising alternative building block for the construction of high performance supercomputers, due to their unique combination of outstanding performance, energy-efficiency, density and cost [5].

The GPU architecture consists of several streaming multi-processors (SMs), each containing a set of streaming processors (sp) that run threads in a SIMD manner. All SMs are connected to an off-chip DRAM memory via a interconnect network. Tesla M2050 has 14 SMs, each equipped with 32 streaming processors, which makes for a total of 448 processing cores [6]. The M2050 employs a dual-issue instruction dispatcher per each SM which can issue two instructions to 32 GPU cores every two clock cycles and thus an average speed of issuing one instruction per clock cycle is achieved. The global memory space is divided into 6 partitions, each with a memory controller.

The CUDA programming model groups GPU threads into a grid of thread blocks. Each thread block is mapped to a SM in a round-robin manner and multiple thread blocks can be running simultaneously on one SM. Each thread is assigned a thread ID (tid), which is used for the data distribution and control condition. Threads are created, managed, scheduled and executed at the granularity of thread warp, which contains 32 threads for most GPUs. The CUDA memory model has an off-chip global memory space, which resides in the DRAM memory and is accessible by all threads.

2.2   Related Work

A commonly introduced metric to characterize a program is arithmetic intensity which accounts operations per data transferred between the processor and the cache. The Roofline performance estimation model [7] introduces operational intensity as another metric which accounts operations per byte that transferred between DRAM and the processor. Zhang and Owen [8] constructed a GPU performance model in a quantitative way to estimate the execution time of arithmetic pipeline, shared memory, and global memory respectively. Performance bottlenecks are derived based on the modeled execution time of each component. Hong and Kim [9] authored an excellent study on analytical GPU performance modeling and using two metrics CWP and MWP to specify a program to be compute-intensive or memory-intensive, which is the most related to our method. However, we classify and predict performance of GPU kernels based on the kernel throughput which complies with the throughput-oriented GPU architecture.

In the past few years, many studies on GPU performance modeling have been proposed. Baghsorkhi et al. [10] proposed a work flow graph (WFG)-based analytical model to predict the performance of GPU applications. The WFG is an extension of a control flow graph (CFG), where nodes represent instructions and arcs represent latencies. Meng et al. [11] proposed a GPU performance projection framework to predict performance in a cross-platform style based on the abstraction of CPU code skeletons.

Hong and Kim [9] proposed the MWP-CWP based GPU analytical model, which shares the most common with our proposed model in the following two aspects: (1) the two analytical models extract parallelism from GPU kernels at the granularity of thread warps and overall execution time is counted on the ability of hiding the latency of global memory accesses by computations. (2) The latency of an uncoalesced global memory transaction can be synthesized as the sum of a base latency and multiple extra delays, each representing the departure delay between uncoalesced global memory transactions. Apart from that, we also see differences between the two models. First, in our work, the departure delay between two uncoalesced global memory accesses turns out to be the DRAM access latency of one memory transaction which can be calculated based on the values provided in the GDDR datasheet instead of profiling. Second, we construct a pipeline model for global memory accesses and utilize the pipeline throughput to describe the memory performance. Third, the computations and memory access operations in the kernels are separated and performances of both parts are represented by the extended compute throughput and memory throughput. As GPU programs are classified into compute-bound and memory-bound categories, the potential performance improving needs to emphasize on enhancing the value of compute throughput or memory throughput. In summary, our model predicts performance of GPU kernels in a more straightforward way and thus is more suitable for the throughput-oriented GPU architectures.

3   Program Classification

In this section, we first redefine compute throughput and memory throughput, and then classify GPU kernels into compute-bound and memory-bound categories.

3.1   Compute Throughput and Memory Throughput

Originally, the compute throughput refers to the throughput of arithmetic pipeline in a SM. We redefine the content of compute throughput as the time interval between warp switches to represent the frequency of memory requests being issued to the global memory interface. As all SMs can issue memory requests to global memory concurrently, the time interval should be divided by #SM, which is the number of SMs in a GPU. It is determined by the efficiency of executing one computation period which may be related to the performance factors of control flow divergence [12] and shared memory bank conflict [10] as we consider shared memory instructions have identical latency with compute instructions.

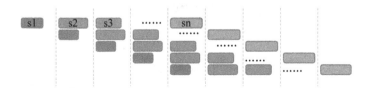

Fig. 1. A pipeline model for global memory accesses

The process of a global memory access includes several operations such as virtual address calculation, on-chip crossbar inter-connect traversal, virtual to physical address translation and physical to raw address translation, and DRAM access per each memory request. The DRAM access time here refers to the latency of reading/writing access to the DRAM chips and thus the latency is just small portion of the whole global memory access cost. In our model, the above operations are further divided into even more subtle steps that can be combined together to compromise a pipeline for memory request servicing, of which the DRAM access takes up the longest stage. According to the global memory coalescing rule implemented, multiple memory transactions may be caused per each request and multiple memory segments need to be transferred between DRAM and SMs, named uncoalesced memory access. In this case, the multiple transactions can be synthesized by one memory transaction with identical steps except a lengthened DRAM access stage due to the increased transferred memory segments. Thus, the global memory accesses can be serviced by the pipeline represented in Fig 1 and the global memory performance can be formulated via the pipeline throughput. The redefined memory throughput actually describes the frequency of memory accesses leaving the global memory.

The duration of each pipeline stage does not need to be equal but a guarantee should be made that DRAM access is the most inefficient among all pipeline stages and thus memory throughput is calculated as the reciprocal of DRAM access time of the synthesized memory transaction. The memory throughput is constraint by the global memory access patterns and partition camping.

For GPU with compute capability 2.0, it can be configured to enable L1 cache or not in SM through a compilation command -Xptxas -dlcm, and corresponded 32-byte or 128-byte transactions will be generated each with a different DRAM access time, denoted as $DRAM_{32B}$ and $DRAM_{128B}$. Let #partition and $comp_p$ each represents the number of memory partitions of the global memory and the number of clock cycles to execute a compute period, and $comp_{inst}$ and mem_{inst} represents the number of compute and memory instructions per each thread, $issue_{lat}$ denotes the Clock cycles needed to issue instructions to the SIMD pipeline while mem_{issue} denotes the Latency per memory transaction. Another two variables tpr_{32B} and tpr_{128B} each represents the number of 32-byte transactions and 128-byte transactions per each memory request. We also let DD represents the departure delay of the synthesized memory transaction .To put it together, we calculate the average DRAM access latency $DRAM_{lat}$ using equation 4. The compute throughput and memory throughput can be obtained using the following equations.

$$comp_p = \frac{comp_{inst}}{mem_{inst}} \times issue_{lat} \tag{1}$$

$$mem_{issue} = \frac{comp_p}{\#SM} \tag{2}$$

$$comp_{thr} = \frac{1}{mem_{issue}} = \frac{mem_{inst} \times \#SM}{comp_{inst} \times issue_{lat}} \tag{3}$$

$$DRAM_{lat} = \frac{DRAM_{32B} \times tpr_{32B} + DRAM_{128B} \times tpr_{128B}}{tpr_{32B} + tpr_{128B}} \tag{4}$$

$$DD = DRAM_{lat} \times (tpr_{32B} + tpr_{128B}) \tag{5}$$

$$mem_{thr} = \frac{\#partition}{DD} \tag{6}$$

3.2   GPU Program Classification

Based on the calculated compute throughput and memory throughput, the kernel throughput limited factors can be concluded and we have the following definitions:

- Compute-bound: it corresponds to the conditions where compute throughput is less than memory throughput, which means that the global memory requests arrive at the global memory interface at a relatively slow speed.
- Memory-bound: this category refers to the situation where the compute throughput is larger than the memory throughput, which means that memory requests arrive at the global memory more quickly than the leaving speed of previously arrived memory requests.

4   Analytical Performance Model

To illustrate how executing quantity of warps on SMs concurrently affects the total execution time, we will illustrate several scenarios covering both compute-bound and memory-bound cases. As the philosophy of the GPU architecture is to cover the long latency operations with interleaving execution of compute operations from a large amount of warps, the final performance is largely dependent on the effectiveness of latency hiding. The total execution time can be decomposed into two parts: duration of compute execution and uncovered memory latency.

4.1   Performance Prediction for Compute-Bound GPU Kernels

Due to a high compute-to-memory-access ratio or perfect global memory access coalescing, the compute throughput is larger than memory throughput, and memory requests can be handled at a faster speed than they arrive at the memory interface. Fig 2 shows an example of compute-bound kernels.

For case 1 in Fig 3a, we assume that each thread has only one memory access and thus one corresponding compute period per warp. Due to the relatively higher throughput of memory requests, the speed of memory requests handling is faster than the speed they are issued, and thus incoming memory requests will not accumulate latency to the final execution time. The resulting latency of case 1 in Fig 3a is 4 compute periods plus one memory period overhead.

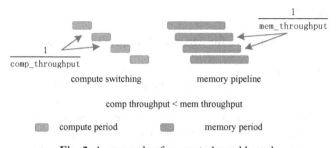

Fig. 2. An example of compute-bound kernels

For case 2 in Fig 3b, there are four warps and each warp has two compute periods and two memory periods. The second compute period can start only after the first memory period of the same warp is finished. The compute throughput and memory throughput are the same as case 1. Since the computation latency is dominant, memory accesses do not contribute to the overall execution time which equals to the sum of 8 compute periods and only one memory period.

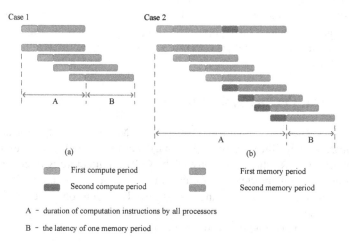

Fig. 3. Total execution time for the compute-bound GPU kernel

To be generally, the performance of compute-bound applications can be calculated using the following equations:

$$comp_{cycle} = \frac{comp_{inst} \times \#warp \times issue_{lat}}{\#SM} \qquad (7)$$

$$exec_{cycle} = comp_{cycle} + mem_{lat} \qquad (8)$$

where #warp represents the number of warps in a kernel which is defined by the kernel launch configurations and mem_{lat} represents the latency of a synthesized memory transaction, as the value is not critical to the final performance, we constrain the latency to be 500 cycles.

4.2   Performance Prediction for Memory-Bound GPU Kernels

Figure 4 shows an example of memory-bound kernels where memory throughput is roughly a half of compute throughput. Equation 5 indicates that the departure delay between memory requests gets longer as more memory transactions are triggered for one memory request because of poor performance in memory coalescing. High throughput of computations will narrow down the interval of warp switching, and as a result, memory requests are issued more frequently to the global memory.

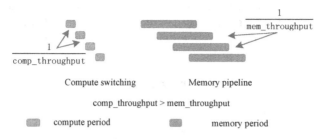

Fig. 4. An example of memory-bound kernels

For case 3 in Fig 5a, there are four warps and each warp has one compute period and one memory period. Since compute throughput is larger than memory throughput, memory access latency cannot be completely overlapped by computation, and thus each warp will accumulate extra latency of $(\frac{1}{mem_{thr}} - \frac{1}{comp_{thr}})$ cycles to the total execution time which equals to the sum of 4 compute periods and 4 extra latencies, which can also be represented as 4 departure delays plus one memory period and one compute period.

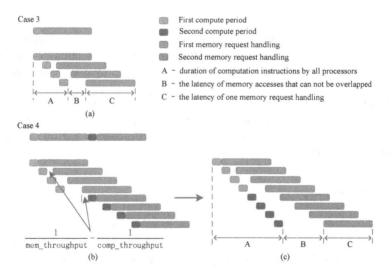

Fig. 5. Total execution time for memory-bound kernels

For case 4 in Fig 5b, there are four warps in each SM and each warp has two compute periods and two memory periods. The second compute period can start only after the first memory period of the same warp is finished. Compute throughput and memory throughput are the same as case 3. Even though idle cycles are introduced to the arithmetic pipeline, the execution time remains stable since the memory access time is dominant. The timing model of case 4 can be equivalently transformed as depicted in Fig 5c by moving the latter compute periods forward. As a result, the latency of memory accesses can only be partially overlapped by the computations. The final execution time is composed of three parts: parallel execution of compute instructions by all process units, uncovered overhead of memory requests and one memory period.

To be generally, the total execution time of memory-bound kernels can be calculated as the following two forms:

$$DD_{sum} = DD \times \#warp \times mem_{inst} \tag{9}$$

$$extra_{lat} = \frac{1}{mem_{thr}} - \frac{1}{comp_{thr}} \tag{10}$$

$$mem_{uncover} = extra_{lat} \times \#warp \times mem_{inst} \tag{11}$$

$$exec_{cycle} = comp_{cycle} + mem_{uncover} + mem_{lat} \tag{12}$$

or

$$exec_{cycle} = \frac{comp_p}{\#SM} + DD_{sum} + mem_{lat} \tag{13}$$

where DD represents the DRAM access time for a single transaction, DD_{sum} represents the overall DRAM access time for all memory transactions in the kernel. The content of $extra_{lat}$ points to the extra latency introduced by one memory access in memory-bound kernels. The $mem_{uncover}$ counts for the latency of global memory that cannot be hidden by computations. Equation 12 and Equation 13 have the same result but from different aspects. Equation 12 calculates execution time from the aspect of latency hiding while Equation 13 calculates execution time based on the memory access efficiency as memory accesses dominant.

5 Methodology

We conduct experiments on one NVIDIA Tesla M2050 GPU and the CUDA programming model, and we believe that the result of this work is still suitable for other chips and programming models as long as modifications are made to the value of input parameters.

To evaluate the effectiveness of our model, we predict performance for a manually written GPU benchmark and a commonly used kernel matrix-multiply.

5.1 Benchmark

The manually written benchmark we used contains 100 iterations, each consisting of one compute period and one memory period. The variable comp_iter controls the amount of compute instructions in a compute period, and the change of its value can simulate optimizations toward computation. Another variable *tran_per_req* presented as a parameter in the calculation of index indicates the number of memory transactions caused by each global memory access, and also its value can simulate optimizations toward memory access pattern. The variable index in the benchmark spreads the footprints of one memory request over multiple memory segments based on the value of *tran_per_req* and data type. For simplicity, single point float numbers are generated in the host CPU and transferred to the GPU global memory, and the generated compute instruction occupies one clock cycle each on Tesla M2050. The number of both the computation and memory access instructions is counted from the assembly code, which is obtained through the cuobjdump tool provided by NVIDIA. As can be concluded from the above assembly code, each iteration of the inner loop will generate 3 compute instructions and there are 7 other instructions in each iteration of the outer loop. The instruction LD.E performs 32 global memory load operations for 32 threads in a warp, which may result in multiple memory transaction according to the performance of memory access coalescing, that is, the value of *tran_per_req*.

5.2   Matrix-multiply

The matrix-multiplication is commonly applied in various applications. The shape of two input matrixes A[M*TILE] and B[TILE*M] are rectangular instead of square shape. The work load of each thread can be decomposed into several memory requests and plenty of computations per each request.

Figure 6 shows two cases of tiled matrix multiplication each corresponds to *TILE_WIDTH*=8 and *TILE_WIDTH*=32. For each iteration of the inner loop, the memory requests per warp of the case in Fig 6(a) consists of 4 addresses across four rows of A and 8 addresses along a row of B tile, which results in 4 32-Byte memory transactions to A and one 32-byte memory transaction to matrix B. The situation has been much improved when the tile width is 32 as each iteration of the inner loop only incurs one 32-byte transaction to A and 4 consecutive 32-byte transactions to B which can be combined into one 128-byte memory transaction, as we will show in the next section.

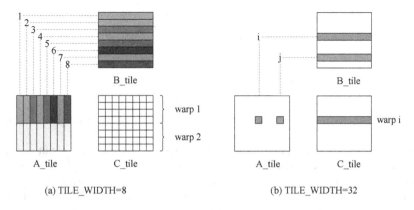

(a) TILE_WIDTH=8   (b) TILE_WIDTH=32

Fig. 6. Matrix multiply : (a) A_tile[8][8] ×B_tile[8][8], (b) A_tile[32][32] ×B_tile[32][32]

6   Experiment Results

6.1   Benchmark

As the address index in the manually written benchmark is carefully assigned that no repetition occurs in the loaded data for each thread, we bring out an experiment for both L1 cache enabled and disabled situations, each corresponds to the compilation command -Xptxas -dlcm=ca and -Xptxas -dlcm=cg, and 128-byte and 32-byte transactions are triggered. We gradually increase the spectrum of address requirement of a single warp to increase the number of memory transactions per each warp's request for a memory-bound program (with higher ratio of memory requests per computation) and the result is concluded in the Fig 7. When *tran_per_req* bellows 8, both the cached and uncached cases follow the same curve and it can be inferred that the 4 32-byte memory transactions are combined into a single 128-byte transaction, even in the uncached conditions. While the *tran_per_req* is above 32, the memory transactions caused by one warp's memory request will not increase. Otherwise, the execution time shows a linear growth to the value of *tran_per_req*, although each with a different value. Based on the memory-bound classification information, the increased latency of the kernel can be attributed to the reduction of the memory throughput, due to the increased memory transactions per each warp's memory request.

For both cached and uncached cases, the DRAM access time can be calculated by dividing the increment of kernel latency by the number of increased memory transactions. The calculated DRAM access latencies for 32-byte and 128-byte memory transaction of Tesla M2050 are 0.67 cycles and 1.53 cycles respectively. The number of instructions is counted in the assemble code.

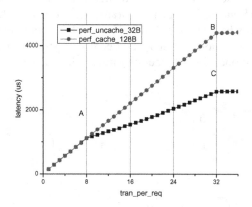

Fig. 7. Measurement of DRAM access time for 32-byte and 128-byte memory transaction

We measured kernel execution time under different compute throughput and memory throughput by varying the value of *comp_iter* and *tran_per_req*. The numbers of compute and memory instructions, as well as memory access pattern specified by the *tran_per_req*, are served as inputs to the performance prediction model. Table 1 lists parameters and predicted performance of two cases of our benchmark, and the results show that the error of prediction is no more than 6.5%.

Table 1. Applying the model for benchmark

Parameter	Case 1	Case 2	Description
comp_iter	100	20	Parameter
tran_per_req	4	8	Parameter
#warp	(64*256)/32=512	(64*256)/32=512	Warp number
$comp_{inst}$	31000	7000	Compute instruction
mem_{inst}	1*100	1*100	Memory instruction
$comp_p$	310	70	Instructions per compute period
mem_{issue}	310/14=22.1	70/14=5	Frequency of memory request issuing
tpr_{32B}	0	0	32-byte transaction per request
tpr_{128B}	4	8	128-byte transaction per request
$DRAM_{lat}$	1.53*4=6.12	1.53*8=12.24	Average departure delay
$comp_{thr}$	1/22.1=0.045	1/5=0.2	Compute throughput
mem_{thr}	1/6.12=0.163	1/12.24=0.082	Memory throughput
classification	Compute bound	Memory bound	Program classification
$comp_{cycle}$	1134393	256641	Execution time of compute instructions
$mem_{uncover}$	0	370688	Uncovered latency of memory accesses
$exec_{cycle}$	1184393	627829	calculated execution time
measured	1267534	642108	Measured execution time
Error	6.5%	2.2%	Prediction error

6.2 Matrix-multiply

We conduct experiments to predict the performance of matrix multiplication C=AB with different matrix scale as depicted in Fig 6.

The case in Fig 6a shows the calculation of a tile of matrix C where A of dimension 1024×8, B of dimension 8×1024, and C of dimension 1024×1024. Each element of C is assigned a thread and 1024×1024 threads are created. The matrix C is decomposed into multiple tiles and each tile contains 8×8 elements. As a result, the threads are organized as 128×128 blocks and each block contains 8×8 threads. Each block calculates the elements of a different tile in C based on a single tile of A and a single tile of B. The 64 threads in a block are organized into two warps, each of which calculates 4 rows of C_tile. As presented in the figure, each iteration of the inner loop will generate 4 32-byte transactions to load A_tile and one 32-byte transaction to load B_tile per warp, thus 40 32-byte memory transactions are generated for each warp.

For the case in Figure 6b, it shows another matrix multiplication C=AB where A of dimension 1024×32, B of dimension 32×1024, and C of dimension 1024×1024. For each warp, an iteration of the inner loop requires one element of A_tile and one row of B_tile, thus one 32-byte transaction of A and four 32-byte transactions of B will be generated. Due to the data locality of L2 cache, the unused element of the last accessed row of A_tile will be used by the next 7 iterations. The generated 4 32-byte transactions for a row data of B_tile can be combined into a 128-byte transaction. As a result, 4 32-byte transactions and 32 128-byte transactions will be generated.

The number of compute instructions per warp can be obtained from the assemble code. The calculated compute throughput and memory throughput is presented in Table 2. Surprisingly, the matrix multiplication code is specified as memory-bound according to our classification method.

Table 2. Parameters for matrix-multiply

	TILE_WIDTH=8	TILE_WIDTH=32
32B trans per warp	40	4
128B trans per warp	0	32
Avg_dep_delay_per_req	(40*0.67)/40=0.67	(4*0.67+32*1.53)/36=1.43
Comp_inst	12*8+26=122	12*32+26=410
Mem_req_issue_dist	122/(40*14)=0.218	410/(36*14)=0.813
1/Comp_throughput	0.218	0.813
1/Mem_throughput	0.67	1.43
Program classification	Memory-bound	Memory-bound

To verify the effectiveness of program classification, we manually add multiple compute instructions in the inner loop by increasing the value of *comp_iter* to the case in Fig 8b. As presented in the Fig 8, the overall latency of the kernel starts to rise at a point around 6 along the x-axis, which means that the kernel is not bounded by the compute operations before that point. We also calculate an expected point at which compute throughput equals to memory throughput, and the result turns out to be *comp_iter*=7, which is pretty close to the measured value.

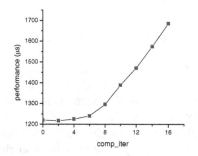 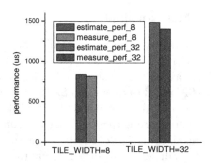

Fig. 8. Verification of program classification for A[1024][32] ×B[32][1024]

Fig. 9. Comparison of estimated and measured latency for two cases

6.3   HotSpot and Gaussian Elimination

We also applied our analytical model to another two GPU programs: HotSpot and Gaussian Elimination, both from the Rodinia benchmark suits [13], which are specifically developed for the GPU-accelerated heterogeneous systems.

HotSpot is an ordinary differential equation solver used in simulating microarchitecture temperature. Every element is computed as a function of 3*3 neighborhood of elements from the input array (as stencil). For each thread's one element computation,

9 elements need to be loaded into the processor unit and thus heavy stresses are assigned to the global memory bandwidth. However, the Hotspot in the version Rodinia 2.4 is optimized throughput caching, by way of utilizing shared memory to store neighborhood data so it can be reused among neighboring threads in the same thread block. As the shared memory accessing has the identical latency as normal compute instruction, shared memory access instructions is treated as compute instructions. There are only two global memory loads and one global memory store instruction in each iteration of a thread, and all three global memory accesses are coalesced due to the shared memory. We calculate the values of compute throughput and memory throughput in the assembly code and the kernel calculate_temp turns out to be compute-bound. We estimate the execution time of all kernel runs using equation (8) and compare the results with the measured latency as listed in Table 3. The input data are also provided in the benchmark suit.

Table 3. Benchmark result for HotSpot

Input size	Measured (s)	Predicted (s)	Error
64	0.021	0.017	19.05%
512	0.040	0.035	12.5%

Gaussian Elimination solves systems of equations using the Gaussian elimination method and contains multiple iterations of two kernels: Fan1 and Fan2. the algorithm must synchronize between iterations, but the values calculated in each iteration can be computed in parallel. For both kernels, parameterized size-strided-accesses to matrix a_cuda and m_cuda lead to uncoalesced accesses which result in tremendous global memory transactions. In the L1 cache-enabled case, 32 128B-memory-transactions will be incurred while the value of size above 32. According to GPU program classification method presented above, the two kernels are defined as memory-bound and we estimate the execution time using equation (12). A comparison of measured and predicted execution time is shown in the Table 4.

Table 4. Benchmark result for Gaussian Elimination

Input size	Measured (s)	Predicted (s)	Error
16	0.000410	0.000324	20.94%
64	0.001643	0.001540	6.27%
512	0.063546	0.056340	11.33%

As can be seen from both benchmarks, the estimated values tend to be constantly smaller than the actual execution time. The inaccuracy in the projected performance can result from various sources, such as synchronization, kernel initialization, CPU execution of loop control instructions, etc. In the following work, all those factors will be considered in our performance model.

7   Conclusion

In this paper, we propose a throughput-aware analytical performance prediction model for the GPU applications. We predict performance of GPU kernels based on the throughput determined by the compute throughput and memory throughput redefined in the paper. Experiment results illustrate high accuracy of our performance prediction model in capturing impaction of performance bottlenecks such as control flow divergence and uncoalesced memory access.

We believe our model has captured the GPU's primary performance factors, and it can provide some useful hints in the future performance optimization. Our work has several limitations that we hope to address in future research: (1) model the cost of double-precision computations and other complex operations, (2) figure out an upper bound of performance based on the model research, (3) automatic memory transaction number detection, (4) model the synchronization barrier's effect on warp-level parallelism.

References

1. Keckler, S.W., Dally, W.J., Khailany, B., et al.: GPUs and the future of parallel computing. IEEE Micro 31(5), 7–17 (2011)
2. Advanced Micro Devices, Inc. AMD Brook+
3. NVIDIA Corporation. CUDA Programming Guide, Version 4.0
4. Stone, J.E., Gohara, D., Shi, G.: OpenCL: A parallel programming standard for heterogeneous computing systems. Computing in Science & Engineering 12(3), 66 (2010)
5. Owens, J.D., Houston, M., Luebke, D., et al.: GPU computing. Proceedings of the IEEE 96(5), 879–899 (2008)
6. Lindholm, E., Nickolls, J., Oberman, S., et al.: NVIDIA Tesla: A unified graphics and computing architecture. IEEE Micro 28(2), 39–55 (2008)
7. Williams, S., Waterman, A., Patterson, D.: Roofline: an insightful visual performance model for multicore architectures. Communications of the ACM 52(4), 65–76 (2009)
8. Zhang, Y., Owens, J.D.: A quantitative performance analysis model for GPU architectures. In: 2011 IEEE 17th International Symposium on High Performance Computer Architecture (HPCA), pp. 382–393. IEEE (2011)
9. Hong, S., Kim, H.: An analytical model for a GPU architecture with memory-level and thread-level parallelism awareness. ACM SIGARCH Computer Architecture News 37(3), 152–163 (2009)
10. Baghsorkhi, S.S., Delahaye, M., Patel, S.J., et al.: An adaptive performance modeling tool for GPU architectures. ACM Sigplan Notices 45(5), 105–114 (2010)
11. Meng, J., Morozov, V.A., Kumaran, K., et al.: GROPHECY: GPU performance projection from CPU code skeletons. In: Proceedings of 2011 International Conference for High Performance Computing, Networking, Storage and Analysis, p. 14. ACM (2011)
12. Cui, Z., et al.: An accurate GPU performance model for effective control flow divergence optimization. In: 2012 IEEE 26th International Parallel & Distributed Processing Symposium (IPDPS). IEEE (2012)
13. Che, S., Boyer, M., Meng, J., et al.: Rodinia: A benchmark suite for heterogeneous computing. In: IEEE International Symposium on Workload Characterization, IISWC 2009, pp. 44–54. IEEE (2009)

Parallelized Race Detection
Based on GPU Architecture

Zhuofang Dai[1,2,3], Zheng Zhang[4], Haojun Wang[3], Yi Li, and Weihua Zhang[3]

[1] Software School, Fudan University, Shanghai, China
[2] Shanghai Key Laboratory of Data Science, Fudan University, Shanghai, China
[3] Parallel Processing Institute, Fudan University, Shanghai 201203
[4] State Key Laboratory of Mathematic Engineering and Advanced Computing,
Zhengzhou 450001, China
{dzf,wanghaojun,liy,zhangweihua}@fudan.edu.cn

Abstract. In order to harness abundant hardware resources, parallel programming has become a necessity in multicore era. However, parallel programs are prone to concurrency bugs, especially data races. Even worse, current software tools always suffer from both large runtime overheads and poor scalability, while most of hardware supports for race detection are not available in parallel programming. Therefore, it has been a challenge that how to introduce a practical and fast race detection tools. Nowadays, GPUs with massive parallel computation resources have become one of the most popular hardware platforms. Hence, the prevalence of GPU architectures has opened an opportunity of accelerating data race detection.

In this paper, we first have a deeply analysis on data race detection algorithms like happens-before and observe that these algorithms have very good computation and data parallelism. Based on the observation, we propose Grace, a software approach that leverages massive parallelism computation units of GPU architectures to accelerate data race detection. Grace deploys detection, the most computation intensive workload, on GPU to fully utilize the computation resource in GPU. Moreover, Grace leverages coarse-grained pipeline parallelism and data parallelism through exploiting the computation resource in multi-core CPUs to further improve performance. Experimental results show that Grace is fast and scalable. It achieves over 80x speedup compared to the sequential version even under a 128-thread configuration.

Keywords: Parallel Acceleration, Data Race, GPU Architecture.

1 Introduction

With the development of computer technology, we have entered multicore era. In order to harness the abundant hardware resources, parallel programming has become more and more prevalent. However, writing robust parallel programs is difficult, largely due to the hard-to-detect concurrency bugs [17].

Among them, data race, is one of the most important and notorious concurrency bugs. A data race manifests when two threads access a shared memory

J. Wu et al. (Eds.): ACA 2014, CCIS 451, pp. 113–127, 2014.

without any synchronization and at least one of them is a write operation. Such bugs, once manifest, will be likely to become a very thorny problem. For instance, in 2003, a data race condition led to a power blackout, which affects about 45 million people in 8 states in Northeastern US [14].

Therefore, over the last couple of years, there have been lots of efforts aiming at providing efficient data race detection mechanisms. In general, prior efforts can be divided into two categories: software-based tools [7–9, 6, 5, 18, 4] and hardware-based supports [3, 2, 1, 16]. Software tools have to instrument program code during execution, which incurs unsatisfactory overheads. Even worse, the detection after instrumentation always contains a large amount of computations and incur large performance overhead and poor scalability. On the other hand, hardware-based supports always require specific hardware extensions for race detection. As these solutions have to depend on specific-modified architectures rather than the general ones today, they cannot be used in practice for now. Therefore, it has been a challenge that how to introduce a practical and fast race detection tools.

Currently, graphics processing units(GPUs) [12] with massive parallel computation resources have become one of the most popular hardware platforms. The prevalence of GPU architectures has opened an opportunity of accelerating data race detection. In this paper, we first have a deeply analysis on data race detection algorithms like happens-before and observe that these algorithms have very good computation and data parallelism. Based on the observation, we propose Grace, a software tool that leverages massive parallelism computation resource of GPU architectures to accelerate data race detection. Grace deploys detection, the most computation intensive workload, on GPU to fully utilize the computation resource in GPU. Moreover, Grace leverages coarse-grained pipeline parallelism and data parallelism through exploiting the computation resource in multi-core CPUs to further improve performance.

We have implemented Grace based on PIN tool. Grace collects traces in the front-end and parallelizes detection by leveraging multicore and GPU in the back-end. Experimental results show that Grace is fast and scalable. It achieves over 80x speedup compared to the sequential version even under a 128-thread configuration. In summary, this paper makes the following contributions:

- A thorough design in terms of data race detection by leveraging parallel acceleration in both CPU and GPU.
- An effective and scalable software tool aiming at race detection.

The rest of paper is organized as follows. We briefly introduce the basic GPU architecture and data race detection logic in Section 2. Then we present the design of Grace in Section 3. In Section 4, we evaluate the performance of Grace. Finally, we discuss related work in Section 5 and make a conclusion in Section 6.

2   Background

To gain insight into exploiting computation resource in multicore and GPU for data race detection, we first give an overview of data race detection algorithm, then we present a brief introduce on GPU architecture. At last, we analyze the basic detection logic to find possible portions that are suitable to be mapped onto GPU.

2.1   Overview of Data Race Detection

Data race is one of the most serious causes of bugs in parallel programming. Nowadays, there are mainly two types of runtime data race detection algorithms: happens-before [11] and lock-set [15]. Happens-before algorithm analyzes happens-before relations between shared memory accesses. If there does not exist a happens-before relation between two shared memory accesses and at least one of them is a write operation, a data race is detected. Lock-set algorithm protects variables with locks and it reports races when shared variables are accessed without a common lock. In this paper, we choose the happens-before algorithm, as we use Helgrind [13], a state-of-the-art happens-before based race detector, as the baseline of accuracy. Extending Grace to support the lock-set algorithm will be our future work.

Happens-Before Algorithm: The happens-before (HB) relation is formally defined as the least strict partial order on events, which can be described by the following three rules:

- HB1: $a \mapsto b$ if a and b are events from the same thread execution and a precedes b.
- HB2: $a \mapsto b$ if a and b are synchronization operations from different threads and the synchronization semantics infers that a precedes b.
- HB3: transitivity, if $a \mapsto b$ and $b \mapsto c$, then $a \mapsto c$.

According to the above rules, a data race is defined as two memory accesses (at least one is write) to the same address without any happens-before relations. The typical happens-before implementation uses logic vector clock, i.e., timestamp, to represent happens-before relations. Each thread has its own timestamp, whose dimension length is the number of threads. Each dimension in the timestamp represents the logic time of the corresponding thread and it is increased based on the happens-before relation. Figure 1 shows an example of the timestamps increase and happens-before relations. There are no races between thread 0 and thread 1 when the timestamp of access "Wr A" for thread 1 is larger than access "Rd A" for thread 0 (this situation is referred to as "Rd A" happens before "Wr A") or vice-versa.

2.2   Overview of GPU Architecture

In typical GPU architectures of NVIDIA [12], GPU consists of hundreds of streaming-processor (SP) cores, which are the basic execution units of GPU.

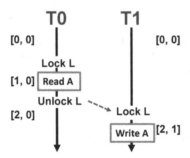

Fig. 1. Happens-before example

Tens of SP cores are grouped into streaming multiprocessors (SM), as shown in Figure 2. In the aspect of memory hierarchy, each SM has a region of on-chip memory, which contains thousands of registers and tens of KB shared memory. The on-chip memory is shared among SPs inside a SM and not visible outside SMs. Different SMs share data through off-chip global memory. In terms of workflow, each SM works as a SIMT engine, it can be assigned a large number of threads at the same time. Every 32 threads are grouped into a warp in NVIDIA GPU and multiple warps are assembled as a thread block. Each SM supports a few blocks to hide memory latency. In addition, GPU provides programmability and there are mature programming models for it such as CUDA. As GPU provides powerful computation ability and great programmability, it has been increasingly used in general purpose computation aiming at improving performance recently [19, 20].

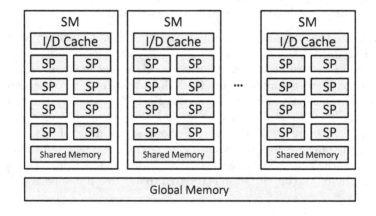

Fig. 2. Overview of GPU architecture

Algorithm 1. Race Detection Algorithm

for all threads **do**
  /* Instrumentation. */
  Record memory and generate timestamp.

  /* History Management. */
  for Each collected trace **do**
    Insert into history buffer.
  end for

  /* Race detection. */
  for Each collected trace address **do**
    for all other threads **do**
      Search same address in this thread's history buffer.
      Compare timestamps to check HB relation.
    end for
  end for
end for

2.3 Observation of Race Detection Logic

To gain insight into possible solution for race detection using GPU, we further analyze the logic of happens-before algorithm. As the algorithm 1 shown, it can be divided into three steps: 1) instrumentation; 2) history management; 3) race detection. In the instrumentation step, memory traces for each thread are collected and attached with timestamps during the program execution. Then, in history management step, each collected trace is written into the history buffer for following detection. At last, in the race detection step, each trace searches those traces with the same address in all other threads' history buffers and its timestamp is compared to those of found traces. A data race is reported if no happens-before relation is found.

To efficiently deploy the algorithm onto the GPU, we profile the execution time of those three steps. We use PIN to instrument the memory traces and implement a sequential happens-before race detector. Then we use Intel VTune to analyze the hotspots. The data [1] shows that the race detection step is the most time-consuming part occupying more than 95% of the whole execution time (evaluated under 4, 8, 16 and 32 threads). In the race detection step, the algorithm needs to search the traces with the same address in the other thread's history information for every memory trace and compare the happens-before relation. Fortunately, such comparisons are totally independent and there are millions of traces in each thread, which means there is abundant fine-grained parallelism in it. Such a computation model is very suitable to GPU architectures and opens the opportunities for Grace to map the race detection step onto GPU.

---

[1] Due to the space constraints, the detailed data are not given out.

3   Design

This section describes the implementation details of Grace. First, we present an overview of Grace. Then we give out detailed parallelism optimizations.

3.1   Algorithm Design

Grace is motivated by the computation-intensive nature of data race detection and the massively available computation resource in GPU. The overall design contains three modules:

- Instrumentation module, which is used to collect traces and generate timestamp during program execution.
- History management module, responsible for receiving traces from instrumentation module, pre-processing traces and sending traces to GPU for bug detection. Since the happens-before algorithm needs to compare the current trace's timestamp with those of previous traces (with the same address) to detect races, a history trace buffer is necessary for recording the previous traces.
- Detection module, handling detection workload. Due to the massive parallelism in concurrency bug detection, Grace offloads the detection process to GPU.

3.1.1   Instrumentation and History Management
As analyzed in Section 2, detection module is the most computation-intensive stage in happens-before algorithm. Therefore, Grace leaves the instrumentation module and history module on CPU while mapping detection module on GPU. Collected traces will be sent to history management module. After a trace arrives history management module, it will be put in the history buffer. The information includes *address*, *type* and *timestamp*. Then, the trace will be sent to GPU for data race detection. Meanwhile, as the transmission between CPU and GPU is costly, we use a centralized history buffer here for batched transmission.

Moreover, we exploit two optimization strategies in history management: one is using hash table to speedup trace traversal. The other is exploiting the fact that read-read traces never raise racy conditions to filter out redundant comparisons in detection.

- **Hashed Strategy:** Managing all traces in a single trace list leads to a long search time during detection, which is quite inefficient. To reduce address search time, the trace buffer is organized as a hash table. Traces are hashed to different entry according to their address. Each entry of the table is a FIFO queue. Such a design brings two advantages in detection process on GPU. One is that same address searching in history buffer is greatly speeded up via hashing location. The other is that the cache locality in shared memory of each SM improves dramatically since the whole history is too large to put into shared memory.

– **Read/Write Distributed Strategy:** As data races never happen between read and read, all read-read comparisons are race-free. To further filter out read-read cases, Grace organizes read and write trace histories separately, as shown in Figure 3. In detection process, GPU accesses traces in different read/write FIFO queue according to hashed address and the read/write types. In other words, the algorithm will not search a read buffer for a read trace.

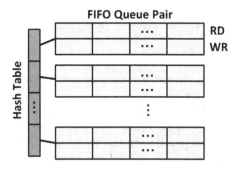

Fig. 3. History management optimizations

3.1.2   Parallelism of Kernel on GPU

When an algorithm is mapped onto GPU, the corresponding kernels are generated by compiler. To make the kernel more efficient, there are two critical factors. One is that the parallelism degree should be large enough. Only then can there be enough number of threads used in overlapping memory latency. The other one is that the size of kernel working set should not be too large as the shared memory of GPU is limited while fetching data from global memory is slow.

To fully utilize GPU computation resource, we gather traces until the parallelism degree is large enough. All gathered traces are partitioned into blocks. The blocks are deployed onto different SMs as shown in Figure 4(a). In each block, each trace is processed by a GPU thread executed on a SP as shown in Figure 4(b). 32 GPU threads are formed into a warp and multiple warps are running on a SM. Therefore, GPU can overlap global memory access latency by warp switch. Based on the mapping model, we collected performance data of different configurations of block size (block number * thread number per block). Due to space constraint, we omit detailed data here. Results show that 256 * 256 is the most efficient configuration. Therefore, we use this configuration in our evaluation.

In order to minimize the kernel size, we leverage the history reorganization and optimize the detection workflow. Each trace does the following steps to detect races as shown in Algorithm 2:

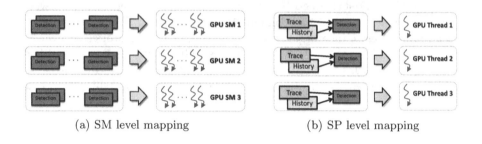

(a) SM level mapping   (b) SP level mapping

Fig. 4. Parallelism mapping onto GPU

- On GPU side, detection kernel spawns large number of threads for the following detection. Each thread fetches one trace according to the index of trace, as shown in Figure 4(a).
- For each trace, detection kernel uses trace's address to find the corresponding history buffer entry in all other threads. If the current trace is a read operation, it will be compared with the write queues to find the nodes with the same address. Otherwise, it will be compared with both the read queues and the write queues.
- The timestamp of the current trace will be compared with the recorded timestamp of the found trace. If there is no happens-before relation, these two memory accesses are identified as a race.

As data transmission between CPU and GPU is costly, we minimize the data transmission in detection process. Except the unavoidable traces transmission from CPU, we postpone the race report process until the whole detection is finished. To support that, Grace collects racy traces in the buffer laying on global memory during detection [2]. After detection, GPU sends the buffer back to CPU as detection report.

3.2   Parallelism Optimizations on CPU

Although GPU accelerates detection stage dramatically, the modules processed on CPU have become the new bottleneck in whole detection. As shown in Figure 5, during the whole detection, CPU execution time (instrumentation module and history management module) has cost about 80% of total time after the detection stage is mapped onto GPU. Meanwhile, as multi-core CPUs are common platforms today, we can leverage them to further improve performance. As a result, to overlap the execution of these three stages, we introduce pipeline parallelism between modules. Moreover, to accelerate the most time consuming stage, we leverage data parallelism.

---

[2] Grace also can report bugs during execution. We leave the report in the end for races classification of the root cause, which can make the report more clearly.

Algorithm 2. Trace Detection Algorithm

localTid = trace.threadID
localAddr = trace.address
for all remoteTid in Threads Expect Itself **do**
    for all remoteTrace in remoteTid's History Buffer **do**
        if remoteTrace.address Is Same As localAddr **then**
            /* Compare timestamps to check HB relation. */
            if HB relation exists **then**
                Return /* No race. */
            else
                Call RaceCollector
            end if
        end if
    end for
end for

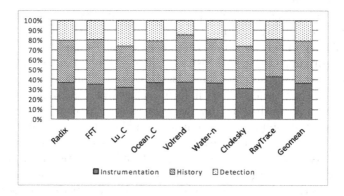

Fig. 5. Execution time percentage of three stages

3.2.1   Pipeline Parallelism

To overlap the execution of these three stages, Grace introduces a pipeline design. In detail, Grace maps the first two stages onto different CPU cores and leverages two communication buffer between three stages, as shown in Figure 6. The communication buffer is designed as a lock-free ring buffer between producers and consumers [21]. Producers write buffer from the head entry of buffer while consumers read buffer from the tail entry. Through such a design, we improve access throughput of the communication buffer. As there will be race conditions during buffer management, some mechanisms should be involved for synchronization. We use semaphores to detect whether the buffer is accessible and to assure atomic access to a buffer entry.

Moreover, the collected traces will occupy the collection buffer until they are transferred to the communication ring buffer. Hence, program execution has to be blocked while collected traces being read. To support parallel trace collection and transmission, Grace uses a rotation buffer mechanism. Grace uses two buffers

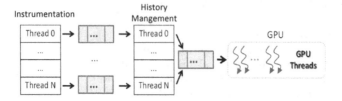

Fig. 6. Buffer design in pipeline parallelism

for trace collection. If one buffer is full and being transmitted, the other continues to collect the incoming traces. If the other is also full, the execution thread has to be blocked until one buffer is available.

3.2.2 Data Parallelism

After the optimizations of pipeline, we focus on history management module, the most time-consuming module (as shown in Figure 5). As every trace has to insert into history buffer, the workload is not trivial. To parallelize the insertion process, we reorganize the whole history buffer. We observe that history insertion is independent for different threads. As traces belong to different threads will not interfere with each other, it forms a natural data parallelism chances here. In order to parallelize history insertion among threads, traces are maintained in different sub-buffers according to their thread ID, as shown in Figure 3. And Grace uses multiple preprocessing threads in history management module, whose number is same as the execution threads of running program. As Figure 7 shows, each history management thread receives traces from the corresponding instrumentation thread according to its thread ID. When the number of physical cores is abundant, Grace deploys each thread pair of instrumentation and history management on a specific physical core for better performance and cache locality. Otherwise, multiple thread pairs are grouped and deployed on a specific physical core.

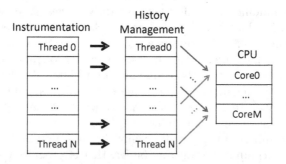

Fig. 7. Mapping between Instrumentation threads and History Management threads

4   Evaluation

In this section, we evaluate the design of Grace from the following three aspects:
1) race detection capability; 2) the performance compared to basic sequential
version; and 3) acceleration scalability with the number of threads increasing.

4.1   Experimental Setup

Our evaluation environment is PIN as front-end, integrated our Grace parallelism
module as back-end. All experiments were run on a Ubuntu server (12.04.2) system with 4 Intel(R) Xeon(R) E5-2660 CPUs with 16 physical cores and NVIDIA
TESLA M2075 GPU. Each CPU frequency is 2.20GHz, with 32KB L1 i-cache,
32KB d-cache and 256KB L2 cache and a 20MB shared last level cache. GPU
contains 448 SPs with 1.15GHz. We use the parallel SPLASH2 [10] benchmarks
suite for evaluation.

4.2   Race Detection Capability

To measure the race detection capability of Grace, we choose Helgrind, a well-
known open source data race detector, as the baseline. Our results show that
Grace is able to detect all bugs found by Helgrind, which is shown in Table 1.

Table 1. Bugs detected by Grace and Helgrind

Benchmark	fft	radix	volrend	lu	ocean	water-n	cholesky	raytrace	sum
Helgrind	0	0	50	0	1	0	3	2	56
Grace	0	0	50	0	1	0	3	2	56

4.3   Detection Speedup

To measure the effectiveness and efficiency of parallelism acceleration of Grace,
we evaluate the race detection speedup compared to the sequential version.
Experimental results show that with GPU acceleration, Grace achieves 68x
speedup. Further, Grace with both CPU and GPU parallel acceleration is over
95x faster than the sequential version under 16-thread configuration.

4.4   Acceleration Scalability

With the number of threads increasing, the workload of Grace increases too.
To illustrate the acceleration scalability of Grace, we evaluate the speedup of
Grace compared to the sequential detection under different number of threads.
As shown in Figure 9, the speedups of 32-thread, 64-thread and 128-thread are
82x, 92x and 166x separately. Grace gains speedup via both GPU parallelism and
CPU parallelism. For 32-thread and 64-thread, the speedups are a bit less than

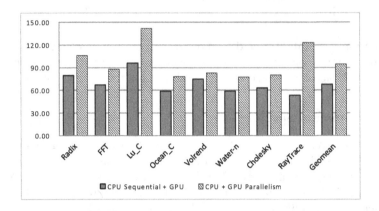

Fig. 8. Grace speedup compared to sequential version

that of 16-thread due to the lack of enough threads in history management in our evaluation platform. In this case, multiple history management threads have to be grouped onto a specific physical core, which would hurt the performance of CPU parallelism to some extent. Therefore, history management module has become bottleneck and hurt the performance improvement brought by CPU parallelism. For 128-thread, the speedup gets a great growth. In the environment with such a large amount of running threads, the workload of detection grows dramatically. Therefore, the speedup gained by GPU parallelism grows largely, which has covered reduction in terms of CPU parallelism.

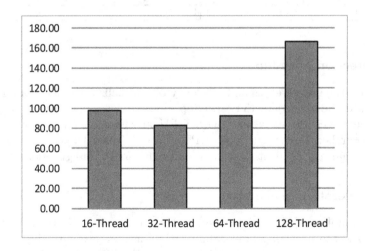

Fig. 9. Acceleration scalability of Grace

5   Related Work

In the following, we will discuss the mostly closest work to Grace.

5.1   Software-based Data Race Detection

Software race detectors can be further categorized into static and dynamic ones, according to when data races are being detected. There are also several efforts in trying to accelerate the software-based detectors.

Software-based detectors can be further divided into static ones and dynamic ones according to their execution environment. Static race detectors, such as RacerX [4], are generally based on static analysis on source code. Due to the possible state space explosion problem, it is usually difficult for static detectors to scale to large programs. Furthermore, due to the lack of runtime information, static detectors usually generate a lot of false positives, which may render the results useless due to the non-trivial manual efforts to filter such false alarms. On the other hand, dynamic race detectors detect data races by constantly monitoring program execution and dynamically analyze the runtime states, which usually has very little false alarms [7, 8]. However, to record and analyze the frequent memory accesses, software-based detectors usually involve significant runtime overhead.

To improve the software detection performance, there are several efforts trying to reduce the runtime overhead by trading accuracy for speed. Examples include sampling-based approach [9] and epoch outcome-based detection [6, 5, 18]. Such a proposal has to make a balance between performance and accuracy.

5.2   Hardware-Based Data Race Detection

As prior software-based detectors usually have limited performance or accuracy, or both, researchers have proposed some hardware-based mechanisms for race detection [3, 2, 1, 16]. These mechanisms always require specific additions aiming at instrumentation inside cores. Moreover, additional computation units are also required for handling detection calculation. In a word, all of these supports require specific hardware additions, which are not parts the general architectures today. As a result, when compared to software solutions, hardware ones cannot be used in practice for now.

6   Conclusion and Future Work

This paper has proposed Grace, an effective and scalable GPU-based race detection tool. Grace leverages a key observation that mainstream dynamic data race detection algorithm has great computation and data parallelism. Further, Grace exploits the abundant computation resources on GPU architecture to accelerate data race detection via both data-parallelism and pipeline-parallelism strategies. Experimental results show Grace is fast and scalable. It achieves over 80x speedup compared to the sequential version even under a 128-thread configuration.

We are continuing our work in two directions. One is to support more types of concurrency bug detection, such as atomicity violation. The other is to support more detection algorithm: such as lock-set algorithm for data race detection.

Acknowledgement. We are grateful to supports from the Key Project of Major Program of Shanghai Committee of Science and Technology under Grant (No. 13DZ1108800), the National High Technology Research and Development Program of China (No. 2012AA010901) and the National Natural Science Foundation of China (No. 61370081). We would like to thank all our anonymous reviewers for valuable feedback on the paper.

References

1. Muzahid, A., et al.: SigRace: signature-based data race detection. ACM SIGARCH Computer Architecture News 37(3) (2009)
2. Zhou, P., Teodorescu, R., Zhou, Y.: HARD: Hardware-assisted lockset-based race detection. In: IEEE 13th International Symposium on High Performance Computer Architecture, HPCA 2007. IEEE (2007)
3. Prvulovic, M.: CORD: Cost-effective (and nearly overhead-free) order-recording and data race detection. In: The Twelfth International Symposium on High-Performance Computer Architecture. IEEE (2006)
4. Engler, D., Ashcraft, K.: RacerX: effective, static detection of race conditions and deadlocks. ACM SIGOPS Operating Systems Review 37(5) (2003)
5. Erickson, J., et al.: Effective Data-Race Detection for the Kernel. In: OSDI, vol. 10 (2010)
6. Veeraraghavan, K., et al.: Detecting and surviving data races using complementary schedules. In: Proceedings of the Twenty-Third ACM Symposium on Operating Systems Principles. ACM (2011)
7. Sack, P., et al.: Accurate and efficient filtering for the intel thread checker race detector. In: Proceedings of the 1st Workshop on Architectural and System Support for Improving Software Dependability. ACM (2006)
8. Flanagan, C., Freund, S.N.: FastTrack: efficient and precise dynamic race detection. ACM Sigplan Notices 44(6) (2009)
9. Marino, D., Musuvathi, M., Narayanasamy, S.: LiteRace: effective sampling for lightweight data-race detection. ACM Sigplan Notices 44(6) (2009)
10. Woo, S.C., et al.: The SPLASH-2 programs: Characterization and methodological considerations. ACM SIGARCH Computer Architecture News 23(2) (1995)
11. Lamport, L.: Time, clocks, and the ordering of events in a distributed system. Communications of the ACM 21(7), 558–565 (1978)
12. http://developer.nvidia.com/nvidia-gpu-computing-documentation
13. http://valgrind.org/docs/manual/hg-manual.html
14. Poulsen, K.: Software bug contributed to blackout. Security Focus (2004)
15. Savage, S., et al.: Eraser: A dynamic data race detector for multithreaded programs. ACM Transactions on Computer Systems (TOCS) 15(4), 391–411 (1997)
16. Devietti, J., et al.: RADISH: always-on sound and complete Race Detection in Software and Hardware. ACM SIGARCH Computer Architecture News 40(3) (2012)

17. Lu, S., et al.: Learning from mistakes: a comprehensive study on real world concurrency bug characteristics. ACM Sigplan Notices 43(3) (2008)
18. Wester, B., et al.: Parallelizing data race detection. In: Proceedings of the Eighteenth International Conference on Architectural Support for Programming Languages and Operating Systems. ACM (2013)
19. Woo, D.H., Lee, H.-H.S.: COMPASS: a programmable data prefetcher using idle GPU shaders. ACM Sigplan Notices 45(3) (2010)
20. Merrill, D., Garland, M., Grimshaw, A.: Scalable GPU graph traversal. ACM SIGPLAN Notices 47(8) (2012)
21. Kogan, A., Petrank, E.: Wait-free queues with multiple enqueuers and dequeuers. ACM SIGPLAN Notices 46(8), 223–234 (2011)

A Novel Design of Flexible Crypto Coprocessor and Its Application

Shice Ni, Yong Dou, Kai Chen, and Lin Deng

National Laboratory for Parallel and Distribution Processing,
National University of Defense Technology,
Deya Road, 109#, Changsha, 410073, P.R. China
{nishice,yongdou,chenkai,denglin}@nudt.edu.cn

Abstract. Accelerating security protocols has been a great challenge in general-purpose processor due to the complexity of crypto algorithms. Most crypto algorithms are employed at the function level among different security protocols. We propose a novel flexible crypto coprocessor architecture that relies on Reconfigurable Cryptographic Blocks (RCBs) to achieve a balance between high performance and flexibility and implement the architecture for security application on FPGA. The pipelining technique is adopted to realize parallel data and to reduce the commication costs. We consider several crypto algorithms as examples to illustrate the design of the RCB in the FC Coprocessor. Finally, we create a prototype of the FC coprocessor on a Xilinx XC5VLX330 FPGA chip. The experiment results show that the coprocessor, running at 216 MHz, outperforms the software-based file encryption running on an Intel Core i3 530 CPU at 2.93 GHz by a factor of 29× for typical encrypt application.

Keywords: flexible crypto coprocessor, reconfigurable crypto block, security protocol, accelerator.

1 Introduction

Cryptography is an essential component in modern electronic commerce. With increasing transactions conducted over the Internet, ensuring security of data transfer is critically important. Considerable amounts of money are being exchanged over the network, either through e-commerce sites (e.g., Amazon and Buy.com), auction sites (e.g., eBay), online banking (e.g., Citibank and Chase), stock trading (e.g., Schwab), and even in governments (e.g., irs.gov). Therefore, many security protocols have been employed to guarantee data privacy and communication channel security, such as virtual private networks [1] and secure IP (IPSec) [2]. Security-related processing can exhaust the processing capacities of many servers.

Accelerating security protocols is a great challenge in the general-purpose processor due to the complexity of crypto algorithms. In general, ciphers use large arithmetic and algebraic modifications, which are inadequate for software implementation. When using a general-purpose processor, even the fastest software implementation of ciphers cannot satisfy the required data rates of bulk data encryption for high-end

J. Wu et al. (Eds.): ACA 2014, CCIS 451, pp. 128–139, 2014.

applications. Most of the modern security protocols widely used today allow for multiple encryption algorithms, whose use is negotiated on a per-session basis, and multicipher and multi-mode schemes are employed to strengthen the secret-key ciphers. Additionally, the security protocol must also support different algorithms and be upgradeable in the field; otherwise, interoperability among different systems cannot be realized, and any upgrade results in excessive cost. However, most hardware implementations suffer from the drawback of the difficulty in the programming model, resulting in upgrading difficulty.

The ultimate solution to this problem would be an adaptive processor that can provide software-like flexibility with hardware-like performance. FPGA chips, which operate at the bit level and serve as custom hardware for different crypto applications, have been considered as a likely option to support efficiently a wide range of cryptographic algorithms and procedures.

Therefore, we propose a novel flexible crypto coprocessor (FC Coprocessor) architecture to achieve a balance between high performance and flexibility and implement the coprocessor for storage of files on FPGA. By utilizing the reconfigure feature of FPGA, we propose the idea of Reconfigurable Cryptographic Blocks (RCBs), which are pipeline implementations of crypto algorithms on the reconfigurable chip, with unified interface ports to the host computer and to one another. For a specific security application, we can adapt the coprocessor architecture and select several corresponding blocks from the library to realize the entire security application on a reconfigurable device.

This paper is organized as follows: Section 2 describes the related works. Sections 3 describe in details the flexible architecture of our proposed coprocessor and several implementations of the RCBs. Section 4 presents the performance of the crypto blocks and their application on FPGA, and Section 5 presents the conclusion.

2   Related Work

Our work encompasses many aspects of cryptographic algorithm accelerations [3–8]. In the following, we summarize some representative works and explain how our work differs from them.

When using a general-purpose processor, even the fastest software implementation of ciphers cannot satisfy the required data rates of bulk data encryption for high-end applications [6–10]. As a result, hardware implementations are necessary for ciphers to achieve this required performance level.

Many studies focused on the hardware structure to reconfigure unit of ciphers. The Cryptographic Optimized for Block Ciphers Reconfigurable Architecture (COBRA) 9 proposed specialized cryptographic elements (named as reconfigurable crypto graphic elements) to construct the COBRA architecture and a methodology to design general-purpose reconfigurable cryptographic elements optimized for block cipher implementation by analyzing the functional requirements of the block ciphers. The Cryptobooster 10 processor adopted modules to implement the IDEA algorithm.

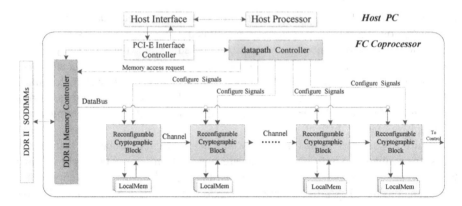

Fig. 1. Block diagram of the hardware design of FC Coprocessor

The Adaptive Cryptographic Engine (ACE) 11 was proposed to provide the speed and flexibility required by IPSec. ACE consists of an FPGA device, a cryptographic library, and a configuration controller. Using the cryptographic library, the FPGA can be configured at run-time using the configuration controller. Various configuration files are available for selection, similar to COBRA; however, only one crypto algorithm is chosen in the meantime.

Most of the times, security protocol needs more than one crypto algorithm block at once, and integrating all crypto blocks needed by the protocols on a chip can decrease the overhead of communications between the host and the accelerator. Therefore, this paper proposes the novel FC Coprocessor architecture that balances high performance and flexibility.

3   Implementation of the Coprocessor

3.1   Architecture

Figure 1 shows the computation platform consisting of a cryptographic coprocessor accelerator and a host. The crypto coprocessor accelerator comprises one FPGA chip, two SDRAM modules, and an I/O channel interface. The interface channel is responsible for transferring the computed data and results between the accelerator and the host.

The core of the FC Coprocessor mainly consists of the memory controller, register files, data-path controller, and reconfigurable integrity blocks for the crypto algorithms. The data-path controller controls the dedicated crypto block and performs the interface operations using external devices such as the memory and an I/O bus interface controller. The RCB executes the various crypto algorithms such as MD5 and SHA-256 (hash algorithm) and other application programs such as the user authentication and IC card interface programs.

The controller module handles the control signal from the data-path controller. When a start signal is received from the top controller, the module orders the RCB to read sequentially the data from the FIFO and to start the pipeline of RCBs. When the pipeline result is ready, the module produces the control signal to write data back to the FIFO.

LocalMem is used to store the local parameters of the symmetric algorithms, such as the S-boxes of AES, RC4, and DES. The S-box design is an important work in progress of these algorithms. RCBs are the pipeline implementations of crypto algorithms, described in details in following section.

The RCB structure is shown in Figure 2. The input data, e.g., plaintext, are transmitted via FIFO, as well as the cipher text. We chose 128 bits as the data width in our implementation because the width of the operands in most crypto algorithms is 128 bits or higher. Through the FIFOs, different blocks with different operand widths can work synchronously.

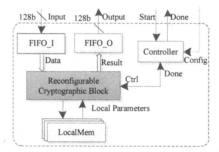

Fig. 2. Block diagram of the hardware design of RCB

A controller module is provided to handle the control signal from the data-path controller. When a start signal is received from the top controller, the module orders the RCB to read the data from FIFO_I sequentially and start the pipeline of RCBs. When the pipeline result is ready, the module produces the control signal to write data back to FIFO_O.

LocalMem is used to store the local parameters of the symmetric algorithms, such as the S-boxes of AES, RC4, and DES. The S-box design is an important work in progress of these algorithms. RCBs are the pipeline implementations of crypto algorithms, described in details in following section.

3.2   Implementations of RCB

RSA

RSA [14] is one of the most popular public-key crypto algorithms. This algorithm is a type of modular exponentiation: $C = M^e \bmod N$. Here, e and N refer to the public-key cryptography, M refers to the plaintext, and C is the calculated cipher text. N, e, and M are large numbers. The width of the operands in the RSA can reach 1,024 bits or higher, indicating that the throughput of the system is too difficult to achieve.

The Montgomery algorithm is used to speed up the modular multiplication and modular exponentiation. The radix-2 Montgomery algorithm without subtraction is presented in [12]. The difficulties of the Montgomery algorithm lie in solving qi and the large-number additions. We propose the following methods to solve these problems:

Solving qi: Before Y is input, we can shift Y to the left of N bits; thus, the calculation of qi would be $q_i = S_i \times n_0' \bmod 2^r$, where $n0'$ is decided by input X. We can truncate the high part of Si because of the mode operation. Then, we can easily and quickly obtain qi.

Large-number additions: Using the CSA contracture, we can split X into Xc and Xs, which indicate the carry of X and the result of X, respectively. Furthermore, the same process with Y can be performed, splitting Y into Yc and Ys. Therefore, the Montgomery algorithm can be modified as shown in Figure 3.

Improved Montgomery Algorithm:

Input: X,Y,N ($0 <= X, Y < 2N$; the length of X,Y,N are all n bits;
and $n_0 n_0' = -1 \bmod 2^r$)

Output: $S = X \times Y \times 2^{-r(n+1)} \bmod N$

1:      $S_0 = 0$;
2:      for ($i = 0$, $i < (n+r)/r$, $i++$)
3:          {
4:                      $q_i = \{S_i + Y \times \text{Equation1}^*\} n_0' \bmod 2^r$;
5:                      $S_{i+1} = \{S_i + Y \times \text{Equation1}^* + q_i N\}/2^r$;
6:          }
7:      return S_n;

*: $\text{Equation1} = 2^{r-1} x_{ri+r-1} + 2^{r-2} x_{ri+r-2} + \cdots + 2^1 x_{ri+1} + 2^0 x_{ri}$.

Fig. 3. Modified algorithm of the general radix-2^r Montgomery algorithm without subtraction from the radix-2 Montgomery algorithm

Figure 4(a) shows that after X and Y_s are input and width_N cycles carry the save addition in the CSA tree, S_c and S_s are sent to the add module to complete the entire addition. Finally, we can derive the result. The whole Montgomery system requires ($n + r$)/$r + n/w$ cycles (w is the width of the data processing in the Adder module).

The full Adder (FA) module completes the final summation operation of the outputs S_s and S_c in the improved Montgomery algorithm. Figure 4(b) shows its construction. The results of the CSA (S_s and S_c) are sent to Registers A and B, respectively. Subsequently, we derive w bits from A and B to send them to the FA, and the resulting w bits are sent to the lower w bit in the result register. The one-bit carry is sent to C_in to prepare for the next w-bit addition. The result register shifts the w bits to the right following the addition of every w bit.

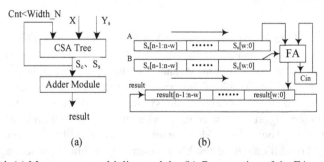

(a)   (b)

Fig. 4. (a) Montgomery multiplier module. (b) Construction of the FA module

MD5

MD5 is a hash algorithm for message digesting, introduced in 1992 by Rivest; it consists of five steps (for more details, please refer to [13]). The core of MD5 is the algorithm used for processing the message. The algorithm consists of four rounds, each of which comprises 16 steps.

The algorithm is performed as follows: first, the values of A, B, C, and D are stored as temporary variables. Then, every step operation is performed for 64 rounds. For each round, a corresponding nonlinear function exists. Finally, the values of the temporary variables are added to the values obtained from the algorithm, and the results are stored in Registers A, B, C, and D. When all message blocks have been processed, the message digest of M is stored in Registers A, B, C, and D.

Message M is divided into 512-bit blocks, which are processed separately. Data dependence does not exist among the pieces of input data. Hence, we can pipeline the data path in 64 cycles.

A one-round process of MD5 is shown in Figure 5. The Const Unit keeps the data of MD5 constant. The registers store the input message block, and a selection module is available that chooses the response corresponding to the value of Xk in every round. FU is a combinational logic consisting of rotate left, adder, and nonlinear functions.

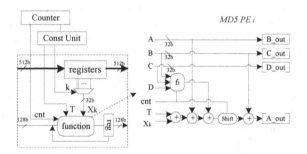

Fig. 5. One round of MD5 algorithm

SHA256

SHA256 15 is another widely used message-digesting algorithm. The SHA-256 algorithm takes a message length of less than 264 bits and outputs a 256-bit long message digest. The digest serves as a concise representation of the message and has the property that any change in the message is very likely to result in a change in the corresponding digest. Initially, we need to initiate several parameters, such as from a to h, as shown in Figure 6, to be used as starting points for the rounds. In the design, parameters a to h are implemented through eight registers whose width are all 32 bits. Subsequently, the message should be scheduled. The next step is an iterative process. Finally, the hash value is updated; the data in registers a to h represent the final result.

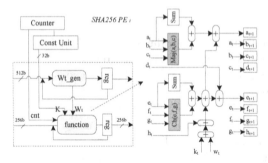

Fig. 6. Iterative progress of SHA256 algorithm

AES

AES [16] was accepted as a FIPS standard in November 2001. The algorithm is composed of four different steps, namely, *byte substitution*, *shift row*, *mix column*, and *key addition*. The number of rounds *Nr* that the algorithm is repeated is related to the key size that the algorithm used. When a key size of 128 bits is used, the number of rounds is equal to 10. Figure 7 shows the unrolled and fully pipelined implementation of the AES algorithm. The *shift row* step is only for interconnection, and the *key addition* is the XORing of the round data and the round key. The mix column step consists of a chain of XORs to permute the elements of the data in each column. The arithmetic of these three stages can be combined in one pipeline stage for each round.

The *byte substitution* is performed on each byte of the state using a substitution table (S-box). In this phase, the input is considered as an element of $GF(2^8)$. First, the multiplicative inverse of $GF(2^8)$ is calculated. Then, an affine transformation over $GF(2)$ is applied. Here, either all substitute values are calculated in advance and stored in the block RAMs or on-the-fly calculation of the values is logically implemented. We implemented the SubBytes block (S-box) with a block RAM, instead of calculating the multiplicative inverse and affine transform, for simplicity and high performance. We used a 1-kbyte block RAM for the S-box, and S-box was used in the implementation of the AES crypto block.

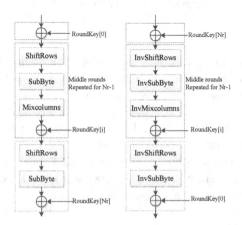

Fig. 7. AES round structure

DES

DES [17] is a block cipher that uses a 64-bit key and operates on 64-bit blocks of data. Because every 8th bit of the 64-bit key is used for parity checking, DES has a 56-bit key. The DES algorithm has 16 rounds of identical operations such as non-linear substitutions and permutations. In each round, 48-bit sub keys are generated, and substitutions using S-box, bitwise shift, and XOR operations are performed.

The 56-bit key length is relatively small by today's standards. For increased security, the DES operation can be performed by three consecutive times, which expands the effective key length to 112 bits. Using DES in this manner is referred to as triple-DES. In this section, we only describe the DES crypto block because the expansion to triple-DES is trivial.

Figure 8 shows one round of the DES algorithm. The left and right halves of each 64-bit input data operand are treated as separate 32-bit data operands L_{i-1} and R_{i-1} . The 32-bit right halves of the data are passed to the next left halves of the data. The left and right halves of each 64-bit input data operand are treated as separate 32-bit data operands L_{i-1} and R_{i}. The 32-bit right halves of the data are passed to the next left halves of the data.

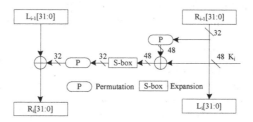

Fig. 8. Structure of one round in DES

RC4

Rivest, of RSA Data Security, Inc., developed the RC4 cipher in 1987; its details were published in 1996 18. RC4 is a public-key encryption system, which is used to encrypt and decrypt messages transferred during a particular communication session. All messages encrypted with the master keys are considered secure.

The core of the RC4 encryption consists of two functions: key schedule algorithm, which is responsible for the initialization of a key-dependent permutation in S, and key stream generator, which generates a sequence of bits that can be XORed with plaintext for encryption and with the cipher text for decryption.

We implement the RC4 algorithm on FPGA using the "read before write" access mode. We can use it to read S[j] and write S[i] in a single cycle, reducing the total number of clock cycles for testing one key.

4   Experimental Results

We implemented the crypto coprocessor on a development board and verified the designs on FPGA. The board was composed of one large-scale FPGA chip, Virtex5 XC5VLX330 from Xilinx, two 4 GB DDRII SODIMM modules, and a PCI-E × 8 interface to the host computer.

Our designed target is the FPGA at its fastest speed grade (-2) using ISE 10.1i.03 implementation flow by Xilinx Synthesis Technology. We used the Mentor Graphics ModelSim 6.5a for the behavioral simulation. The software platform included a host PC with Intel Dual-Core i3 530 CPU at 2.93 GHz and 8.0 GB DDR3 1333 memory at level O3 compiler optimization [19].

4.1   Performance of RCB

In this section, we present and analyze the performance of the FC Coprocessor. We compared the representative operation mode of the algorithms in the test. By the term "performance," we mean the throughput of the blocks measured by the minimum time that elapsed between the completions of two independent encrypting operations, which is smaller than the instruction latency because the circuit is pipelined.

➤   *Performance of the RCB*
Table 1 shows the details of the FPGA synthesis results for the basic RCBs. The AES crypto block was implemented with full pipelined-based architecture, and its S-boxes were implemented with FPGA's block RAM. We also chose the pipelining technique for the MD5, SHA256, and DES crypto blocks. Resource cost is usually related to the width of the operand, such as RSA. Because of the mode of operation, the RC4 algorithm block was selected to exploit the sub-pipelining technique.

The achievable maximum frequency of the RCBs is 308 MHz. Compared with the same circuit implemented directly on silicon (ASIC), the FPGA implementation, emulated with a very large number of configurable elementary blocks and network of wires, is typically one order of magnitude slower. However, the performance of the FPGAs improved using custom hardware for applications equipped with multiple RCBs working in parallel.

Table 1. Resource and frequency of the algorithms on FPGA

Algorithms	Slice LUT	BRAM	Freq.(MHz)	Perf.(Gbps)
AES 128	14833	32	307.89	39.4
RC4	1215	1	320.62	0.83
SHA-256	11,047	55	214.34	10.9
MD5	12,662	20	248.08	53.3
RSA-1024	24,996	1	308.36	2.2×10^{-3}

➢   *Performance comparison with an i3 core*

Table 2 shows that we can obtain better performance compared with the parallel programs running on Intel multi-core processor. We compare the performance of the RCBs with the corresponding parallel program of the multi-core processor. The speedup factor for the RCBs is between 2 and 72. The DES hardware implementation achieves 20.2 Gbps, a factor of 72 times better than the general processor. The AES in the CBC mode results in a performance of 39.4 Gbps and achieves a speedup of 15.8 times. The throughput of the 1,024-bit RSA encryption is 2.2 Mbps.

Table 2. Performance (gigabit per second) comparison with the general processor

Algorithms	Ours (Gbps)	CPU (Gbps)	Speedup
AES-128	39.4	1.16	15.8
RC5	5.6	0.08	66.7
SHA256	10.9	0.12	68.3
MD5	53.3	2.24	29.2
RSA-1024(Sign)	2.2×10^{-3}	1.2×10^{-3}	2.1

➢   *Performance comparison with related works*

In Table 3, we compare the performance of our design with existing designs. From the result, we obtain a better throughput in most algorithms. The performance of AES and SHA256 in our design is approximately the same. For RC4 and MD5 algorithms, the frequency of our design is higher; therefore, the throughput is higher than that of the related works.

Table 3. Performance comparisons with other designs

Algorithms	Imple.	Area (slice)	Freq. (Mhz)	Perf. (Gbps)
AES-128	Ours	14,833	307.89	39.4
	1	20,720	240.9	30.8
RC4	Ours	915	353.78	0.91
	21	9170	60.8	0.055
SHA256	Ours	11,047	214.34	10.9
	22	4,219	163.80	10.4
MD5	Ours	12,662	248.08	53.3
	23	26,758	66.48	32.0
RSA-1024	Ours	24,996	308.36	2.2×10^{-3}
(Sign)	24	6,826	--	0.3×10^{-3}

4.2   Coprocessor Application in File Encryption

To test and verify the method and architecture proposed in this paper, we used the processor to implement SSL ciphered communication in the Virtex5 FPGA. In addition, we evaluated the feasibility of the SSL accelerator based on one-chip architecture using FPGA.

To test and verify our proposed architecture, we adopt the coprocessor to implement an accelerator on the FPGA that can encrypt the file storage. We analyze the encryption procedure of the common files such as in word or pdf format, which adopts the RC4 and MD5 algorithms to encrypt the user password. Therefore, we select the corresponding RCBs of MD5 and RC4 described above. Next, we build the control circuit and RCBs as the processor.

The processor costs 15,264 slices and 32 BRAM, which runs at 216 MHz. We compare the computation time on FPGA with the parallel programs running on Intel multi-core processor. According to the results shown in Table 4, the coprocessor outperforms the software-based encryption procedure running four threads by a factor of 29.4×.

Table 4. Performance comparison of file encryption (the result is measured by running the program for 10^6 times)

Algorithms	Implements	Time(s)	Performance (Mbps)	Speedup
	1 Thread	26.7	2.39	1
RC4+MD5	4 Threads	9.2	7.03	**10**
	Ours	0.91	70.33	**29.4**

5   Conclusion and Future Work

In this paper, we have presented the design and implementation of a novel crypto coprocessor with flexible architecture and reconfigurable crypto blocks. The RCBs of the crypto processor accelerated the private and public key crypto algorithms. The crypto processor was evaluated by constructing an acceleration system for the encryption procedure of file storage. The high performance and flexibility of the crypto processor design enables its use in various security applications.

For our future work, we plan to develop additional high-performance public-key crypto blocks. To facilitate our crypto processor, we will exploit the high-level synthesis toolchain based on existing architecture for security protocols.

For future work, we plan to develop additional high-performance public-key crypto blocks. To facilitate our crypto processor, we will exploit the high-level synthesis toolchain based on existing architecture for security protocols.

Acknowledgments. This work was supported by the National Science Foundation of China (61125201 and 60921062).

References

1. Freier, A.O., Karlton, P., Kocher, P.C.: Introduction to SSL. IETF draft (1996), https://developer.mozilla.org/zh-CN/docs/Introduction_to_SSL#The_SSL_Protocol
2. Kent, S., Atkinson, R.: Security Architecture for the Internet Protocol. RFC 2401 (November 1998)

3. Taylor, R.R., Goldstein, S.C.: A High-Performance Flexible Architecture for Cryptography. In: Koç, Ç.K., Paar, C. (eds.) CHES 1999. LNCS, vol. 1717, pp. 231–245. Springer, Heidelberg (1999)
4. Antão, S., Chaves, R., Sousa, L.: AES and ECC Cryptography Processor with Runtime Configuration. In: Proceedings of ADCOM (2009)
5. Hodjat, A., Verbauwhede, I.: A 21.54 Gbits/s Fully Pipelined AES Processor on FPGA. In: Proc. FCCM 2004 (2004)
6. Mazzeo, A., Romano, L., Saggese, G.P., et al.: FPGA-based Implementation of a serial RSA processor. In: Proc. DATE 2003 (2003)
7. Michail, H.E., Athanasios, P., et al.: Top-Down Design Methodology for Ultrahigh-Performance Hashing Cores. IEEE Transactions on Dependable and Secure Computing 6(4), 255–268 (2009)
8. Kakarountas, A.P., Michail, H.: High-Speed FPGA Implementation of Secure Hash Algorithm for IPSec and VPN Applications. The Journal of Supercomputing 37, 179–195 (2006)
9. Elbirt, A.J., Paar, C.: An Instruction-Level Distributed Processor for Symmetric-Key Cryptography. IEEE Transactions on Parallel and Distributed Systems 16(5) (2005)
10. Mosanya, E., Teuscher, C., Restrepo, H.F., Galley, P., Sánchez, E.: CryptoBooster: A Reconfigurable and Modular Cryptographic Coprocessor. In: Koç, Ç.K., Paar, C. (eds.) CHES 1999. LNCS, vol. 1717, pp. 246–256. Springer, Heidelberg (1999)
11. Prasanna, V.K., Dandalis, A.: FPGA-based Cryptography for Internet Security. In: Online Symposium for Electronic Engineers (2000)
12. Li, M., Ji, X., Liu, B.: Analysing and Researching Montgomery Algorithm. Science Technology and Engineering 6, 1628–1631 (2006)
13. Rivest, R.L.: The MD5 Message-Digest Algorithm. RFC 1321, MIT Laboratory for Computer Science and RSA Data Security, Inc. (April 1992)
14. Rivest, R., Shamir, A., Adleman, L.: A Method for Obtaining Digital Signatures and Public-Key Cryptosystems. Communications of the ACM 21, 120–126 (1978)
15. NIST Federal Information Processing Standards Publication, FIPS PUB 180-2 (2002)
16. National Institute of Standards and Technology. Advanced Encryption Standard (AES). Federal Information Processing Standards Publications – FIPS 197 (2001)
17. FIPS PUB 46-3, Data Encryption Standard (DES), Reaffirmed (1977)
18. Rivest, R.L.: The RC5 Encryption Algorithm. In: Preneel, B. (ed.) FSE 1994. LNCS, vol. 1008, pp. 86–96. Springer, Heidelberg (1995)
19. OProfile. OProfile Website (2012), http://oprofile.sourceforge.net/news/
20. Bouhraous, A.: Design feasibility study for a 500Gbits/s advanced encryption standard cipher/decipher engine. IET Computers & Digital Techniques 4(4), 334–348 (2010)
21. Kwok, S.H.M., Lam, E.Y.: Effective Uses of FPGAs for Brute-Force Attack on RC4 Ciphers. IEEE Transactions on VLSI Systems 16(8) (August 2008)
22. Michail, H.E., et al.: On the Exploitation of a High-Throughput SHA-256 FPGA Design for HMACACM. Transactions on Reconfigurable Technology and Systems 5(1) (2012)
23. Wang, Y., Zhao, Q., Jiang, L., Shao, Y.: Ultra-High Throughput Implementations for MD5 Hash Algorithm on FPGA. In: Zhang, W., Chen, Z., Douglas, C.C., Tong, W. (eds.) HPCA 2009. LNCS, vol. 5938, pp. 433–441. Springer, Heidelberg (2010)
24. Blum, T., Paar, C.: High-Radix Montgomery Modular Exponentiation on Reconfigurable Hardware. IEEE Transaction on Computer 50(7) (2001)

A PGSA Based Data Replica Selection Scheme for Accessing Cloud Storage System

Bang Zhang, Xingwei Wang, and Min Huang

College of Information Science and Engineering, Northeastern University, Shenyang, 110819
Key Laboratory of Network Control Systems,
Chinese Academy of Sciences, Shenyang, 110016, China
cucumberbb@163.com, {wangxw,mhuang}@mail.neu.edu.cn

Abstract. The data replica management scheme is a critical component of cloud storage system. In order to enhance its scalability and reliability at the same time improve system response time, the multiple data replica scheme is adopted. When a cloud user issues an access request, a suitable replica should be selected to respond to it in order to shorten user access time and promote system load balance. In this paper, with network status, storage node load and historical information of replica selection considered comprehensively, a PGSA (Plant Growth Simulation Algorithm) based data replica selection scheme for cloud storage is proposed to improve average access time and replica utilization. The proposed scheme has been implemented based on CloudSim and performance evaluation has been done. Simulation results have shown that it is both feasible and effective with better performance than certain existent scheme.

Keywords: cloud storage, multiple data replica, replica selection, PGSA (Plant Growth Simulation Algorithm).

1 Introduction

Cloud storage is developed from cloud computing [1]. With the support of clustering, networking, virtualization, distributed operating system and distributed file system and others, it collects huge amount of heterogeneous storage devices in network and make them work cooperatively by application software, providing the unified storage system to enable users to store and access data transparently without the need to know where the data physically locate. The users only need to acquire online storage space through storage service provider without setting up their own data storage center, thus avoiding repeated construction of storage systems as well as saving the investment on hardware and software infrastructure.

Cloud storage is generally composed of massive storage devices distributed over different data centers. These devices are connected through network and have different reliability and performance with temporary even permanent faults happened occasionally. The network status also has influence on the timeliness and dependability of data

J. Wu et al. (Eds.): ACA 2014, CCIS 451, pp. 140–151, 2014.

access. In the face of huge amount of access requests from massive cloud users, deploying multiple replicas of one single data object in cloud storage system is generally needed in order to get timely, reliable and efficient data access services, and thus improve cloud storage system response time to user access and enhance system QoS (Quality of Service) and user QoE(Quality of Experience) [2-6]. A multiple data replica scheme can deploy right quantity of replicas for suitable data objects in due time and due place. It needs an efficient management mechanism to realize the suitable placement of multiple replicas, the suitable selection of the specific replica for user access and consistency maintenance among replicas, etc. In this paper, we discuss how to select the suitable data replica to respond to the user access request to the cloud storage system when multiple data replicas exist. In fact, the problem of data replica selection can be divided into two sub-problems: data replica location and suitable replica selection. The former refers to locate one or more replicas by the data's logical name. The latter refers to select the suitable one from multiple replicas in order to minimize, for example, the user access cost and thus help improve the overall system performance. In this paper, our research focus is put on the latter.

There are many factors which have major influences on the suitable replica selection, including network status, performance of the storage node where the data replica resides, and cloud user access cost to the replica, etc. A replica selection scheme is said to be good if it can shorten the cloud user access time to data as much as possible with the above factors taken into account thoroughly and comprehensively.

Some of the data replica selection mechanism has been proposed. In [7], an adaptive replica selection strategy was presented to employ network bandwidth information and account for its fluctuation in the wide-area environment, taking advantage of multiple replicas and concurrent data transfers. In [8], a two phased replica selection scheme was proposed. In the first coarse-grain phase, replicas with low latency (located at the uncongested network segments) and replicas with high latency (located at the congested network segments) were distinguished. In the second fine-grain phase, the replicas admissible for user access requirements were selected through applying a modified minimum cost and delay policy. In [9], a balanced QoS replica selection strategy was proposed to select a suitable replica which was the closest to the user with almost equal values of QoS parameters (such as availability, time and security).In [10], a workload-driven replica selection algorithm was proposed to minimize query latency in terms of the average query span, i.e., the average number of machines that were involved in processing of a query. In [11], based on the min-max balancing workload method, a dynamic replica selection strategy was proposed to upgrade the efficiency of execution in data grid environments. In [12], a new replica selection strategy was presented. It used the concept of association rules of data mining approach to the most stable network segments and could adapt its replica selection criteria dynamically so as to satisfy user access requirements and reduce system response time. In [13], an ant algorithm based replica selection scheme was proposed. The calculation formula of the probability of a replica being selected was devised, and the candidate replicas were predicted based on the historical replica accessed records. It could help balance the access loads among replicas dynamically. In [14], a hybrid replica selection strategy was proposed. It tried to combine the advantages of genetic algorithm and ant algorithm to find the suitable replica for the user access request. By speeding up the convergence to the optimum, the system response time to access was improved.

Inspired by the above research, a data replica selection scheme for accessing cloud storage system is proposed in this paper. It comprehensively considers network status, performance and load of the storage node where the replica resides, and historical information of replica selection. It tries to select the suitable data replica to respond to the cloud user access request based on the idea of PGSA (Plant Growth Simulation Algorithm) [15], so that the QoE of the user to use the cloud storage system can be improved in terms of replica utilization and average access time.

2   Problem Formulation

The suitable replica selection scheme is one of critical components of the data replica management scheme in cloud storage system. It selects the suitable replica from multiple candidates to respond to the cloud user access request. A good replica selection strategy should at first determine the related factors which have significant influence on the QoE of the user to access data, and then a suitable replica selection algorithm should be devised based on these factors. In this paper, the following major factors are considered when the suitable replica is selected to respond to the user request [13].

(1) Network status. It is an important factor to be considered when replica selection is done, because, for example, the available bandwidth affects the data transmission time, the end-to-end delay affects user access time, and the packet loss rate affects the data transfer reliability. Therefore, in the process of replica selection to respond to the cloud user request, the replicas which locate in those network segments in good conditions should be chosen preferentially. In addition, under the environment of cloud storage, the distance between the cloud user and the storage node where the replica resides should be considered when making the replica selection decision. It affects the data transfer latency and further influences the system response time. Thus, choosing the nearer replica to the user is more appropriate when responding to the access request.

(2) Storage node performance. It mainly refers to the node's data access speed, computing capability and networking capacity to the external network.

(3) Storage node access load. In general, the more heavy the access load of a storage node, the weaker its ability to respond to the cloud user access request, thus the replica which resides in the light-loaded storage node is preferred when selecting the suitable in replica.

(4) Historical information. The historical information of a specific replica being chosen to respond to the cloud user access request can reflect the user QoE on using this replica to certain degree and represent the measurement of the system on the effect of setting up this replica in a sense. The more the specific replica being selected to respond to the user requests, the more suitable and valuable it being setup. Thus, in this paper, the ratio of the times of a replica being chosen to respond to the user requests to the total times of its corresponding data object being accessed is also considered to be a reference to the process of suitable replica selection.

In summary, selecting suitable data replica can reduce the cloud user access latency and the network resource consumption, it can effectively achieve load balance among storage nodes where replicas reside at the same time improve the reliability of data access, etc. Therefore, how to select the suitable data replica from multiple candidates to respond to the cloud user access request is critical to the effective and efficient data replica management. The purpose of the proposed suitable data replica selection scheme in this paper is to achieve fast and reliable data access as well as efficient use of replicas with the above mentioned factors taken into account thoroughly.

3   Algorithm Design

PGSA is an intelligent optimization algorithm using the plant phototropism mechanism [15]. Based on the characteristics of the plant phototropism, it uses the plant growth environment as the problem solution space and determines the corresponding plant morphactin concentration according to the objective function value of the problem solution. The greater its difference from the root (i.e., the initial solution), the bigger the plant morphactin concentration, and thus the higher the plant growth chance. Therefore, it simulates the plant growth dynamic model to converge to the global optimum rapidly. In this paper, we use morphactin concentration to represent the data replica's fitness to the user access request, and select the suitable data replica by adjusting and comparing its morphactin concentration.

3.1   Calculation of Replica Morphactin Concentration

We refer to the basic idea of PGSA to devise the proposed suitable replica selection scheme. It mainly uses the morphactin concentration as the criteria to decide which replica being selected. When a new data replica R_j is set up in the cloud storage system, the Eqn. (1) is used to calculate the initial morphactin concentration of the replica.

$$\tau_j(0) = f_j \Big/ r_j \tag{1}$$

where the size of the R_j is denoted by f_j and the access speed of the storage node in which R_j resides is denoted by r_j.

After the replica setup, its morphactin concentration is adjusted when it being selected and accessed, and its calculation is defined in the following Eqn. (2):

$$\tau_j^{new} = \rho \tau_j^{old} + \Delta_{\tau_j} \tag{2}$$

where the proportion of the historical morphactin concentration information is denoted by ρ and the variation of the morphactin concentration is denoted by Δ_{τ_j}.

In fact, the morphactin concentration adjustment is involved in the following three different cases.

When a data replica has been selected to respond to the user request, its morphactin concentration will be reduced and the reduction is defined in the following Eqn. (3).

$$\Delta_{\tau_j} = -\left(f_j \Big/ bw_j + dl_j \right) \tag{3}$$

where the available bandwidth of the storage node in which R_j resides, is denoted by bw_j and the transfer latency between the storage node and the user is denoted by dl_j. The reason why the morphactin concentration is reduced is that load balance should be considered, once a replica was selected to respond to a user request, its probability of being selected to respond to other user requests should be decreased in order to prevent it being overloaded.

After a replica selected, if it is accessed successfully, its performance is considered good, thus as a kind of encouragement, its morphactin concentration is increased to make its probability of being selected to respond to user requests in the future higher, and the increase is defined in the following Eqn. (4).

$$\Delta_{\tau_j} = \vartheta_e \cdot \left(f_j \big/ bw_j + dl_j \right) \tag{4}$$

where the reward factor is denoted by ϑ_e.

If the access to the selected replica failed, it means that the selected replica does not work normally at present, its morphactin concentration is decreased to make its probability of being selected to respond to user requests in the future lower, and the decrease is defined in the following Eqn. (5).

$$\Delta_{\tau_j} = -\vartheta_p \cdot \left(f_j \Big/ bw_j + dl_j \right) \tag{5}$$

where the penalty factor is denoted by ϑ_p.

3.2   Calculation of Replica Selection Probability

The change of a replica's morphactin concentration affects the probability of its being selected to respond to user requests. In this paper, the replica selection probability are determined by two parts: p_j and p_j. The former is derived from the replica morphactin concentration and the node load, reflecting the influence of the status of the network and the node where the replica resides, i.e., the instant information on the selection decision. The latter is based on the historical information, reflecting the influence of the historical access frequency to the replica on the decision of whether it being selected in the future to respond to user requests.

In order to reflect the load status of the node where the replica resides, in this paper we divide the node load into 3 levels, i.e., light-loaded, moderate-loaded, and heavy-loaded. At the same time, a load factor is introduced to characterize the node load and defined as follows.

$$t(\lambda_j) = \begin{cases} e^{-b} & \lambda_j \in [0, \lambda_j^{\text{light}}] \\ e^{-b^2} & \lambda_j \in (\lambda_j^{\text{light}}, \lambda_j^{\text{heavy}}] \\ e^{-b^3} & \lambda_j \in (\lambda_j^{\text{heavy}}, \lambda_j^{\text{max}}) \end{cases} \tag{6}$$

where λ_j indicates the current access volume of the storage node in which R_j resides, λ_j^{light} and λ_j^{heavy} are boundary values of light-loaded and heavy-loaded respectively, λ_j^{max} is the upper bound of the access volume which the storage node can accept, b is a constant greater than 1. The calculation of p_j is defined as follows.

$$p_j = \frac{\tau_j + \alpha t(\lambda_j)}{\sum_{j=1}^{k}(\tau_j + \alpha t(\lambda_j))} \tag{7}$$

where α is the adjustment coefficient determined by experience or experiment.

For p_j', it is set be the ratio of the times of a replica being chosen to respond to the user requests to the total times of its corresponding data object being accessed.

Taking p_j and p_j' into account comprehensively, the probability of a replica being selected is defined as follows.

$$p_j'' = \beta p_j + (1-\beta)p_j' \tag{8}$$

where β is a weighting coefficient to reflect the relative importance of the instant information and historical information on replica selection decision.

The selection probability of each replica is calculated by Eqn. (8) and then the roulette method is used to select the specific replica. The selection process is described as follows.

Assume that there are k replicas of the specific data object in the cloud storage system, the selection probability of each replica is $p_j^{''} (1 \leq j \leq k)$, then we have $ps(j) = p_0^{''} + p_1^{''} + \cdots + p_j^{''}$, $1 \leq j \leq k$. Generate a random number r between $r \in [0, ps(k)]$, if $ps(j-1) < r \leq ps(j)$, then R_j is selected.

3.3   Algorithm Description

Based on the above discussion, the algorithm of the PGSA based suitable replica selection scheme is described as follows.

Step 1: Initialization: for each data object in the cloud storage system, generate k growing points corresponding to k replicas, and use Eqn. (1) to calculate the initial morphactin concentration of each growing point; input the user request set.

Step 2: Take one user request out of the input set and determine the specific growing points corresponding to the data object requested by the user.

Step 3: Calculate the selection probability of each replica corresponding to the growing point by the Eqn. (8), use the roulette method to select the matched growing point, i.e., the suitable replica to the specific user request.

Step 4: Do the regeneration process of growing point to update the corresponding morphactin concentration.

Step 4.1: Update the corresponding replica's morphactin concentration to the growing point selected in Step 3 by Eqn. (2).

Step 4.2: Access the selected replica as the response to the user request. If succeeded, use the Eqn. (4) to update the replica's morphactin concentration morpheme as encouragement; otherwise, use the Eqn. (5) to update it as punishment.

Step 5: Check whether the user request set becomes empty: if empty, the algorithm ends, otherwise go to Step 2.

4   Performance Evaluation

The simulation experiment of and performance evaluation on the proposed scheme in this paper have been done on the CloudSim [16]. The main functions of the proposed scheme, which have been implemented by simulation, are listed in Table. 1.

Table 1. Main functions of the proposed scheme

Name	Description
void get_ replica_info (…)	Get information about replica.
double cal_ morphactin (…)	Calculate morphactin concentration for a replica.
double cal_ probability (…)	Calculate probability of a replica being selected.
void roulette(…)	Use roulette method to select a replica.
double tuning (…)	Reduce a selected replica's morphactin concentration.
double reward (…)	Increase a successfully accessed replica's morphactin concentration.
double penalty(…)	Decrease an access failed replica's morphactin concentration.

In order to evaluate the performance of the PGSA based data replica selection scheme proposed in this paper (simply call it P scheme below), it is compared with the ant algorithm based one proposed in [13] (simply call it A scheme below) in terms of replica utilization and average access time.

4.1   Replica Utilization

Replica utilization (RU) is defined as the ratio of the response of a replica to the access requests to the corresponding data object. Apparently, the sum of RUs of all replicas of the same data object is 1. From Fig. 1, it can be seen that the RU distribution of P scheme is more balanced than that of A scheme. This is because when replica selection decision made, P scheme considers not only the performance of the storage node where the replica resides and the network status, but also the storage node load and the historical information of replica access, once the above factors changed, it will re-select the suitable replica; in addition, after a replica selected, its morphactin concentration will be adjusted and thus influence its chance to be selected in the future, promoting the selection balance among replicas. By contrast, A scheme does not take the above factors into account thoroughly, leading to a little poor RU distribution.

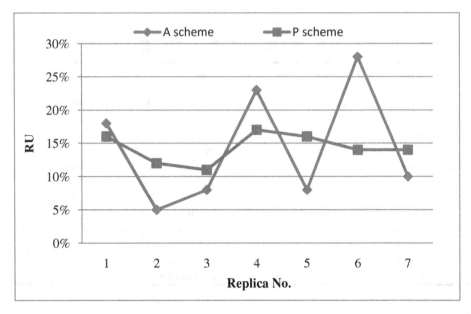

Fig. 1. Replica utilization distribution

4.2   Average Access Time

A user request's access time is defined as the time interval from it being issued to the end of the selected replica access, and the average access time (AAT) is defined as the average value of the access time of the simultaneously arrived user requests. From Fig. 2, it can be seen that the AAT of P scheme is better that of A scheme. This is because P scheme tries to achieve balance between the replica access time and the load of the storage node where the replica resides, thus it often selects the replica with smaller access cost and lower corresponding storage node load. Meanwhile, it uses roulette method to determine the selected replica by probability, this can further balance the access load among replicas, in the long run, it helps reduce AAT significantly. It also can be seen that, as the increase of the amount of replicas, P scheme has more chance to select the suitable replica from more replicas, each replica's access load is further reduced and becomes more balanced, thus AAT is reduced further. By contrast, A scheme is inflexible in reasonable apportion of replica access load and lacks dynamic adjustment ability, leading to the bigger AAT.

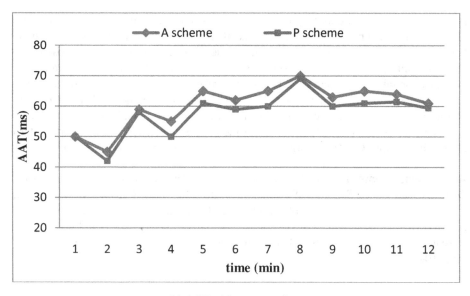

(a) AAT with seven replicas

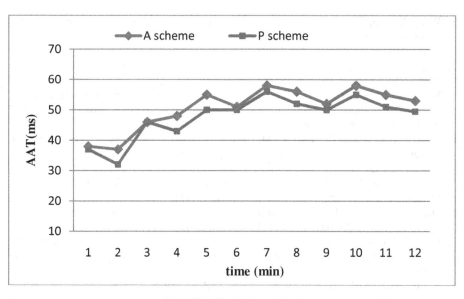

(b) AAT with eleven replicas

Fig. 2. Average access time

5   Conclusions

The data replica management scheme is an important method to improve the efficiency of cloud storage system and a good data replica selection scheme is critical to improve its performance. It can not only help balance system load and shorten user access time, but also help improve replica utilization and make them work well. In this paper, based on the basic idea of PGSA, a data replica selection scheme for cloud storage is proposed with network status, performance and load of storage node and historical information of replica selection taken into account. It has been implemented based on CloudSim and performance evaluation has been done. Simulation results have shown that it has good performance in terms of replica utilization and average access time. In the near future, we will make the prototype implementation of the proposed scheme over the Northeastern University Campus Cloud platform in order to verify and enhance its practicability.

Acknowledgements. This work is supported by the National Science Foundation for Distinguished Young Scholars of China under Grant No. 61225012 and No. 71325002; the Specialized Research Fund of the Doctoral Program of Higher Education for the Priority Development Areas under Grant No. 20120042130003; the Fundamental Research Funds for the Central Universities under Grant No. N110204003 and No. N120104001.

References

1. Wang, X., Sun, J., Li, H., Wu, C., Huang, M.: A reverse auction based allocation mechanism in the cloud computing environment. Applied Mathematics & Information Sciences 7(1L), 75–84 (2013)
2. Lin, C., Hu, J., Kong, X.: Survey on models and evaluation of quality of experience. Chinese Journal of Computers 35(1), 1–15 (2012)
3. Wang, X., Cheng, H., Li, K., Li, J., Sun, J.: A cross-layer optimization based integrated routing and grooming algorithm for green multi-granularity transport networks. Journal of Parallel and Distributed Computing 73(6), 807–822 (2013)
4. Wang, X., Cheng, H., Huang, M.: Multi-robot navigation based QoS routing in self-organizing networks. Engineering Applications of Artificial Intelligence 26(1), 262–272 (2013)
5. Xie, X., Wang, X., Wen, Z., Huang, M.: A QoS routing protocol for cognitive networks. Chinese Journal of Computers 36(9), 1807–1815 (2013)
6. Qu, D., Wang, X., Huang, M.: An aware ant routing in mobile peer-to-peer networks. Chinese Journal of Computers 36(7), 1456–1464 (2013)
7. Gui, B., Yi, K.: A global dynamic scheduling with replica selection algorithm using GridFTP. Challenges in Environmental Science and Computer Engineering 1, 106–109 (2010)
8. Almuttairi, R.M., Wankar, R., Negi, A., Rao, C.R., Agarwal, A., Buyya, R.: A two phased service oriented Broker for replica selection in data grids. Future Generation Computer Systems 29(4), 953–972 (2013)
9. Jaradat, A., Amin, A.H.M., Zakaria, M.N.: Balanced QoS replica selection strategy to enhance data grid. In: International Conference on Networking and Information Technology, vol. 17, pp. 356–364 (2011)
10. Ashwin Kumar, K., Deshpande, A., Khuller, S.: Data placement and replica selection for improving co-location in distributed environments. Cornell University

11. Cheng, K., Wang, H., Wen, C., Lin, Y., Li, K., Wang, C.: Dynamic file replica location and selection strategy in data grids. In: IEEE International Conference on Ubi-Media Computing, pp. 484–489 (2008)
12. Almuttairi, R.M., Wankar, R., Negi, A., Chillarige, R.R., Almahna, M.S.: New replica selection technique for binding replica sites in data grids. Energy, Power and Control, 187–194 (2010)
13. Sun, M., Sun, J., Li, M., Yu, C.: Research of replica selection scheme based on ant algorithm in data grid. Computer Engineering and Application 43(1), 145–147 (2007)
14. Han, Z., Lin, Z., Wang, R.: A novel replica selection strategy based on combination algorithm in data grid. Journal of Nanjing University of Posts and Telecommunication (Natural Science) 31(5), 78–82 (2011)
15. Ding, X., You, J.: Plant growth simulation algorithm, pp. 1–59. Shanghai People's Publishing House, Shanghai (2011)
16. Calheiros, R.N., Ranjan, R., Beloglazov, A., et al.: CloudSim: a toolkit for modeling and simulation of cloud computing environments and evaluation of resource provisioning algorithms. Software: Practice and Experience 41(1), 23–50 (2011)

Location-Aware Multi-user Resource Allocation in Distributed Clouds

Jiaxin Li[1], Dongsheng Li[1], Jing Zheng[2], and Yong Quan[3]

[1] National Key Laboratory for Parallel and Distributed Processing,
National University of Defense Technology, Changsha, China
[2] Information Center of Logistics Department, Beijing, China
[3] School of Computer Science, National University of Defense Technology,
Changsha, China
{licyh,dsli.lee,jing.z,healthyquan}@gmail.com

Abstract. Resource allocation for multi-user across multiple data centers is an important problem in cloud computing environments. Many geographically-distributed users may request virtualized resources simultaneously. And the distances from users to allocated resources have much impact on the quality of service (QoS) in multiple data centers environment. Most existing methods do not take all these factors into account when allocating resources. They usually result in poor runtime performance of users' virtual computing environment and the remarkable difference of users' QoS. In this paper, we propose RAMD, a resource allocation algorithm based on multi-stage decision in multiple data centers. The RAMD algorithm allocate VMs to users, taking into account the correlation and interaction between multiple users, so as to minimize the sum of all users' service distances (i.e. determined by user location and network distance of virtual machines). Experimental results show that the algorithm can effectively deal with the cloud resource allocation for multi-user across multiple data centers. It can improve the runtime performance of users' virtualized resources and reduce the difference of QoS.

Keywords: resource allocation, data centers, location-aware, multi-user, multiple data centers.

1 Introduction

With the development of cloud computing, the integration and interaction of geographically distributed data centers has become important service mode in clouds [1]. Multiple data centers (MDC) can rationally schedule data center resources to users according to their requirements and provide efficient services for users located in different regions. Thereby it can enhance the user experiences, improve the overall resource utilization rate of cloud data centers and reduce the operating costs of cloud service providers. MDC also can meet some certain requirements about elasticity and fault tolerance.

J. Wu et al. (Eds.): ACA 2014, CCIS 451, pp. 152–162, 2014.

In reality, cloud computing system usually consists of some data centers which are distributed in different geographical areas. These data centers connect with each other by dedicated network with high reliability and high transmission rate [2]. Compared to traditionally centralized Internet data center (IDC), users in different regions can access to the close data centers in MDC environments. The services user requested can be provided by data centers nearby, it can reduce access latency and network load, meanwhile, improve communication efficiency. And for some high-bandwidth applications, it helps to reduce network costs [3]. Moreover, users' requests may come at any time (many users may request virtual machines simultaneously or in the same period of time), so the cloud resource allocation for multi-user is rather universal and typical. This paper will study the cloud resource allocation mechanism for multiple users in multiple data centers environment.

However, most existing studies, e.g. [4-14], mainly focus on resource allocation mechanisms in centralized data center, and there are few studies involving the MDC. On the other hand, they usually implement virtual machine (VM) allocation for a single user at a time without considering methods for multiple users.

Though the study [15] considered the resource allocation problem in distributed cloud data centers and proposed a resource allocation algorithm based on the maximum clique problem in order to minimize the network diameter (i.e. the maximum distance among VMs), but it was only fit for the particular cases in which all the network traffic between any VMs were known. Moreover, it did not consider that resource allocation for multi-user can be performed simultaneously and user locations can have impact on the QoS in multiple data centers environment.

Resource allocation methods in single data center (or centralized IDC) can usually be directly extended to the MDC environment. However, due to the fact that the merger of many data centers will be considerable larger (i.e. simply suppose that a MDC consists of many single data centers, without regard to topological structure among the IDCs), it is easy to lead to a low performance when using previous methods. In addition, the purpose of introducing the MDC is to facilitate the users in different regions to acquire service nearby. And that particularity has not be considered with previous extended algorithms. We take the positional relationship between users and data centers as the researching point, and aim to balance the network distance of users' VMs and the distance between users and data centers. So we propose a resource allocation algorithm based on multi-stage decision in MDC environments, called RAMD, which taking into account the correlation and interaction between multiple users and using a multi-stage strategy to implement the resource allocation, so as to minimize the sum of all users' service distances.

The main contribution of this paper is shown as below. Firstly, we defined the problem of location-aware multiple-user resource allocation. Secondly, we designed the resource allocation algorithm based on multi-stage decision in MDC environments. Finally, we perform experiments to evaluate the RAMD algorithm and verify that the algorithm can effectively deal with the cloud resource allocation for multi-user across multiple data centers.

The rest of this paper is organized as follows. Section 2 describes the resource allocation problem in MDC environments. Section 3 proposes the selection algorithm of MDC based on user location for single user request. Section 4 illustrates the RAMD algorithm. Section 5 evaluates the algorithms by simulation experiments. Section 6 introduces the related work. Section 7 presents the conclusion.

2   Problem Description

In MDC environments, users may request virtual machine resource simultaneously or in the same period of time. Since users can request the number of data centers, the number of racks, or the number of physical machines to place their VMs, here we take the number of IDCs that users want to place VMs at least as an example (i.e. users decide the number of IDCs to place first, then if the MDC environment could not satisfy this requirement, it will automatically select more IDCs to place). We divide the resource allocation method based on MDC into two steps as follows:

i) For all user requests, determine which IDCs to place VMs in the MDC and how many VMs to place in each IDC. By default, we equalize the number of VMs in each IDC for every user to reduce the traffic between data centers.

ii) Allocating VMs in each IDC. In this case, we can use resource allocation algorithms in centralized data center, e.g. [4]. The paper does not discuss this owing to limited space.

Our work in this paper is to solve the resource allocation problem in step i). For every user, we will consider the user location and the network distance of multiple IDCs that would be selected to place VMs. Our goal is to make all users in different regions select the IDCs that meet their requirements.

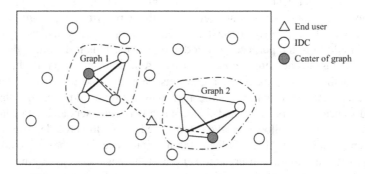

Fig. 1. Example of geographically distributed data centers

Figure 1 shows an example diagram of geographically distributed data centers. Assuming that the current end-user wants to place requested VMs into four IDCs, the figure shows two possible options: Graph 1 and Graph 2. The gray nodes indicate the centers of the graphs respectively. Graph 1 is far from the end-user but gets a small network diameter, while Graph 2 is close to the end-user but gets a large network diameter. How to find the IDCs that meet the conditions in the MDC and effectively balance the relationship of both sides are our research points.

In MDC environments, we define communication delay or network hops between IDCs to be their network distance. Assuming that the number of total IDCs is m, then all IDCs constitute an undirected complete graph $G_M = (V_M, E_M, C_M^V, D_M^E)$. Here the subscript M means the MDC; V_M specifies the node set of IDCs; E_M specifies the edge set of IDCs; C_M^V specifies the set of the number of available VMs; D_M^E specifies the set of the network distances between IDCs.

Assuming that there are n user requests of $U=\{P_U, K, m_U\}$, where P_U specifies the user location, K specifies the number of VMs requested by the user, m_U specifies at least the number of IDCs requested by the user (we suppose the number of actually selected IDCs is $s(>=m_U)$, so we place $\lfloor K/s \rfloor$ or $\lceil K/s \rceil$ VMs in each IDC, the value sequence of s is m_U, m_U+1, m_U+2, ..., until meet the conditions). For each user request U, our goal is to look for all sub-graphs $G_U^i=(V_U^i, E_U^i, C_U^{Vi}, D_U^{Ei})(i=1,2,...)$ which satisfy the user request in the undirected complete graph G_M. Here the subscript U means user request; V_U specifies the node set of $/V_U/$ IDCs that satisfy the user request, exists $V_U \subseteq V_M$; E_U specifies the edge set of V_U, exists $E_U \subseteq E_M$; C_U^V specifies the set of allocated VMs to V_U for the user (the value is $\lfloor K//V_U^i/ \rfloor$ or $\lceil K//V_U^i/ \rceil$), exists $C_U^V \subseteq C_M^V$; D_U^E specifies the set of the network distances between IDCs in V_U.

Definition Service Distance (SD): For a user, we define the distance between the user and G_U^i (i=1,2,...) to be the Service Distance (SD_i) of the user. The computational formula is as follows.

$$SD_i = \sigma * Distance\left(P_U, G_U^i\right) + (1-\sigma) * Diameter\left(G_U^i\right), \ i = 1, 2, ... \tag{1}$$

Here, $Distance(P_U, G_U^i)$ specifies the distance between the user location and the center of the graph G_U^i, $Diameter(G_U^i)$ specifies the network diameter of G_U^i, σ specifies the balance factor, the default value is taken as 0.5.

We define the optimization target to be minimizing the sum of users' service distances for all n user requests.

$$Minimize\ TSD = \sum_{t=1}^{n} SD^{(t)} \tag{2}$$

Here $SD^{(t)}$ specifies the service distance of the user t.

3   Selection Algorithm of MDC

Since our goal is to determine which IDCs to place in MDC for every user request. We will take into account the correlation and interaction between multiple users and propose a multi-stage strategy to implement the resource allocation in Section 4.

In this section, we will consider the user location and the network distance of multiple IDCs that would be selected to place VMs for single user request. Then we propose a selection algorithm of MDC base on user locations and the algorithm is shown in Figure 2.

Looking for all sub-graphs $G_U^i = (V_U^i, E_U^i, C_U^{Vi}, D_U^{Ei})$ (i = 1, 2, ...) which satisfy a user request in the undirected complete graph G_M is a NP-hard problem. So we design an approximation algorithm to solve it.

Algorithm 1. GetGuAndDiameter(v, G_M, U)

Input: v: the initial node to be extended; $G_M=(V_M, E_M, C_M^V, D_M^E)$: the MDC; $U=\{P_U, K, m_U\}$: the user request;

Output: $G_U^i=(V_U^i, E_U^i, C_U^{Vi}, D_U^{Ei})$: the sub-graph that satisfied the user request; Diameter(G_U^i): the network diameter of G_U^i;

1   $G_U^i \leftarrow \{v\} \cup \{C_U^{Vi}(v) \leftarrow \min\{\lfloor K/m_U \rfloor, C_M^V\}\}$;
2   $Q \leftarrow \{$all vertex connected to v$\}$;
3   Diameter $\leftarrow 0$;
4   last $\leftarrow K - C_U^{Vi}$;
5   **for** $z = 1$ to m_U **do**
6   tmp_dia $\leftarrow$ MAX_VALUE;
7   **for** u $\in$ Q **do**
8   **if** ($z<m_U$ && $C_M^V(u) >= \lfloor K/m_U \rfloor \parallel z==m_U$ && $C_M^V(u) >=$ last)
                                    and $D_M^E(u, G_U^i) <$ tmp_dia **then**
9   tmp_dia $\leftarrow D_M^E(u, G_U^i)$;
10   tmp_v $\leftarrow$ u;
11   **end if**
12   **end for**
13      $G_U^i \leftarrow G_U^i \cup \{tmp_v\} \cup \{C_U^{Vi}(tmp_v) \leftarrow \min\{\lfloor K/m_U \rfloor, C_M^V(tmp_v),$ last$\}\}$;
14      $Q \leftarrow Q \cup \{$all vertex connected to tmp_v$\}$;
15   Diameter $\leftarrow \max\{$Diameter, tmp_dia$\}$;
16   last $\leftarrow$ last $- C_U^{Vi}($tmp_v$)$;
17   **if** last $== 0$ **then**
18   **break**;
19 **end for**
20 **return** G_U^i, Diameter;

Fig. 2. Selection algorithm of MDC

Algorithm 2. FindCenterOfGraph(G_U^i)

Input: $G_U^i=(V_U^i, E_U^i, C_U^{Vi}, D_U^{Ei})$: the sub-graph that satisfied the user request;

Output: vc: the center of G_U^i;

1   min $\leftarrow$ MAX_VALUE;
2   **for** each v in V_U^i **do**
3   now $\leftarrow 0$;
4   **for** each u in V_U^i **do**
5   **if** v$\neq$u **and** $D_U^{Ei}(v,u) >$ now **then**
6   now $\leftarrow D_U^{Ei}(v,u)$;
7   **end if**
8   **end for**
9   **if** now $<$ min **then**
10   min $\leftarrow$ now;
11   vc $\leftarrow$ v;
12   **end if**
13 **end for**
14 **return** vc;

Fig. 3. The algorithm to find center of graph

The selection algorithm of MDC (Algorithm 1) calculates a sub-graph $G_U{}^i$ that satisfies the user request U by a node of IDCs at a time. The algorithm uses a method based on minimum spanning tree (MST) to extend nodes. The initial node set of the sub-graph $G_U{}^i$ includes a node of IDCs, every time it selects the node that has shortest network distance to $G_U{}^i$ and the number of its available VMs is not less than $\lfloor K/m_U \rfloor$ to join into the set (and determines $\lfloor K/m_U \rfloor$ or $\lceil K/m_U \rceil$ VMs to be placed), until m_U IDCs to be selected. If it exists unallocated VMs (i.e. $last \neq 0$), then we selects the final IDC (the number of its available VMs is not less than $last$) according to previous procedure. If it does not exist a solution, we will iteratively replace m_U with m_U+1 to solve it (pseudo-code omitted this step). At the end, the algorithm returns the subgraph $G_U{}^i$ and the network diameter. The time complexity is $O(mm_U)$.

The center of the graph represents the node that gets the minimum value of the maximum of the distance to other nodes in the graph. We regard it as the center of the multiple IDCs that be selected for VMs placement. The algorithm to find the center of the graph is shown in Algorithm 2.

4   Resource Allocation Algorithm Based on Multi-stage Decision

Location-aware multiple-user resource allocation in MDC cloud environments is also a NP-hard problem. The paper defined the optimization target to be minimizing the sum of all users' service distances for all user requests. In order to achieve that target, we use above approximation algorithm (Section 3) to work out the resource allocation schemes to all user requests. Then we propose a resource allocation algorithm based on multi-stage decision in MDC environments. RAMD takes full advantage of the feature to multi-user.

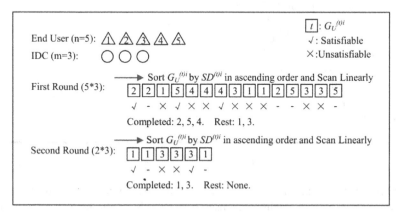

Fig. 4. Example of RAMD

As shown in Figure 4, there are 5 users and 3 IDCs. In the first round of the allocation process, the algorithm first calculates all possible allocation schemes (total is 5*3) for all users (Described in Section 3), and sorts all schemes by the service distance in ascending order, then uses linear scanning from left to right to select feasible schemes. For example, it first selected the first scheme of user 2, and skipped the second scheme of user 2 (because of user 2 was already allocated). Then it met the scheme of user 1 and would determine whether the number of available VMs in IDCs can satisfy it or not. If it was not satisfied then skipped it, or selected it. Repeat this process. After the first round, it completed the allocation of the users 2, 5 and 4. In the second round of the allocation process, used the same method to allocate the remaining users 1 and 3. Until it completed resource allocation for all users.

Algorithm 3. MinTSD_MultistageDecision(G_M, U)

Input: G_M=(V_M, E_M, C_M^V, D_M^E): the MDC; $\{U^{(t)}=\{P_U^{(t)}, K^{(t)}, m_U^{(t)}\} \mid t=1,2,\ldots,n \}$: all user requests;

   Output: Z: set of allocation schemes; *TSD*: sum of users' service distances;

1    $Z \leftarrow \emptyset$; $TSD \leftarrow 0$;

2    $Q \leftarrow \{ U^{(t)} \mid t=1,2,\ldots,n\}$;

3   **while** $Q \neq \emptyset$ **do**

4   **for** t:each U in Q **do**

5   **for** i:each IDC v in V_M **do**

6   **if** $C_M^V(v) >= \lfloor K^{(t)} / m_U^{(t)} \rfloor$ **then**

7                    $G_U^{(t)i} \leftarrow$ **GetGuAndDiameter(v, G_M, $U^{(t)}$)**;

8                    $SD^{(t)i} \leftarrow \sigma*Distance(P_U^{(t)}, G_U^{(t)i}) + (1-\sigma)*Diameter(G_U^{(t)i})$;

9   **end if**

10   **end for**

11   **end for**

12   Sort all $G_U^{(t)i}$ by $SD^{(t)i}$ in ascending order;

13   **for** each $G_U^{(t)i}$ **do**

14   **if** $U^{(t)} \in Q$ and $C_U^{V(t)i} \subseteq C_M^V$ **then**

15                $Q \leftarrow Q - \{U^{(t)}\}$;

16                $C_M^V \leftarrow C_M^V - C_U^{V(t)i}$;

17                $Z \leftarrow Z \cup \{ G_U^{(t)i} \}$;

18                $TSD \leftarrow TSD + SD^{(t)i}$;

18   **end if**

19   **end for**

20   **end while**

21   **return** Z,TSD;

Fig. 5. The RAMD algorithm

RAMD (Algorithm 3) uses a multi-stage strategy to implement resource allocation. The set Q specifies all unallocated user requests. At each stage, it figures out all possible allocation schemes $\{G_U^{(t)i}\}$ for all unallocated user requests, and sorts all these schemes by service distance $SD^{(t)i}$ in ascending order. Then it uses linear scanning from left to right to select feasible schemes that are unallocated ($U^{(t)} \in Q$) and can be allocated ($C_U^{V(t)i} \subseteq C_M^V$). The time complexity of lines 4~11 is $O(nm)*O(mm_U)$, line 12 is $O(nmlg(nm))$ and lines 13~19 is $O(nm)$, so the total time complexity of the algorithm is $O(n*(O(nm)*O(mm_U) + O(nmlg(nm)) + O(nm))) = O(n^2m^2m_U)$, a polynomial complexity.

5   Experimental Results

In this section, we will evaluate the performance of these algorithms through experiments, including the RAMD algorithm, Random algorithm and Greedy algorithm.

When a user selects its multiple data centers to place VMs, Random algorithm each randomly selects an IDC that the number of available VMs satisfies the user request until m_U IDCs to be selected, while Greedy algorithm selects the allocation scheme that satisfies the user request and be of minimum service distance.

Table 1. Experimental setup

	1	2	3
#IDCs (variable m)	10	100	1000
#VMs in a IDC	10000	1000	100
total #VMs	10^5	10^5	10^5
coordinate range of IDCs and users	[0~10^4, 0~10^4]	[0~10^4, 0~10^4]	[0~10^4, 0~10^4]

Table 1 shows the simulation experimental setup, which includes 3 types of MDC. The total #VMs is 10^5, #IDCs are 10, 100, 1000 respectively. And the coordinate values of IDCs and user locations are randomly distributed in [0~10^4, 0~10^4].

Assuming that the number of VMs of all user requests (variable K) is randomly distributed in [1, 500] and the number of IDCs of all user requests (variable m_U) is randomly distributed in [1, 10]. So the number of user requests is about 400 (i.e. until the number of available VMs in multiple data centers is not sufficient). We report the results as average of 100 runs.

Figure 6 shows the experimental results. Compared to the random algorithm and the greedy algorithm, the RAMD algorithm can get the better service performance (determined by the average of users' service distances). Moreover, the greater the number of IDCs in MDC, the better the service performance for same algorithms. The reason is that the more IDCs to be densely distributed, the better to acquire service nearby for users and reduce the network diameter of multiple IDCs that are selected to place VMs.

Since the random algorithm and the greedy algorithm allocate virtualized resources according to the order of users' arrival sequence, the random algorithm may make the difference between users' service performance large, while the greedy algorithm may make the difference between users that come early or later obvious. RAMD can improve the runtime performance of users' virtualized resources and reduce the difference of users' service performance (i.e. users' QoS).

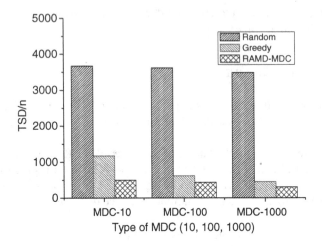

Fig. 6. Experimental results of the three algorithms in MDC

6   Related Work

Most existing studies mainly focus on resource allocation in single centralized data center, and there are few studies involving the MDC [4-14]. On the other hand, they usually implement virtual machine (VM) allocation for a single user at a time without considering methods for multiple users [6] [7].

In MDC environments, resource allocation methods can usually be directly extended from the methods (e.g. [4],[8]) of single data center or centralized IDC. But due to the fact that the merger of multiple data centers will be considerable larger, it is easy to lead to a low performance. Another method divided the resource allocation top-down into two steps: the IDC selection and the allocation within IDC [15], then took different methods in each step to deal with the resource allocation problem.

To consider the issue of resource allocation for multiuser across MDC environments, many studies mainly focus on minimizing overall communication costs between VMs within single IDC or centralized IDC (e.g. [4]). And the network-aware resource allocation [15] aims to minimize the network diameter. However, we consider that user location can impact on the QoS and define the optimization target to be minimizing the sum of all users' service distances.

7   Conclusion

Cloud resource allocation problem for multi-user in multiple data centers is one of hot topics in cloud computing. To solve the resource allocation problem in MDC cloud environments, existing methods usually lack enough consideration. For example, resource allocation for multi-user can be performed simultaneously and user locations can have impact on the quality of service in multiple data centers environment. These usually result in poor runtime performance of users' virtualized resources and the difference of QoS for users is obvious. In this paper, we proposed RAMD, a resource allocation algorithm based on multi-stage decision in multiple data centers. The RAMD algorithm allocates VMs to users, taking into account the correlation and interaction between multiple users, so as to minimize the sum of all users' service distances. The algorithm uses a multi-stage strategy to implement the resource allocation. At each stage, it works out all possible allocation schemes for all unallocated user requests and sorts all these schemes by service distance in ascending order, then uses linear scanning from left to right to select feasible schemes that are unallocated and can be allocated. Experimental results show that the algorithm can effectively deal with the cloud resource allocation for multi-user in multiple data centers. It can improve the runtime performance of users' virtualized resources and reduce the difference of QoS.

Acknowledgments. This work is sponsored in part by the National Basic Research Program of China (973) under Grant No. 2011CB302600, the National Natural Science Foundation of China under Grant No. 61222205, the Program for New Century Excellent Talents in University, and the Fok Ying-Tong Education Foundation under Grant No. 141066.

References

1. Lu, X., Wang, H., Wang, J., Xu, J., Li, D.: Internet-based virtual computing environment: beyond the data center as a computer. Future Generation Computer Systems 29(1), 309–322 (2013)
2. SCOPE Alliance. Telecom grade cloud computing (2011), http://www.scope-alliance.org
3. Gottlieb, A.: Beware the network cost gotchas of cloud computing. Cloud Computing Journal (June 2011)
4. Meng, X., Pappas, V., Zhang, L.: Improving the scalability of data center networks with traffic-aware virtual machine placement. In: 2010 Proceedings of IEEE INFOCOM, pp. 1–9. IEEE (March 2010)
5. Hyser, C., Mckee, B., Gardner, R., Watson, B.J.: Autonomic virtual machine placement in the data center. Hewlett Packard Laboratories, Tech. Rep. HPL-2007-189, 2007-189 (2007)
6. Padala, P., Hou, K.Y., Shin, K.G., Zhu, X., Uysal, M., Wang, Z., Merchant, A.: Automated control of multiple virtualized resources. In: Proceedings of the 4th ACM European Conference on Computer Systems, pp. 13–26. ACM (April 2009)
7. Mylavarapu, S., Sukthankar, V., Banerjee, P.: An optimized capacity planning approach for virtual infrastructure exhibiting stochastic workload. In: Proceedings of the 2010 ACM Symposium on Applied Computing, pp. 386–390. ACM (March 2010)
8. Menasce, D., Bennani, M.N.: Autonomic virtualized environments. In: 2006 International Conference on Autonomic and Autonomous Systems, ICAS 2006, p. 28. IEEE (July 2006)
9. Song, Y., Li, Y., Wang, H., Zhang, Y., Feng, B., Zang, H., Sun, Y.: A service-oriented priority-based resource scheduling scheme for virtualized utility computing. In: Sadayappan, P., Parashar, M., Badrinath, R., Prasanna, V.K. (eds.) HiPC 2008. LNCS, vol. 5374, pp. 220–231. Springer, Heidelberg (2008)

10. Song, Y., Wang, H., Li, Y., Feng, B., Sun, Y.: Multi-tiered on-demand resource scheduling for VM-based data center. In: Proceedings of the 2009 9th IEEE/ACM International Symposium on Cluster Computing and the Grid, pp. 148–155. IEEE Computer Society (May 2009)
11. Zhou, W., Yang, S., Fang, J., Niu, X., Song, H.: Vmctune: A load balancing scheme for virtual machine cluster using dynamic resource allocation. In: 2010 9th International Conference on Grid and Cooperative Computing (GCC), pp. 81–86. IEEE (November 2010)
12. Wood, T., Shenoy, P., Venkataramani, A., Yousif, M.: Sandpiper: Black-box and gray-box resource management for virtual machines. Computer Networks 53(17), 2923–2938 (2009)
13. Padala, P., Hou, K.Y., Shin, K.G., Zhu, X., Uysal, M., Wang, Z., Merchant, A.: Automated control of multiple virtualized resources. In: Proceedings of the 4th ACM European Conference on Computer Systems, pp. 13–26. ACM (April 2009)
14. Xu, W., Zhu, X., Singhal, S., Wang, Z.: Predictive control for dynamic resource allocation in enterprise data centers. In: 10th IEEE/IFIP Network Operations and Management Symposium, NOMS 2006, pp. 115–126. IEEE (April 2006)
15. Alicherry, M., Lakshman, T.V.: Network aware resource allocation in distributed clouds. In: 2012 Proceedings IEEE INFOCOM, pp. 963–971. IEEE (March 2012)

Parallel Rank Coherence in Networks for Inferring Disease Phenotype and Gene Set Associations

Tao Li, Duo Wang, Shuai Zhang, and Yulu Yang

Department of Computer Science and Information Security,
Nankai University
Tianjin, China
{Litao,yangyl}@nankai.edu.cn,
{duow,zhangshuai}@mail.nankai.edu.cn

Abstract. The RCNet (Rank Coherence in Networks) algorithm has been used to find out the associations between the gene sets and disease phenotypes. However, it suffers from high computational cost when the size of dataset is very large. In this paper, we design three mechanisms to solve the RCNet algorithm on heterogeneous CPU-GPU system based on CUDA and OpenMP programming model. The pipeline mechanism is much suitable for the collaborative computing on CPU and dual-GPUs, which can achieve more than 33 times performance gains. The work plays an important role in reconstructing the disease phoneme-genome association efficiently.

Keywords: disease phenotype, gene set, RCNet, CUDA, OpenMP.

1   Introduction

It is well known that phenotypes are determined by genetic material since Gregor Mendel discovered that phenotypes were inherited from ancestors in the 19th century. The associations between the candidate gene sets and disease phenotypes have been the research focus in the bioinformatics and medical informatics fields [1,2,3]. The knowledge of determined disease phenotype-gene associations has been quickly accumulated in many databases in the last decades such as the Online Mendelian Inheritance in Man (OMIM) database [4].

To understand the relations between the disease phenotypes and gene sets, many network-based approaches are proposed based on the observation that genes associated with the same or related diseases tend to interact with each other in the gene network [5,6,7,8]. These approaches prioritize disease genes by the disease modules and gene modules in the networks. But they cannot fully utilize the disease phenotype network and known relations in the global analysis. A heterogeneous network is created from the gene network, disease phenotype network and the association network of the gene and disease phenotype in the label propagation algorithm [9]. But it is difficult to obtain the optimal parameters and the results due to they cannot fully utilize the information of the networks.

J. Wu et al. (Eds.): ACA 2014, CCIS 451, pp. 163–176, 2014.

The RCNet (Rank Coherence in Networks) algorithm is different from the gene set enrichment analysis with statistical methods, such as hypergeometric statistics, McNemar's test, permutation test and other non-parametric methods [10,11,12]. It analyzes the associations between a gene set and all phenotypes using the topological information in the disease phenotype network and the gene network. It can provide adequate global dependency by analyzing all the phenotypes [13]. Hence much reliable information can be utilized to compute the relationship scores when ranking all the phenotypes. However, the RCNet algorithm faces high computational cost and needs to improve the large data processing efficiently.

Due to being powerful and cost-effective, GPUs have been used in a vast range of scientific applications, including the DNA analysis [14], protein sequence processing [15], MapReduce [16], etc. GPU has a large number of stream multiprocessors (SMs) and high memory bandwidth, and its computing power has been significantly improved and growing beyond Moore's law in the recent years [17]. GPGPU (General Purpose GPU) computing mainly adopts CPU-GPU heterogeneous model, which is based on CUDA (Compute Unified Device Architecture) to give full play in handling floating-point arithmetic [18].

In this paper, the RCNet algorithm is analyzed quantitively and parallelized using the OpenMP and CUDA model to accelerate the association inference between the gene sets and disease phenotypes. The computing intensive operations including the matrix normalization, correlation coefficient calculation, summation of each row and column have been implemented on single- and dual-GPU(s) with three parallel mechanisms. They are evaluated with the gene network, disease phenotypes network and disease phenotype-gene association network from OMIM database. The data transfer optimization mechanism can achieve 12.9 times speedup on GTX 480 GPU, while the collaborative pipeline mechanism on dual-GPUs can obtain 33.8 performance gains.

The rest of the paper is organized as follows. Section 2 shows the RCNet algorithm. Section 3 presents the different parallel mechanisms using the CUDA and OpenMP programming models. Section 4 analyzes the results of the RCNet alogirhtm with different implementation. Conclusion and future work are shown in Section 5.

2   RCNet Algorithm

The RCNet algorithm is a general network-based approach to infer associations between disease phenotypes and gene sets, which can be defined as the query process in the disease phenotype network and the gene network. A list of disease phenotypes are expected to retrieve with the highest predicted association with the gene set by querying the networks with a given gene set.

2.1   Problem Definition

A heterogeneous network has been constructed in the RCNet algorithm from the gene network (GNet), disease phenotypes network (PNet) and disease phenotype-gene association network (ANet). The PNet and ANet are from OMIM, where the ANet contains 1393 associations between 1126 disease phenotypes and 916 genes. The GNet is from the human protein-protein interaction (PPI) networks [21]. Each node in the heterogeneous network represents a disease phenotype or a gene set. A link to the gene set of one or several phenotypes can be obtained by query a sequence of gene set in the heterogeneous network.

The GNet, PNet and ANet are represented as adjacency matrix $G_{(n \times n)}$, $P_{(m \times m)}$ and $A_{(n \times m)}$ respectively, where n is the number of genes and m is the number of disease phenotypes. The query gene set is represented as a binary vector $g = [g_1, g_2, \cdots, g_n]^T$ and $g_i = 1$ if gene i is in the query gene set, otherwise 0. Similarly, the list of target phenotype is represented as another binary vector $p = [p_1, p_2, \cdots, p_m]^T$ and $p_j = 1$ if phenotype j is a target phenotype. The purpose is to find the p that gives the highest rank coherence with the query gene set g.

2.2   RCNet Algorithm

The RCNet algorithm measures the query gene set g and a phenotype set p whether have coherent associations with the known disease-gene associations. The Laplacian scores $\tilde{g}$ and $\tilde{p}$ are required in this process. The score $\tilde{g}$ ranks the genes by their relevance to the query gene set g. The score $\tilde{p}$ ranks the disease phenotypes by their relevance to the hidden target phenotypes p. Given A, the RCNet($\tilde{g}$, $\tilde{p}$, A) tests whether the association can connect the genes and phenotypes in $\tilde{g}$ and $\tilde{p}$ with similar scores.

Computing Graph Laplacian Scores

In order to fully utilize the network topology information, the global correlation score between the query gene set g and all the genes based on the graph Laplacian of the gene network $G_{(n \times n)}$ should be got at first. Then the Laplacian score can be used to capture the information of the interaction between the nodes in the network.

The Laplacian sore is a second order differential operator in the n-dimensional Euclidean space, defined as the divergence (∇f) of the gradient $(\nabla \cdot f)$. Thus, if f is a twice-differentiable real-valued function, then the Laplacian of f is defined by $\nabla f = \nabla^2 f = \nabla \cdot \nabla f$. The Laplacian score use the modular information in the network to capture the interactions between the different nodes. At first, the matrix G of GNet is normalized as $\overline{G} = D_G^{-1/2} G D_G^{-1/2}$, where D_G is a diagonal matrix with diagonal elements $D_{G_{i,j}} = \sum_j G_{i,j}$. The Laplacian score vector can be derived from the following optimization formula (1) [19].

$$\min_{\tilde{g}} \sum_{i,j} \overline{G}_{i,j} \left(\tilde{g}_i - \tilde{g}_j \right)^2 + \frac{1-\alpha}{\alpha} \sum_i \left(\tilde{g}_i - g_i \right)^2. \tag{1}$$

The first term in formula (1) is a smoothness penalty, which gives interconnected genes similarity scores and the second term ensures consistency with the query gene set. The factor $\alpha \in (0,1)$ is used to balance the weight ratio of the two components. The closed-form solution for the formula (1) is

$$\tilde{g} = (1 - \alpha)(I - \alpha \bar{G})^{-1} g. \tag{2}$$

The iterative algorithm can be used to calculate the closed-form solution with the following rules in time step t to avoid computing the inverse of $(I - \alpha \bar{G})$.

$$\tilde{g}^t = (1 - \alpha) g + \alpha \bar{G} \tilde{g}^{t-1}. \tag{3}$$

Formula (4) is used to measure the relevance between the phenotypes and the target phenotype. The closed-form solution is as formula (5), where $\bar{P}$ is the normalized P and $\beta \in (0,1)$ is the balancing parameter.

$$\min_{\tilde{p}} \sum_{i,j} \bar{P}_{i,j} \left(\tilde{p}_i - \tilde{p}_j \right)^2 + \frac{1-\beta}{\beta} \sum_i \left(\tilde{p}_i - p_i \right)^2. \tag{4}$$

$$\tilde{p} = (1 - \beta)(I - \beta \bar{P})^{-1} p, \tag{5}$$

The Laplacian score calculation is equivalent to a weighted summation of performing random walk on the graph from one step to infinite step. Note that G and P can be normalized as a stochastic matrix. Therefore, G and P are enabled to be directed graphs. Other scoring functions also can be used to achieve the same goal such as counting the direct neighbors of the query gene set or find the shortest distance from the query gene set to other genes [5]. However, the direct-neighbor function doesn't generate enough information, and the shortest-path function cannot fully explore the neighborhood information too.

Process of the RCNet Algorithm

A score against the query gene set g for each case is computed by going through each phenotype if only to get the most relevant disease phenotype. For this method, two functions are proposed to measure the RCNet.

$$\text{RCNet}_{\text{corr}} \left(\tilde{g}, \tilde{p}, A \right) = \text{corr} \left(A \tilde{p}, \tilde{g} \right), \tag{6}$$

$$\text{RCNet}_{\text{lap}} \left(\tilde{g}, \tilde{p}, A \right) = -\sum_{i,j} A_{i,j} \left(\tilde{p}_i - \tilde{g}_j \right)^2. \tag{7}$$

In formula (6), RCNet$_{\text{corr}}$ checks the consistency between $A\tilde{p}$ and $\tilde{g}$ by using the Pearson correlation coefficient. The adjacent gene and phenotype in disease phenotype-gene association network are checked in formula (7) whether they have a similar score. The smaller the disagreement, the higher the relevance is. The pseudocode of the RCNet algorithm is given below.

RCNet Algorithm

Input $g, \overline{G}, \overline{P}, A, \alpha, \beta$

$\tilde{g} = (1-\alpha)(I - \alpha\overline{G})^{-1} g$.

Initialize $p^{(0)} \leftarrow 0, s^{(0)} \leftarrow 0$.

Iterate n times

(1) $p_i \leftarrow 1$

(2) $\tilde{p} \leftarrow (1-\beta)(I - \beta\overline{P})^{-1} p$

(3) $s_i \leftarrow corr(A, \tilde{p}, \tilde{g})$ or $-\sum_{i,j} A_{i,j} (\tilde{p}_i - \tilde{g}_j)^2$

(4) $p_i \leftarrow 0$

End Iterate

$j \leftarrow \arg\max_i s_i$

$p_j \leftarrow 1$

return p

The main calculation of the RCNet algorithm includes matrix normalization (MN), matrix-vector multiplication (MVM), calculation of the correlation coefficient of two column vectors (CCV), calculation of the sums of each row and column of the matrix (SRC). The RCNet score is computed in the iterations of each configuration of p. The time complexity of the algorithm is $O(m^2 + n^3)$ for one phenotype if $(1-\beta)(I - \beta\overline{P})^{-1}$ can be preprocessed. The total cost is exponential of m if all possible configuration of p are explored.

3   Parallel Implementation of RCNet

3.1   CUDA Programming Model

CUDA is based on the extensions of the C programming language, which virtualizes the underlying hardware of NVIDIA's GPUs at multiple levels and abstracts the view for programmers from actual hardware operation [18]. It has been designed with the scalability to use the increased resources of each new GPU generation. CUDA's abstraction provides an easy-to-program model for developers from a wide variety of application domains.

On the heterogeneous CPU-GPU platform, the CPU and its system memory is referred as the host and the GPU and its device memory is referred as the device. It uses the master-slave programming model, where the GPU operates as a slave processor under the control of a master or host processor. A function executed on the device is typically called a CUDA kernel, which is usually expressed using data parallel scheme. When a kernel issued, many threads will be created and organized in the form of an array into a thread block. These thread blocks are composed of a grid. The dimension of the grid and thread block can be specified through CUDA API functions. Each thread will be assigned a unique thread index, by which we can control the corresponding thread to process the data on the GPUs.

Fermi architecture has some advantages such as supporting double-precision floating-point, 64-bit addressing, unified virtual address and so on. Kepler architecture has some new technologies such as new streaming multiprocessor design, dynamic parallelism, Hyper-Q, etc. The memory hierarchy of GPU can be divided into three layers by access permission of thread. An underlying memory owned by single thread including registers and local memory is the innermost layer. A middle memory shared by the threads in the same thread block, which only includes the shared memory is the inner layer. The outermost memory can be accessed by all threads in any grids including global memory, constant memory and texture memory. The page-locked host memory that Fermi architecture supported can be accessed by a kernel directly. The operating system guarantees that it will never page this memory out to the disks, which ensure its residency in the physical memory. Knowing the physical address of a buffer, GPU can use direct memory access (DMA) to transmit data between the host and device. The page-locked host memory enjoys roughly a twofold performance advantage over standard pageable host memory when data are transmitted between the host and device. Furthermore, GPU can handle large scale data sets exceeding the device memory size limit by using the page-locked host memory.

3.2   CUDA Implementation Mechanisms

There are three computating intensive operations in the RCNet algorithm, which are analyzed using gcov, gprof and Intel vtune tools. These operations are the SRC, the CCV and the MN. Their time overheads are 46.17%, 31.16% and 19.06% respectively of the whole time to execute the RCNet algorithm serially. These three operations involve many basic matrix operations such as the sums of the matrix, matrix normalization and matrix multiplication. It is very suitable for the GPU to compute in parallel because of the homogeneous data distribution and regular memory access.

Three mechanisms based on different storage schemes are proposed as CUDA implementation mechanism (CIM), Data transfer optimization mechanism (DTOM) and Pipeline mechanism (PM). All the data sets are stored in host memory and transferred from host memory to global memory when necessary in the CIM. The SRC, MN and CCV are all executed on the GPU. The CPU conducts the known information excluding between 2007 and 2010 of the ANet and the partial GNet and PNet excluding. In the DTOM, the PNet, ANet are stored in the GPU device memory and the GNet in the host memory. The known information excluding between 2007 and 2010 of the ANet is executed on the CPU. The GPU conducts the SRC, MN, the partial GNet and PNet excluding and CCV operations. In the PM, the ANet, GNet and PNet are stored in GPU device memory and the task assignment as same as the CIM.

CUDA Implementation

Each computing intensive operation has many inner iterations, which has no data dependencies in each iteration. GPU is good at highly parallel numerical calculation of the graphics class or non-graphical class. It can accommodate thousands of threads to run in parallel. Data parallel programming on GPU is very suitable for parallel computing of no logical relation data. The CIM is proposed to make use of this advantage and directly implement the operations using corresponding kernels on GPU.

The algorithm steps are listed in Fig.1. The computing intensive steps are accelerated on GPU in this mechanism. Separate kernels are designed to implement the MN and CCV operations. The SRC operation is divided into SR kernel for calculating of the sums of each row of the matrix and SC kernel for calculating the sums of each column of the matrix.

Firstly, CPU conducts the calculation for excluding the known information between 2007 and 2010 from the ANet. And the ANet (before 2007) will be pitched and transferred to the GPU global memory. The SR kernel creates some blocks by the amount of the rows of ANet matrix. Each block executes an iteration to calculate the sum of one row elements of ANet matrix. There are 256 threads launched in each block. Each thread calculates the sum of the elements by striding 256 elements. The SRC operation is shown in Fig.2.

Secondly, the MN kernel creates thread blocks by the amount of the rows of the ANet matrix. Each thread block normalizes each row of the matrix. At the end of MN kernel, the zero-columns and zero-rows will be excluded from ANet matrix.

Finally, CPU excludes the useless information for the next calculation step about the GNet and PNet. The PNet matrix and the transposed GNet matrix will be transferred to the GPU global memory. The CCV kernel creates thread blocks by the amount of the rows of the transposed GNet matrix. Each thread block calculates the correlation coefficient of gene set G_j (one row vector of the transposed GNet matrix) and the phenotype set P_i. Then one prediction vector (PV) will be calculated by one thread block. These PVs will be transferred from the GPU global memory to the host memory. At last, the prediction matrix is composed on CPU. The CCV kernel is shown in Fig.3.

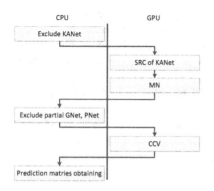

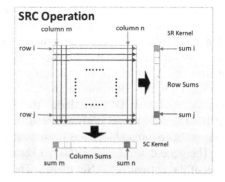

Fig. 1. Calculation steps on CPU and GPU   **Fig. 2.** SRC Operation

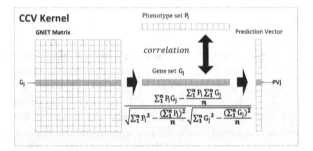

Fig. 3. CCV Kernel

Data Transfer Optimization Mechnism

There is not enough device memory to store the PNet, GNet and ANet matrices in GTX 480 GPU. So the GNet is stored in the host memory. GPU needs to get the data's physical address before accessing them. And the operating system may page these data out to disk or relocate their physical address by updating the operating system's pagetables. The page-locked host memory can be used to solve this problem.

In this mechanism, the computing intensive operations of MN, SR calculation, SC calculation and excluding the known ANet information between 2007 and 2010 will be implemented by four corresponding kernels. The SRC operation for the ANet matrix is divided into the SR calculation kernel and the SC calculation kernel. Before calculating CCV, the target gene set, target disease phenotype, the mean value and variance of the vector of the target gene set need to be get. So the operation of CCV calculation is designed to three kernels as follows: the vector of disease-gene obtaining kernel, the statistic obtaining kernel and the correlation coefficient computation kernel. At first, the PNet matrix and ANet matrix are transferred to the page-locked host memory. Then they will be pitched and transmitted to GPU global memory. The columns of the GNet matrix are non-contiguous in the memory, since the matrix elements are allocated column-by-column in traditional C++ language. And the GNet matrix is accessed column-by-column in the RCNet algorithm. So, it would cause frequent context switch when copying one column each time. The efficiency of memory access would or will be decreased distinctly. The GNet matrix is transposed so that the elements in each columnneed to be accessed only once. The contiguous memory space is allocated for thethe elements in each column. After that, the GNet matrix and ANet matrix are transmitted to the GPU global memory.

Secondly, the SR kernel and SC kernel will be called to calculate SRC of ANet matrix. And then GPU excludes the known ANet information between 2007 and 2010. The MN kernel creates thread blocks by the amount of the rows of the ANet matrix. Each thread block has been arranged to normalize one row of the matrix.

The gene-disease vector (GDV) kernel creates thread blocks by the amount of the row of the normalized ANet matrix. Then each thread block computes the dot product of one row of the matrix and one phenotype vector, and transmits the GDV to another kernel which is used to obtain the statistics. Because the GDV is stored in a contiguous memory, one thread block and multiple threads are created to calculate the statistics. Then the result will be transmitted to the correlation calculation kernel. This kernel creates thread blocks by the amount of the row of the GNet matrix and assigns the assignments to different thread blocks. Each thread block calculates the disease phenotype-gene vector and the correlation coefficient of each gene set in the query gene sets. These predictive PVs will be transmitted from the GPU global memory to host memory. Then the predictive ANet matrix will be stored on specified location.

Pipeline Mechanism

The NVIDIA Visual Profiler is used to analyze the RCNet implementation on single GPU, which spends much time on accessing the PNet matrix in the page-locked host memory. In order to solve this memory access bottleneck, the PM on dual GPUs is proposed. All the data sets are stored in the GPU global memory to prevent the program from accessing the page-locked host memory frequently. Based on the dual-GPUs, the problem is divided into several subtasks and a suitable scheduling sequence is given for these subtasks. These subtasks can run on dual-GPUs at the same time. So the overlap of computation and data transfer can be achieved.

In this mechanism, some computing intensive operations are implemented by the MN kernel, SR kernel, SC kernel, excluding KANet kernel and GDV calculation kernel. The CCV calculation is implemented by the statistic obtaining kernel and PV calculation kernel. Fig.4 lists the task assignment and execution steps on the dual-GPUs. GPU 0 transmits the GDV to the GPU 1 through the PCIE. Then GPU 0 goes to the next cycle of computation instead of waiting for the computing completion of GPU 1. Thus GPU 0, GPU 1 and the CPU will calculate concurrently with overlap of calculation and data transfer.

3.3   OpenMP Implementation of RCNet

OpenMP (Open Multi-Processing) is an API that supports shared memory multiprocessing programming. It uses the fork-join model of parallel execution. There are many inner loops in SRC calculation, CCV calculation, MN and no data dependences in them. So these operations can be paralleled by OpenMP respectively.

In the design of ANet calculation, the ANet matrix is stored by row-by-row, so the physical address of the adjacent elements of each column are discontinuity. On this occasion, it will increase the time overhead of accessing the CPU memory if we use multi-threads to calculate SC. So only the operation of SR calculation can be accelerated by OpenMP. Each core of CPU is arranged to calculate the sum of one row of the matrix. When normalizing the matrix, each core of the CPU is arranged to calculate one row of the ANet matrix until all the rows of the matrix have been accessed.

In the CCV calculation, all the elements of the GNet matrix will be accessed column-by-column. The matrix will be transposed in advance for the sake of decreasing CPU memory accessing time. And it will be accessed row-by-row only once in the whole process. The correlation coefficient of the vector of gene-disease and one row of the matrix will be calculated by each core of CPU until all the elements of the matrix has been accessed.

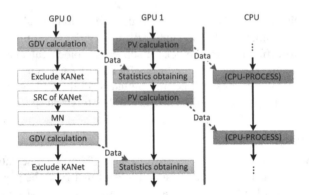

Fig. 4. Task assignment on dual-GPUs

In this mechanism, the data sets will just be read by every core of CPU and the writing operations on these data sets are at different physical address. Therefore, there are no competitions for the resources.

4   Experiment and Discussion

4.1   Experimental Platform and Dataset

The experiments are conducted on the quad-core processor Intel® Core^{TM}i7-2600 with four cores, clock of 3.4 GHz, 64-bit instruction sets, 16GB RAM and 32GB/s maximum memory bandwidth. The GPUs are NVIDIA GeForce GTX 480 and GTX 780 with 1.5GB and 6GB global memory respectively. Ubuntu desktop 12.04 operating system runs on this platform.

All the data sets are from the OMIM database. There are five PNets [20] and each is an undirected graph with 5080 vertices representing OMIM disease phenotypes with the size of approximate 200MB.The five GNets are derived from the human protein-protein interaction (PPI) networks [21] and each of them is an undirected graph with 12456 vertices representing OMIM genes with the size of approximate 1GB. There is only one ANet (Ver. 2010) with the size of approximate 400MB. And it contains 1393 associations between 1126 disease phenotypes and 916 genes.

4.2   Correctness Verification

The implementation approaches between the parallel mechanism and the serial mechanism have some adjustments, since the hardware architecture and instruction set of the GPU and CPU are different. To guarantee the result of the parallel mechanism can meet the accuracy requirement in reality, the accuracy error between the results of different parallel mechanisms and the result of the serial implementation of the RCNet algorithm is calculated.

The relative error measurement is adopted to calculate the accuracy error. In this measurement, the maximum difference of the data in the same location between the results of the different implementation mechanisms and the mechanism of serial implementation of the RCNet algorithm are adopted to evaluate the accuracy error. The formula is $\max\left(abs\left(A2_{i,j} - A_{i,j}\right)\right)$ $\left(i = 1, 2, \cdots, n. j = 1, 2, \cdots, m\right)$, where $A_{(n \times m)}$ represents the results of the mechanism of serial implementation of RCNet and $A2_{(n \times m)}$ based on the GPU.

The results show that there is no accuracy error of the result of OpenMP compared with the result of the serial implementation. While the results of CUDA parallel mechanisms have approximately five millionths level relative accuracy error compared to that of the serial implementation. However, the level of accuracy error will not affect its practical applications in the bioinformatics and medical informatics fields.

4.3   Performance Comparison and Analysis

CUDA-Based Implementation

NVIDIA Visual Profiler is used to collect and analyze the GPU computing performance. Table 1 lists the profiling results of different parallel mechanisms based on current CUDA: HtoD (Host to Device) includes the time overhead of data sets transfer from host memory to device memory and the intermediate results transferring from host to device. DtoD (Device to Device) includes the time overhead of intermediate results transferring from GPU 0 to GPU 1. DtoH (Device to Host) includes the time overhead of results transferring from device memory to host memory. It can be observed that the DTOM and PM achieved an ideal effect on reducing the data sets transfer time overhead.

Table 1. Time overhead of data transfer

CUDA Mechanisms	HtoD(s)	DtoD(s)	DtoH(s)
CIM	2318.41	0.00	2241.05
DTOM	0.23	197.17	0.63
PM	5.26	141.99	2.67

The time overhead of the three computing intensive operations including MN, CCV calculation, SRC calculation and their data sets transfer time overheads are counted in different mechanisms. Fig.5 lists all the analysis results. Four threads are launched in the OpenMP mechanism. It can be observed that the three computing intensive operations in the DTOM and PM had obtained an ideal effect.

OpenMP-Based Implementation

Different numbers of threads are launched to evaluate the performance of the implementation mechanism. Table.2 lists the experimental results.The time overhead is the least when the amount of threads is equal to the cores of CPU. There will be a competition for resource when the amount of the threads exceeding the cores of the CPU because all the threads may read or write the same variables at the same time.

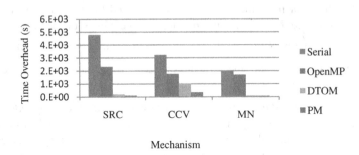

Fig. 5. Hotspots time overhead of different mechanisms

Table 2. Results with variable threads

Threads	1	2	4	8	16
Time(s)	17475.0	13626.6	13308.0	13375.8	13408.8

Comparison and Analysis

Fig.6 lists the whole time overhead and speedup results of different mechanisms. The OpenMP mechanism had created 4 threads to calculate. The PM on dual GPUs achieves the best performance and its speed-up ratio is 33.8. A nice performance with a 12.94 speedup is achieved of the DTOM.

The time overhead of CIM is 15744.6 seconds, which shortens about 9.9% of the time overhead compared to the serial implementation mechanism. The time overhead of DTOM decreases to 1350 seconds from 15744.6 seconds of the serial implementation mechanism. It proves that 92.27% time overhead is saved compared to the mechanism of CUDA implementation. The time overhead of PM on dual GPUs is 516.6 seconds, which is proved 97.04% time overhead saved compared to the serial implementation mechanism. The PM achieves a higher performance than other mechanisms.

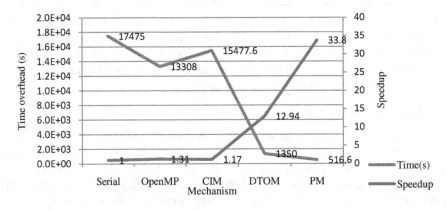

Fig. 6. Time overhead and speedup of different mechanisms

With the size of the data sets increasing, the PM cannot store all the data sets in the GPU. So the DTOM has more universal applicability and scalability than the PM since partial data sets are stored on host memory in the whole process. The DTOM is tested on NVIDIA GTX 780 GPU, which has 6GB global memory. The DTOM's time overhead is 829.67s, which is only about 360 seconds more than the DTOM of putting all the data sets on the GPU. This result has proved that the DTOM's universal applicability and scalability.

The performance of sub-process belonging to the mechanism based on single GPU obtains a significant improvement by creating enough threads. The experiment result of dual-GPUs proves the reasonable of the mechanism of computation and data transfer overlap, which stores all the data sets in the GPU global memory instead of the page-locked host memory. This mechanism breaks the bottleneck of the PCIE bus bandwidth and obviously decreases the time delay of data transmission. Finally its performance is 1.61 times compared to the mechanism of single GPU.

5   Conclusion

The disease-causing genes prediction process encounters the challenge of slow processing speed. Several parallel implementation mechanisms are proposed for inferring disease and gene set associations based on the OpenMP or CUDA programming model. The experimental results show that the PM on dual GPUs can be efficiently used to inferring the disease-causing genes, which ensures the accuracy of the prediction results. This mechanism greatly reduces the prediction time and achieves 33.8-fold speedup. It will have an impact on accelerating the research progress of inferring the disease-causing genes.

Acknowledgment. This work is supported by the National Natural Science Foundation of China under Grant No. 61212005, 61379146, 61272483, the Fundamental Research Funds for the Central Universities under Grant No. 65012101, and Fund of National University of Defense Technology No.JC13-06-03.

References

1. Bustamam, A., Burrage, K., Hamilton, N.A.: A GPU Implementation of Fast Parallel Markov Clustering in Bioinformatics Using EIIPACK-R Sparse Data Format. In: Advances in Computing, Control and Telecommunication Technologies (ACT), Jakarta, pp. 173–175 (2010)
2. Tumeo, A., Villa, O.: Accelerating DNA analysis applications on GPU clusters. In: Application Specific Processors (SASP), Anaheim, CA, pp. 71–76 (2011)
3. Membarth, R., Hannig, F., Teich, J., Korner, M., Eckert, W.: Generating Device-specific GPU code for Local Operators in Medical Imaging. In: Parallel & Distributed Processing Symposium (IPDPS), Shanghai, pp. 569–581 (2012)
4. McKusick, V.: Mendelian inheritance in man and its online version, OMIM. Am. J. Hum. Genet. 80, 588–604 (2007)

5. Franke, L., van Bakel, H., Fokkens, L., de Jong, E.D., Egmont-Petersen, M., Wijmenga, C.: Reconstruction of a functional human gene network, with an application for prioritizing positional candidate genes. Am. J. Hum. Genet. 78(6), 1011–1025 (2006)

6. Köhler, S., Bauer, S., Horn, D., Robinson, P.N.: Walking the interactome for prioritization of candidate disease genes. Am. J. Hum. Genet. 82(4), 949–958 (2008)

7. Linghu, B., Snitkin, E.S., Hu, Z., Xia, Y., Delisi, C.: Genome-wide prioritization of disease genes and identification of disease-disease associations from an integrated human functional linkage network. Genome Biol. 10(9), R91 (2009)

8. Wu, X., Jiang, R., Zhang, M.Q., Li, S.: Network-based global inference of human disease genes. Mol. Syst. Biol. 4 (2008)

9. Hwang, T., Kuang, R.: A heterogeneous label propagation algorithm for disease gene discovery. In: Proc. of SIAM International Conference on Data Mining, pp. 583–594 (2010)

10. Huang, D., Sherman, B.T., Lempicki, R.A.: Systematic and integrative analysis of large gene lists using david bioinformatics resources. Nat. Protoc. 4(1), 44–57 (2009)

11. Subramanian, A., Tamayo, P., Mootha, V.K., Mukherjee, S., Ebert, B.L., Gillette, M.A., Paulovich, A., et al.: Gene set enrichment analysis: a knowledge-based approach for interpreting genome-wide expression profiles. Proc. Natl. Acad. Sci. USA 102(43), 15545–15550 (2005)

12. Martin, D., Brun, C., Remy, E., Mouren, P., Thieffry, D., Jacq, B.: GOToolbox: functional analysis of gene datasets based on gene ontology. Genome Biol. 5(12), R101 (2004)

13. Hwang, T., Zhang, W., Xie, M., Liu, J., Kuang, R.: Inferring disease and gene set associations with rank coherence in networks. Bioinformatics 27(19), 2692–2699 (2011), doi: 10.1093/bioinformatics/btr463

14. Encarnaijao, G., Sebastiao, N., Roma, N.: Advantages and GPU implementation of high-performance indexed DNA search based on suffix arrays. In: High Performance Computing and Simulation, Istanbul, pp. 49–55 (2011)

15. Xiao, S., Lin, H., Feng, W.-C.: Accelerating Protein Sequence Search a Heterogeneous Computing System. In: Parallel & Distributed Processing Symposium, Anchorage, AK, pp. 1212–1222 (2011)

16. Stuart, J.A., Owens, J.D.: Multi-GPU MapReduce on GPU Clusters. In: Parallel & Distributed Processing Symposium, Anchorage, AK, pp. 1068–1079 (2011)

17. Owens, J.D., Luebke, D., Govimdaraju, N., Harris, M., Krüger, J., Lefohn, A., et al.: A survey of general-purpose computation on graphics hardware. Computer Graphics Forum 26(1), 80–113 (2007)

18. NVIDIA, http://www.nvidia.com/object/cuda_home_new.html

19. Zhou, D., Bousquet, O., Lal, T.N., Weston, J., Schölkopf, B.: Learning with local and global consistency. In: Advanced Neural Information Processing Systems, Cambridge, MA, vol. 16, pp. 321–328 (2004)

20. van Driel, M., Bruggeman, J., Vriend, G., Brunner, H.G., Leunissen, J.A.: A text-mining analysis of the human phenome. Eur. J. Hum. Genet. 14, 535–542 (2006)

21. Chuang, H.-Y., Lee, E., Liu, Y.T., Lee, D., Ideker, T.: Network-based classification of breast cancer metastasis. Molecular Systems Biology 3 (2007)

Dynamic Power Estimation with Hardware Performance Counters Support on Multi-core Platform

Xin Liu[1,2], Li Shen[1,2], Cheng Qian[1,2], and Zhiying Wang[1,2]

[1] State Key Laboratory of High Performance Computing, NUDT, Changsha, China, 410073
[2] School of Computer, National University of Defense Technology, Changsha, China, 410073
{liuxin12,lishen,qiancheng,zywang}@nudt.edu.cn

Abstract. Power estimation has attracted a plenty of attentions for its significant guidance for OS scheduling and the development of power-efficiency optimization design. Previous researches indicate that power consumption can be estimated via monitoring related hardware events, such as retirement of instructions, cache access, etc. However, these models based on hardware events will introduce an error around 5%. In this paper, a more accurate hardware events directed power model is proposed. We identified the most appropriate events to respond to the major power consumption components. By analyzing the hardware events in processor through performance counters, a unified run-time power estimation model is introduced. Our model has been verified through real-time measurement and shown to be 3.01% and 1.99% inaccurate for PARSEC and SPLASH-2 benchmark suites. Our power estimation model can serve as a foundation for intelligent, power-aware systems that can dynamically balance power assignment and smooth peak power at run-time.

Keywords: Dynamic Power, Power Estimation, Performance Counters.

1 Introduction

Until recently, benefiting from the increasing of clock rate and shrinking of transistor size, the performance of microprocessors has been developing in an amazing speed. However, power is becoming an issue that restricts the further development. First, if the excess thermal produced by high power cannot be sent out in time, device temperature would rise up, which usually leads to an unreliable system. Second, current high performance processors are reaching the limitation of conventional cooling techniques. Powerful radiator fan even water-cooling has to be employed to guarantee processors to work normally. Third, electric cost is another important factor that we must take into account in the age of environment-friendly and energy-saving. For example, the electric charge of Tianhe-2, the first one of top500 ranking in June and November 2013[1], is over hundreds of thousands of US dollars each hour. Therefore, Green computing has attracted more and more attentions and how to improve power efficiency becomes a hot topic. In order to raise the awareness of Power-Aware Computing instead of pursuing performance blindly, Green500 [2] lists the most energy-efficiency supercomputer twice a year according to the ratio of performance and power consumption.

J. Wu et al. (Eds.): ACA 2014, CCIS 451, pp. 177–189, 2014.
© Springer-Verlag Berlin Heidelberg 2014

With multi-thread or multi-core becoming dominant, power density further increases. Modern operating system also introduces a variety of power saving mechanisms, such as DVFS (Dynamic Voltage and Frequency Scaling), which is widely used to reduce power and temperature. Usually, the schedule is based on the worst case. For example, on some multi-core platforms, all processor cores share a same frequency and voltage domain. If one core is overheating because of hot tasks, their frequency will be brought down. Other cold cores have to bear the negative influence. To reduce the performance impairments, an alternative is thread schedule or migration instead of throttling. Appropriately energy-aware dispatching tasks among cores can obtain optimal performance per watt or maximal performance under a power-limited system. Obviously, the precondition of energy-aware schedule is to realize how much power a task will consume at present and in the future. Even for platforms supporting different frequency and voltage domain among cores, power consumption of each core is also an important factor which will influence frequency adjustment.

Some researchers try to optimize power efficiency according to CPU temperature. "HybDTM" [3] and "ThreashHot" [4] implement task schedule according to real time temperature to take full advantage of computing resource and avoid overheating. However, temperature does not work as effectively as power in reflecting the run-time characteristics of workloads for the delay before temperature changing. Hot core with high temperature may be coursed by a heavy load a moment ago not right now. Russ Joseph [5] tried to measure real hardware power by placing a shunt resistance between computer's power supply and motherboard power terminal. But the extra instrument consumes power itself and the measurements are limited by its accuracy. What's more, tiny change cannot be detected nimbly. Imprecise power would misguide the scheduler and lead to downgrade of power efficiency which is opposite to the original goal.

Power consumption can also be estimated via monitoring hardware events [6,7,8], such as the number of unhalt cycles, instructions retired, cache miss/hit at each level. Compared with power model based on simplified simulations [21], it can be implemented and evaluated on real hardware. To collect hardware events, almost all modern processors offer special hardware performance counters, which are commonly used in commercial toolsets such as Intel's performance analysis software VTune. These counters monitor the occurrence of hardware events with almost no performance penalty which catches valuable insights into various performance aspects of application. The only overhead is to record and reset counters. These counters were designed for performance tuning separately at the beginning and accessing them will not increase the burden of pipeline or other resource. However, Frank finds a strong linear correlation between some hardware events and processor's dynamic power [6]. Having understood when and how these events occur, we can build a power estimation model with the explored hardware events using a mathematical method. Hardware-based performance monitor not only can help pinpoint where the power is consumed; it can also offer input for power estimation model. A good profile can provide a lot of useful information about the behavior of a running program and guides to optimization strategy. In practice, the operating system scheduler can benefit from power profiles to optimize the thread assignments, avoiding unbalanced situations when one core is overloaded but others are idle. Also, developers can understand the behavior of applications and undertake a relevant performance tuning. Current estimation models have its own limitations in different aspects. For example, the model depends on applications closely, or process method is too intricacy. Most importantly, some of them are far from accurate. This paper's goal is to overcome these weaknesses and demonstrate an easy, application-independent model with high-accuracy.

We propose a two-stage power estimation approach, as shown in Fig. 1. We assume this approach is implemented on a four-core platform as a monitor program. The monitor program is bound to core 0 and be responsible for gathering information of real power, performance counter values and temperature. Applications can run on core 1 to 3. The first stage is offline profiling, in which the monitor program takes sample of hardware events, core temperature and total power periodically. All related data is stored into a log file. Then, a statistical method is applied with above log file as input to construct both static and dynamic power model. In the second stage, online estimation, processor monitors appropriate events and calculates the power with the model obtained in the offline phase.

The rest of this paper is organized as follows. Section 2 reviews the related works. Section 3 describes how to build the parameter model in offline stage. Section 4 presents the details of experiment implementation, then analyses the error of model with actual measurement. And section 5 summarizes the conclusion.

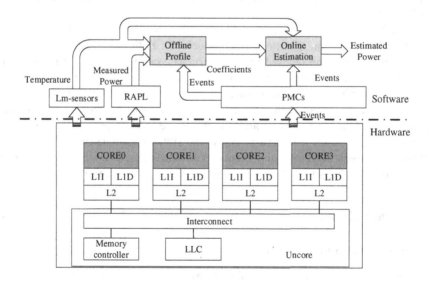

Fig. 1. Framework of our approach

2 Related Work

Frank Bellsoa's work [6] shows the linear correlation of hardware events and energy. Then, they use hardware activity to establish thread-specific energy consumption model. Since then, a lot of work has been done for power estimation based on hardware performance counters.

Performance monitor counters (PMCs) based power estimation models in prior work can be divided into two categories [7]. The top-down method uses a reduced set of events, aiming to build a fast and simple model with little overheads, while the bottom-up approach breakdowns the power components based on microarchitecture. The latter one produces more accurate power model by gathering more information to reflect the power characteristics of applications, at the cost of increasing the complexity of modeling. Our model makes a balance between accuracy and cost, and can be viewed as a moderation on both sides.

Karan Singh et al. [24] achieves a run-time per-core power estimation of multithread and multi-program workloads using the top-down method [7]. They categorize the processor's hardware event into four classes (because their environment platform has only four performance counters). Then the topmost one is chosen in each class which is the most correlated to power. With the runtime data from executing microbenchmark, they build a piece-wise linear mode and achieve median errors of 3.9%, 5.8% and 7.2% for the SPEC-OMP, NAS and SPEC2006 benchmark suites respectively. However, comparing with ours, their model is uniform and relies on the application, and they can't thoroughly explain the cause to fragment. Our uniform model catches a better precision with errors of 3.01% and 1.99% for PARSEC and SPLASH2 respectively.

Isci and Martonosi [8] decompose CPU into 22 power breakdowns based on function unit which is a typical bottom-up approach [7]. Following that, they present a per-unit power estimation devised from performance counters. They train sub-model with a set of specialized micro-benchmark to stress the correlated power units one by one. Plenty of hardware events can reflect more power characteristics, making contribution to the prediction accuracy. However, their process of modeling is complicated and quite dependents on particular architecture. Since modern processor is becoming more and more intricate, it is hard to define the suitable granularity for each power breakdown and seek corresponding events. We treat things as a whole and combine different units on a higher level view to avoid cumbersome per-unit model.

3   Power Model

3.1   Hardware Event Selection

Hardware events for building model directly decide the precision of final estimation model. The accuracy of performance monitoring hardware is discussed in article [20], the overhead from interface may influence the accuracy. As a result, taking too many events into consideration would result in a bad estimation. On the contrary, insufficient of events would make the model unable to catching enough information of power characteristics. It's a great challenge for us to select the events that are most representative for system power with the least redundancy. Events with high correlation to power consumption usually come from power-hungry components. For a good

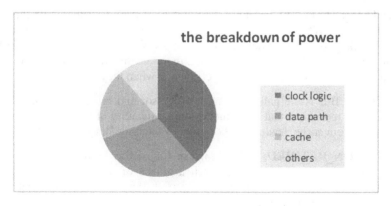

Fig. 2. The breakdown of power in microprocessor

model, the events should reflect the work of most energy component as far as possible. In a microprocessor, clock logic unit is the largest consumer of processor power. It includes clock driver, clock tree, clock load and so on [23] (Fig. 2). Data path is the second leading cause of power consumption, which includes all kinds of complex execution unit, register file with high access frequency and bus. What we need to do is to extract the most representative event set for them with little redundancy. First of all, we pick out events which are related to these component. Then, events were filtered based on Pearson correlation coefficient to total dynamic power. Pearson correlation shows the linear relationship between two sets of data. Events with the coefficient between -0.1 and 0.1 are cast out, which means no linear relationship exits. Finally, through stepwise multiple linear regression, redundant events were filtered, with 9 typical events left finally which are described below. These selected hardware events are belong to four different groups based on the distribution of power above, as listed in Table 1. The groups represent different causes of power in a microprocessor.

Table 1. Selected hardware events

Unit	Event
Clock logic	UNHALTED_CORE_CYC
Data path	INSTRUCTION_RETIRED MISPREDICTED_BRANCH_RETIRED BUS_CYCLE DTLB_MISS
Cache	MEM_UOP_RETIRED:ALL_LOADS MEM_UOP_RETIRED:ALL_STORES ICACHE:MISSES PERF_COUNT_HW_CACHE_L1D:MISS
Others	OFFCORE_REQUESTS:ALL_DATA OFFCORE_REQUESTS_BUFFER

UNHALTED_CORE_CYC: Counts the number of thread cycles while the core is not in a halt state. When CPU is in idle state, OS halts it by a HLT instruction then gates the clock signal to save power. So, the running power is significantly different between unhalt and halt. In Intel processors, there are several C-states [9] in device, core or package level to improve energy efficiency when they are idle.

BUS_CYCLE: Bus is the path to connect processor and memory. For the speed of processor is far more than that of memory, a great quantity of bus cycle means target data is absent from cache, leading to the action of fetching memory.

INSTRUCTION_RETIRED: This event can be used to reckon the activity of instruction retired component. We can catch a glance of the throughput of pipeline through the number of retired instructions. Due to branch instructions with wrong prediction don't accomplish executing, they are ignored by this event.

MISPREDICTED_BRANCH_RETIRED: Branch instructions usually predict executing direction in advance by demanding branch history buffer (BHB) or branch target buffer (BTB). Once mistaken is detected, the pipeline would be flushed and rerun in the opposite direction. For the modern processor especially those with long pipeline, overhead coursed by wrong prediction is greater.

MEM_UOP_RETIRED:ALL_LOADS/ALL_STORES: Loading or storing operation would lead to memory access which usually brings stalls into pipeline and decreases throughput. These two events represent the access times of load and store buffer as well as L1 cache.

ICACHE:MISSES/DCACHE:MISSES: Represent number of L1 instruction cache and L1 data cache misses respectively. The sum of which is the access to L2 private cache that reflects the access frequency of the L2 cache.

OFFCORE_REQUESTS/OFFCORE_REQUESTS_BUFFER: With the growing size of uncore-cache and the integration of other SOC components, uncore must not be overlooked [10]. We record the requests sent to uncore which are mostly triggered by L2 cache miss.

DTLB_MISS: Processors that utilizes page or segmented virtual memory need to access memory twice for each load or store operation. To ensure better performance, translation look-aside buffer (TLB) is used to improve virtual address translation speed [19]. A TLB miss will result in walking the page tables and performing the translation of virtual address.

3.2   Event-Based Power Estimate Model

It was difficult to build a pinpoint power model without information of processor's circuit. While we try to model the major power customers in the processor. We assume power consumed by these units for each access is a constant. To count the access of component, the related hardware events are supervised. The total dynamic power of unit U_i can be calculated by formula (1).

$$P(U_i) = Act_i * avgP_i \tag{1}$$

Where Act_i represents U_i's access frequency which is a measurement of the utilization rate. Simply summing up the power of all the major power-sapping components can obtain the total dynamic power using formula (2):

$$P_{dynamic} = \sum_{i=1}^{k} P(U_i)$$ (2)

We can get Act_i by dividing the sample interval with the value of corresponding event counter (formula 4). Treating activities as independent variables and dynamic power as dependent variable, we perform a multi-linear regression analysis to gain coefficients of the model. Finally, we can obtain the following linear model:

$$P_{dynamic} = \sum_{1}^{cores} (\sum_{i=1}^{eventnum} Act_i * W_i) + C$$ (3)

$$Act_i = S_i / Sampling\ Interval$$ (4)

Where W_i is the coefficient calculated from linear regression, acting as the average power cost by unit U_i. Act_i is the occurrence of event i per second. It's the measurement of component activity. S_i is sampled data for event i from performance counter. The limited number of events cannot reflect the total power. C is a constant represents the partition out of our monitor.

4   Experimental and Analysis

We select Intel i5 2300 processor as baseline platform to evaluate the correctness and performance of our model. System configurations are listed in Table 2. Intel i5 2300 has 4 single-threaded cores and its own private L1 and L2 caches. Its L1 cache is typical Harvard structure with divided instruction and data cache. The last level cache inside the physical package is an inclusive, unified data and instruction cache, shared by all processor cores. The processor provided the interface to real time power for its Sandy Bridge architecture which a RAPL (Running Average Power Limit) [14] module has been integrated into. All the experiments run on the Ubuntu Linux 13.04 operating system, whose kernel version is 3.8.0.

Table 2. Configuration of processor

Processor	Intel i5 2300
# of Core	4
# of thread	4
L1 Caches	64KB Instruction, 64KB Data, Private
L2 Cache	256KB, Private
L3 Cache	6MB, Shared
Size	32mn
TDP	95W
Clock speed	2.8Ghz max,1.6Ghz min

4.1   Experiment Environment Setup

Hardware Events Collection

In order to gather events data, we have to configure MSR (Model Specific Register) which refers to event coding and mask. Fortunately, performance monitor tools or libraries like PAPI [11], Perfmon [12], Perfsuit [13] are commonly used to monitor hardware counters. They provide APIs that are accessible and well documented for users. Here, we use libpfm4, a library with a flexible performance interface for Linux. With this lightweight interface, we can control counters easily and collect profiles on a per-thread or per-CPU basis. It helps converting an event name, expressed as a string to the event encoding, so as to avoid complex configuration register setting.

The sampling interval which refers to the numbers of events monitored has an indirect influence on estimation accuracy. A trouble appears in our model when we have to catch the values of 11 events for all cores with only 4 performance counters. Therefore, one counter is configured to monitor the events in a fixed core and record one event value at a time. We rotate through all these selected events and assign each event a time slice of 20ms. This multiplexing assumes that program behavior is fairly constant with respect to the sampling intervals, because of the guarantee by temporal locality. There is a tradeoff between inaccuracy with a longer sampling interval and an increasing overhead for continually sampling.

Real Time Power Measurement

RAPL is first introduced to Intel's Sandy Bridge architecture, which allows users to monitor and control power consumptions. With the support of RAPL[14], we can measure the real time power in different domains hierarchy, such as package, DRAM controller and CPU core, even make a power budgeting. We bound the monitor program to core0, and other applications to be tested running on core1 to core3. The measured power can be described as below:

$$P_{measured} = P_{dynamic} + P_{idle} \qquad (5)$$

$$P_{idle} = P_{os} + P_{monitor} + P_{static} \qquad (6)$$

Where the idle power (P_{idle}) contains the static power (P_{static}), the dynamic power of OS (P_{os}) and the monitor ($P_{monitor}$).

We subtract P_{idle} from $P_{measured}$ to obtain the dynamic power. It's difficult and beyond the research scope for us to decouple OS power, monitor power and static power separately. However, to treat the two parts ahead as a constant is reasonable. As OS dynamic power is tiny by contrast, we ignore it directly. Power consumed by monitor is stable, because it only performs sampling and data storing periodically. Static power is a function of voltage and temperature, but the voltage keeps unalterable in our experiment for which we just consider the changes coursed by the temperature. Lm-sensors is used to detect the temperature, which is a user space tool to sense temperatures, voltages and fans. Then we built the model of idle power (formula 7). In spite of exponent relationship in theory, linear approximation within a small range of temperature is acceptable [15]. In fact, measurements of the changing range of temperature in our experiment is within 15 degree centigrade. To avoid the unknown interference from the Turbo Boost [9], we turned down this mechanism in the BIOS in advance.

$$P_{idle} = C_1 * T + C_2 \tag{7}$$

Both C_1 and C_2 are constant. T is the average temperature of all cores.

Benchmark Selection

Training Set
The model would be more precise, if the behavior of training set can explore the full space of the selected events. We use benchmarks from SPEC CPU2006 [16] benchmark suite to build model. This training set covers computing domains form workstation, scientific and enterprise involving CPU and memory bound workload that stresses different subsets of system components. Prediction would lose precision if some scenarios are absent for considering.

Testing Set
To guarantee the fairness of evaluation, a different benchmark group is used for test and verity. PARSEC [17] benchmark suite enjoys widespread use in evaluating CMPs. It's composed of multithread programs and focus on emerging workloads. Some researchers [18] have proved PARSEC is fundamentally different from SPLASH2 [19] benchmarks in the view of architectural characteristics, such as instruction footprint and working set size. As a result, they complement each other well to give a credible comprehensive. So the combination is a good choice to test model.

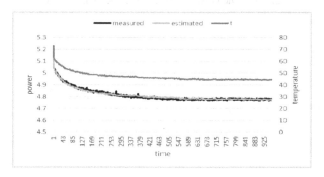

Fig. 3. (a) Idle power

4.2   Results and Error Analysis

To model the idle power, we run a heavy workload for quick heating up the chip, then stop all applications except the monitor, to keep track of the idle power and temperature of each core until the temperature is no longer falling down. Idle power result

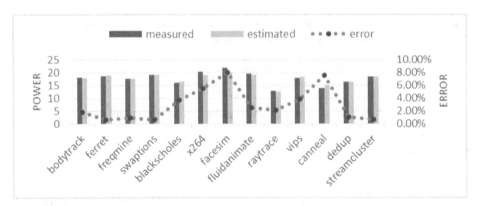

Fig. 3. (b) The power of PARSEC and estimation errors

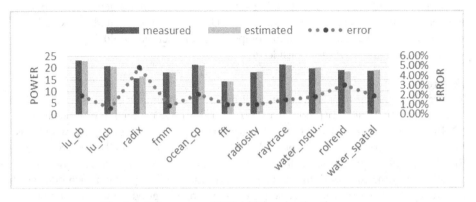

Fig. 3. (c) The power of SPLASH2 and estimation errors

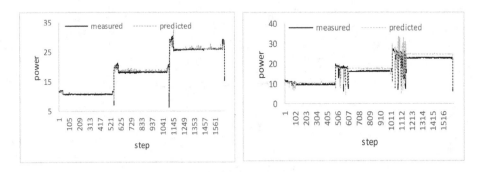

Fig. 4. The power phase of Blackscholes(left) and Streamcluster(right)

is shown in Fig 3(a). It drops with the reducing of core temperature. Although a linear fitting is so simple, it really produces a great result with a percentage error of 0.78%. For dynamic power, we run multi-thread workload with 2 threads, then compare predicted power to the measured one. The result (Fig3 b, c) shows that our model tracks the power consumption well. There is an average error of 3.01% and 1.99% for

PARSEC and SPLASH-2 have respectively. 80% of the applications have less than 5% error. Moreover, the model adapts power phase of running programs well, which can be shown in Figure 4. Because the phase behavior can be detected by hardware event directly [22], which our model is exactly based on. Some benchmarks are estimated unsatisfactory such as facesim, with an error up to 8%.

Reasons may lead to errors are analyzed below:

- The estimation model is built with a simple multi-liner regression which ignores the non-linear element to the power which would be a potential reason to cause the major error.
- Coarse-grained model for some complex components are not elaborate enough. For example, the estimation model can't distinguish between ADD and DIV instruction which certainly cost different mount of power. The disability to differentiate instruction type ignores this influence to ALU.
- Insufficiently training in the phase of model learning coursed by incomplete training set. We exercise model with SPEC2006 benchmarks which are designed to stress ALU and memory hierarchy. Adding some I/O bound program for training seems to be more comprehensive.
- The multiplex technology subdivides the usage of the counting hardware over time to simultaneously monitor more performance events which may cause some lose in prediction precision.
- Dynamic power model is built based on idle power. Errors in idle power would be delivered to dynamic power model, even to be magnified.

In spite of some errors, our estimation fits actual value well. Especially, it can follow the changes of power phase accurately. The prediction is application independent and need no other pretreatment of tested application. Moreover, the modeling methodologies used in this work can also be popularized to any other platform with performance counter, which indicates the generality of this work.

4.3   Contrastive Analysis

We compare our model with previous works in Table 3. Top-down method is easy and low overhead compared with Bottom-up method which is more accurate. However, our method incorporates the advantages of both of them. Filtering events with a Top-Down method at first, then determining the final events through mathematical statistics from the bottom up, we effectively avoid the model for each feature separately, greatly reducing the complexity of modeling. We make use of 11 events and acquire a more precise model with the average error of 2.5% on the Intel I5 processor.

Table 3. Comparison between different models

Model	Method	Platform	# of events	Average Error	Application-independent
Karan's model[24]	Top-Down	AMD Phenom 9500	4	5.63%	No
TDC[7]	Top-Down	Intel Core TM 2 Duo	4	4.53%	Yes
BU[7]	Bottom-Up	Intel Core TM 2 Duo	9	2.53%	No
Isci's model[8]	Bottom-Up	P4	22+	Around 3W	Yes
MICRO[25]	Bottom-Up	Intel Core TM 2 Duo	20	2.85%	Yes
Our model	integrated approach	Intel I5	11	2.5%	Yes

5   Conclusions and Future Work

This paper proposes a general framework for estimating microprocessor's power through performance counters and implements a light-weight and accuracy power estimate model. Its accuracy has been validated by PARSEC, SPLASH2 with average errors of 3.01% and 1.99%. In addition, the framework provides power breakdown for the components which helps to locate the hot point. What's more, our model needs no priori understanding of the tested applications.

To further demonstrate the platform-independent of proposed methodology, we plan to transplant it to other platform such as AMD processor. Still further, we will focus on exploring new power model for CPU+GPU or CPU+MIC heterogeneous architectures which are more and more commonly adopted in high performance computing

References

1. TOP 500 SUPERCOMPUTER SITES, http://www.top500.org/list/2013/06 (accessed December 12, 2013)
2. THE GREEN500 SITES, http://www.green500.org (accessed December 12, 2013)
3. Kumar, A., Shang, L., Peh, L.S., et al.: HybDTM: a coordinated hardware-software approach for dynamic thermal management. In: Proceedings of the 43rd annual Design Automation Conference, pp. 548–553. ACM (2006)
4. Yang, J., Zhou, X., Chrobak, M., et al.: Dynamic thermal management through task scheduling. In: IEEE International Symposium on Performance Analysis of Systems and Software, ISPASS 2008, pp. 191–201. IEEE (2008)
5. Joseph, R., Martonosi, M.: Run-time power estimation in high performance microprocessors. In: Proceedings of the 2001 International Symposium on Low Power Electronics and Design, pp. 135–140. ACM (2001)

6. Bellosa, F.: The benefits of event: driven energy accounting in power-sensitive systems. In: Proceedings of the 9th Workshop on ACM SIGOPS European Workshop: Beyond the PC: New Challenges for the Operating System, pp. 37–42. ACM (2000)
7. Bertran, R., Gonzàlez, M., Martorell, X., et al.: Counter-Based Power Modeling Methods: Top-Down vs. Bottom-Up. The Computer Journal 56(2), 198–213 (2013)
8. Isci, C., Martonosi, M.: Runtime power monitoring in high-end processors: Methodology and empirical data. In: Proceedings of the 36th Annual IEEE/ACM International Symposium on Microarchitecture, p. 93. IEEE Computer Society (2003)
9. Intel® 64 and IA-32 Architectures Software Developer's Manual. Volume 3A: System Programming Guide, Part 1
10. Gupta, V., Brett, P., Koufaty, D., et al.: The forgotten 'uncore': On the energy-efficiency of heterogeneous cores. In: USENIX Annual Technical Conf. (2012)
11. Performance Application Programming Interface, http://icl.cs.utk.edu/papi/ (accessed December 2, 2013)
12. Perfmon2 improving performance monitoring on Linux, http://perfmon2.sourceforge.net (accessed December 2, 2013)
13. PerfSuite@SourceForge website, http://perfsuite.sourceforge.net (accessed December 2, 2013)
14. David, H., Gorbatov, E., Hanebutte, U.R., et al.: RAPL: memory power estimation and capping. In: 2010 ACM/IEEE International Symposium on Low-Power Electronics and Design (ISLPED), pp. 189–194. IEEE (2010)
15. Liu, Y., Dick, R.P., Shang, L., et al.: Accurate temperature-dependent integrated circuit leakage power estimation is easy. In: Proceedings of the Conference on Design, Automation and Test in Europe. EDA Consortium, pp. 1526–1531 (2007)
16. Henning, J.L.: SPEC CPU2006 benchmark descriptions. ACM SIGARCH Computer Architecture News 34(4), 1–17 (2006)
17. Bienia, C., Kumar, S., Singh, J.P., et al.: The PARSEC benchmark suite: Characterization and architectural implications. In: Proceedings of the 17th International Conference on Parallel Architectures and Compilation Techniques, pp. 72–81. ACM (2008)
18. Bienia, C., Kumar, S., Li, K.: PARSEC vs. SPLASH-2: A quantitative comparison of two multithreaded benchmark suites on chip-multiprocessors. In: IEEE International Symposium on Workload Characterization, IISWC 2008, pp. 47–56. IEEE (2008)
19. Arpaci-Dusseau, R.H., Arpaci-Dusseau, A.C.: Operating Systems: Three Easy Pieces [Chapter: Faster Translations (TLBs)] (2014)
20. Korn, W., Teller, P.J., Castillo, G.: Just how accurate are performance counters? In: IEEE International Conference on Performance, Computing, and Communications, pp. 303–310. IEEE (2001)
21. Brooks, D., Tiwari, V., Martonosi, M.: Wattch: a framework for architectural-level power analysis and optimizations. ACM (2000)
22. Isci, C., Martonosi, M.: Phase characterization for power: evaluating control-flow-based and event-counter-based techniques. In: HPCA, pp. 121–132 (2006)
23. 张骏, 樊晓桠, 刘松鹤. 多核, 多线程处理器的低功耗设计技术研究. 计算机科学 34(10), 301–305 (2007)
24. Singh, K., Bhadauria, M., McKee, S.A.: Real time power estimation and thread scheduling via performance counters. ACM SIGARCH Computer Architecture News 37(2), 46–55 (2009)
25. Bertran, R., Gonzalez, M., Martorell, X., et al.: Decomposable and responsive power models for multicore processors using performance counters. In: Proceedings of the 24th ACM International Conference on Supercomputing, pp. 147–158. ACM (2010)

Double Circulation Wear Leveling
for PCM-Based Embedded Systems

Guan Wang, Fei Peng, Lei Ju, Lei Zhang, and Zhiping Jia*

School of Computer Science and Technology, Shandong University, Jinan, China
jzp@sdu.edu.cn

Abstract. Phase change memory (PCM) has emerged as a promising candidate to replace DRAM in embedded systems with its attractive features. However, the endurance of PCM greatly limits its adoption in embedded systems. It can only sustain a limited number of write operations. To solve this issue, we propose a simple, novel, and effective wear leveling technique, called Double Circulation Wear Leveling (DCWL), to evenly distribute write activities across the PCM chips. The basic idea is to periodically move the hot region across the whole PCM chips. When a movement of the hot region is triggered, several small areas in the hot region move to the right. The experimental results show that our wear leveling technique can effectively improve the lifetime of PCM chips compared with the previous work.

Keywords: PCM, Wear Leveling, Endurance, Non-volatile Memory.

1 Introduction

PCM is a promising non-volatile memory technique [1,2,3]. There are several characteristics compared with DRAM and NAND flash. The most typical feature of PCM is non-volatile, which is similar to NAND flash, but it has advantages over NAND flash in density, energy, endurance and read/write speed. In particular, PCM is bit-alterable and byte-addressable, and unlike NAND flash, does not require erase operations for overwrites. Low standby power is another feature of PCM, which is superior to DRAM, because PCM does not need the refresh power. Although PCM has better endurance than NAND flash, its write endurance is still limited [4]. A single level PCM cell (SLC) can endure 10^7 to 10^9 writes before it permanently fails [3]. On the other hand, a program in embedded systems usually distributes write traffic in an extremely unbalanced way. Repeated write operations to the same address may break PCM in dozens of seconds, which poses challenges for the adoption of PCM, so appropriate management for PCM is important and necessary. Furthermore, the access latency of PCM is much closer to DRAM, and combined with its density advantage, PCM is an ideal candidate to replace DRAM as the main memory [5].

In order to increase the lifetime of PCM, a series of reducing write operations and implementation of wear leveling studies are carried out. For reducing

---

* Corresponding author.

J. Wu et al. (Eds.): ACA 2014, CCIS 451, pp. 190–200, 2014.

writes on PCM, various effective techniques have been done, e.g., removing redundant writes [6], write truncation [7], software optimizations proposed by [8,9] and Flip-N-Write [10]. Flip-N-Write is a simple read-modify-write technique to write either flipped or unflipped in order to reduce writes. Whereas, the lifetime of PCM is not directly proportional to the total number of writes on PCM, but to depend on the location that is written most frequently. Therefore, these techniques are inability when the writes in a program are non-uniformity. To evenly distribute write traffic on PCM, row shifting and segment swapping [6] has been proposed to achieve wear leveling, in which a mapping table is employed to record writes on each row or segment. It requires a huge space overhead. To avoid the space overhead, random-based swapping techniques, such as Start-Gap [11], security refresh [12] and PCM-aware swap algorithm [13], are proposed to dynamically randomize the mapping on PCM chips for achieving wear leveling. Start-Gap [11] method first randomizes the mapping from logical to physical addresses to distribute write traffic with high spatial locality. Then, by combining a rotation-based wear leveling utilizing start and gap registers, logical to physical address mapping is changed. Curling-PCM [14] is a kind of wear leveling algorithms oriented particular embedded application. The basic idea is to periodically move the hot region across the whole PCM chips. There are also other kinds of wear leveling algorithms, such as age-based PCM wear leveling [15] and bloom filter-based dynamic wear leveling [16].

In this paper, we propose a simple, novel, and effective wear leveling technique, called Double Circulation Wear Leveling (DCWL), to evenly distribute write activities across the PCM chips so that the endurance of PCM-based embedded systems is enhanced. Our basic idea is to periodically move the hot region across the whole PCM chips. When a move of the hot region is triggered, several small areas in the hot region move to the right. In such a way, write traffic to hot areas can be evenly distributed to the whole PCM chips, so the PCM wear leveling can be improved. DCWL is very simple and requires only five additional registers to perform wear leveling. The experimental results show that DCWL can effectively improve the lifetime of PCM chips compared with the previous work.

This paper makes the following contributions:

- We propose a simple, novel, and effective wear leveling technique, called Double Circulation Wear Leveling (DCWL), to evenly distribute write activities across the PCM chips. The effectiveness of our techniques is demonstrated by comparing with previous work using workloads.
- We develop a simulator to simulate PCM-based embedded systems, and based on which, we conduct a series of experiments to demonstrate the effectiveness of our techniques.

The rest of the paper is organized as follows. Section 2 introduces the background and motivation. Double Circulation Wear Leveling is proposed in Section 3. Section 4 reports the experimental results. Finally, in Section 5, we conclude this paper and discuss future work.

2   Architecture and Motivation

In this section, we first present the architecture of PCM-based embedded systems. Then, we discuss the motivation of our work.

2.1   Architecture of PCM-Based Embedded Systems

In [17], the architecture of PCM-based embedded systems has been presented. DRAM serves as the main memory, NOR flash is used to store code with eXecution-In-Place, and NAND flash is used as the secondary storage to store user data. As PCM has superior read/write performance compared with NOR flash, it has been utilized as NOR flash replacement. In [4], NOR flash is replaced with PCM, which is used to store the code and meta-data. In our paper, the architecture of PCM-based embedded systems is shown in Figure 1. PCM replaces the conventional DRAM as the main memory of embedded systems, and is used for storing data from execution process of program [14]. The embedded systems adopt the SRAM-based Scratch Pad Memory (SPM) as its on-chip memory, which is widely used for reducing the speed gap between the processor and the PCM-based main memory. In this architecture, the flash-based storage drive is used as the secondary storage to store user data [18].

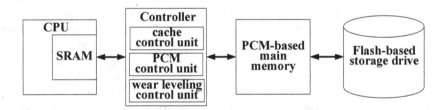

Fig. 1. Architecture of PCM-based embedded systems

2.2   Motivation

Despite the studies in PCM wear leveling, most existing work is based on counting the number of writes per line or page [6], which may introduce non-negligible hardware overheads. Other approaches such as Start-Gap [11] require simple additional hardware changes, but move cold regions only. Application-specific features such as fixed update frequencies and access patterns in embedded systems are not fully utilized, so Curling-PCM [14] has been proposed, which is a kind of wear leveling algorithms oriented particular embedded application. As shown in Figure 2, we still note some extraordinary large write counts. The reason behind is that the frequency of moving hot regions is not large enough to perfectly and evenly distribute all write activities across the PCM chips. If we reduce the number of writes required before conducting a move, write activities will become more evenly distributed. But small thresholds may lead to frequent and

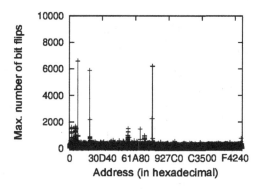

Fig. 2. Distribution of write activities with Curling-PCM [14]

excessive copy operations, thus increasing the total number of bit flips. To solve this conflict, we propose a wear leveling algorithm that is suitable in distributing unbalanced writes in PCM evenly across the whole PCM chips.

3   Double Circulation Wear Leveling

In this section, we present our wear leveling technique, called Double Circulation Wear Leveling (DCWL), which is a simple and effective wear leveling technique. Many methods in PCM wear leveling have been proposed in the general computing field. Most of the previous work is based on recording the write counts of each line or page, which may introduce big hardware overhead. Other approaches such as Start-Gap [11] require simple hardware.

The basic idea is to periodically move predefined hot areas across the whole PCM chips. When a movement of the hot region is triggered, several small areas in the hot region move to the right. In this way, write traffic to hot areas can be evenly distributed to improve wear leveling. In DCWL, we mainly need to solve the following three problems: (1) How to identify and allocate PCM space for hot and cold regions; (2) When to move the hot region and several small areas in the hot region; (3) How to implement the address mapping after moving the hot region.

To identify hot and cold regions, for the data and code of an application that will be put into PCM chips, we can first obtain the number of writes for the data and code by analyzing memory accesses of an application. Then, all hot areas where there exist more writes are grouped together and put into a region called as hot region, and all other areas are put into a region called as cold region. Since the identified starting logical address and length of the hot region will not change.

To evenly distribute writes of the hot region, it is periodically moved across the PCM chips. When the hot region reaches to the bottom, it will continue to move and exchange its contents of the first entries of the PCM chips. A move

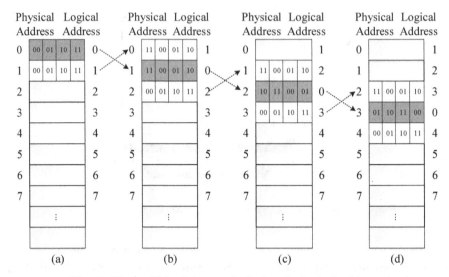

Fig. 3. The mapping between logical and physical addresses

of the hot region is triggered when the number of writes reaches a predefined threshold. To achieve this, in DCWL, besides the register for storing the number of writes, we need one register to record the starting physical address of the hot region, and one register to record the logical address of the first cold region entry after the hot region to implement the address mapping after moving the hot region. To achieve better wear leveling, we divide each region into multiple sub-regions with fixed number of PCM entries. When a move of the hot region is triggered, several small areas in the hot region move to the right. We also need two registers which are the number of hot region moves and the number of hot region circulation in order to implement the address mapping after moving sub-regions inside the hot region.

Moving the hot region will cause mismatches of logical-to-physical address mappings. One example is shown in Figure 3. With the initial PCM layout, logical and physical addresses match each other exactly. Then with the continuous movements of the hot region, as shown in Figure 3(b)-(d), the mapping between logical and physical addresses keeps changing. In DCWL, two steps address mappings are needed. First step is based on the following equations.

$$
HPA = \begin{cases}
(HLA + R\_HStart) \bmod Len \\
\qquad\qquad\qquad\qquad \text{if } LA \in hot\ region \\
(HLA + R\_HStart + Len - R\_CStartL) \bmod Len \\
\qquad\qquad\qquad\qquad \text{if } LA < R\_CStartL \\
(HLA + R\_HStart + HLen - R\_CStartL) \bmod Len \\
\qquad\qquad\qquad\qquad \text{if } LA \geq R\_CStartL
\end{cases} \tag{1}
$$

From the equation (1), there are three cases for the address translation. In Case 1, when a given logical address is within the hot region, the high addresses of physical address (HPA) is obtained by adding the high addresses of logical address (HLA) to the starting physical address of the hot region (R_HStart). Note that in this paper, we assume that the hot region starts at the first physical PCM entry. In Case 2, a given logical address is not in the hot region and is less than the first logical address following the hot region ($R\_CStartL$). In this case, the physical address can be obtained by adding the starting physical address of the hot region, the total length of hot and cold regions (Len), and subtracting $R\_CStartL$. Finally, in Case 3, a given logical address is not in the hot region and is greater than or equal to $R\_CStartL$. The physical address calculation is same as that in Case 2 except that it is the hot region length ($HLen$), instead of total length (Len) is added. Note that one needs to modulo Len after did the above calculations.

$$
LPA = \begin{cases}
(LLA + M\_Num \times SLen) \bmod HLen \\
\qquad\qquad\qquad\qquad\qquad \text{if } LA \in hot\ region \\
(LLA + (C\_Num + 1) \times SLen) \bmod HLen \\
\qquad\qquad\qquad\qquad\qquad \text{if } LA < R\_CStartL \\
(LLA + C\_Num \times SLen) \bmod HLen \\
\qquad\qquad\qquad\qquad\qquad \text{if } LA \geq R\_CStartL
\end{cases} \tag{2}
$$

Second step is shown in the equation (2). As shown in Figure 3, each region is divided into four sub-regions. We require one register to record the number of hot region moves (M_Num), another register to record the number of hot region circulation (C_Num). When the hot region moves to the bottom of the whole region, the number of hot region circulation adds one. The low addresses of physical address (LPA) also need to change, when the hot region moves. There are three cases for the address translation. In Case 1, when a given logical address is within the hot region, LPA is obtained by adding the low addresses of logical address (LLA) to the multiplication of M_Num and the sub-region length ($SLen$). In Case 2, a given logical address is not in the hot region and is less than $R\_CStartL$. LPA can be obtained by adding LLA to the multiplication of C_Num plus one and $SLen$. Finally, in Case 3, a given logical address is not in the hot region and is greater than or equal to $R\_CStartL$. LPA can be obtained by adding LLA to the multiplication of C_Num and $SLen$. Note that one needs to modulo $HLen$ after did the above calculations. We can get the real physical addresses combining the changed low addresses (LPA) with the high addresses (HPA).

4   Experiments

To evaluate the effectiveness of DCWL, we conduct various experiments with application traces. In this section, we first introduce the schemes for comparison, and then we describe experimental setup. Finally, the experimental results with analysis of DCWL algorithm are presented.

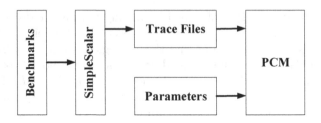

Fig. 4. The simulation framework

4.1   Schemes for Comparison

Since the maximum number of bit flips will directly determine the lifetime of a PCM chip, wear leveling algorithms are required to further evenly distribute the write activities across the whole PCM chips. Therefore, we use DCWL to distribute the write activities, compared against both Start-Gap [11] and Curling-PCM [14].

Start-Gap [11] is a well-known wear leveling scheme. An additional empty line which is called the Gap is moved up periodically after the number of writes to PCM reaches a predefined threshold. In our experiment, one line contains four bytes, and the threshold is set to 100 writes.

Curling-PCM [14] is another wear leveling scheme. The basic idea is to periodically move the hot region across the whole PCM chips. In this scheme, the hot region contains roughly 2,000 lines, and the threshold for triggering a movement of the hot region is set to 20,000 writes.

In our Double Circulation Wear Leveling scheme, the hot region contains almost 2000 lines. Therefore we set DCWL to move this region periodically. The threshold for triggering a movement of the hot region should be set carefully. Small thresholds may lead to frequent and excessive copy operations, and large thresholds can not perform good wear leveling. Through the experiment the threshold is set to 20,000 writes by which we obtain good results overall.

4.2   Experimental Setup

To accelerate development, we first collect application trace data by SimpleScalar [19]. Trace files are then fed into our simulator with related parameters (e.g., wear leveling thresholds) to obtain experimental results. Figure 4 explains the experimental work flow. We adopt the architecture shown in Figure 1 for our simulator. The system specification used in our experiment is shown in Table

Table 1. Experimental setup

	Description
CACHE	size:16KB, block size:32B, LRU
PCM	size:32Mb, read latency:48ns, write latency:150ns

1. Experimental benchmarks adapt Mibench [20], which is a free, commercially representative embedded benchmark suite.

4.3   Experimental Results and Discussion

Based on the above experimental setup, we record the total number of bit flips of all PCM cells and the maximum number of bit flips in each PCM cells. We compare our results with two wear leveling approaches: Start-Gap [11] and Curling-PCM [14]. In addition, we also compare our results with the two schemes: no wear leveling (No-WL) that does not adopt wear leveling, and the ideal case that all the writes are distributed evenly over the PCM space.

Table 2. Comparison of the maximum number of bit flips

Benchmark	No-WL	Start-Gap	Curling-PCM	DCWL
basicmath	2035628	607	227	96
bitcount	490317	4562	1396	419
crc32	71598	463	193	107
dijkstra	1463800	1874	490	112
FFT	4259	600	258	128
patricia	63048	1392	547	332
qsort	3019	602	506	221
blowfish	92570	1628	770	395
susan	1985	863	336	80

Table 2 shows the maximum number of bit flips among all PCM cells for each benchmark. A PCM cell can survive only a limited number of writes before it loses ability to change the state. Hence, the lifetime of PCM depends on the maximum number of bit flips. The results show that DCWL can effectively reduce the maximum number of bit flips. Compared with no wear leveling (No-WL), Start-Gap and Curling-PCM, DCWL can reduce by 98.27%, 81.16%, 57.81% respectively on average. Start-Gap cannot effectively and evenly distribute the hot traffic and cool down hot areas, because it only moves empty line. Curling-PCM distributes most write activities across the whole PCM chips. However, there are still some extraordinary large write counts. The reason behind is that the frequency of moving hot regions is not large enough to perfectly and evenly distribute all write activities across the PCM chips. DCWL can solve this problem perfectly. Because of the movement inside the hot region, write activities will become more evenly distributed.

Figure 5 shows the lifetime of PCM on these wear leveling schemes. Compared with Start-Gap [11], the lifetime of DCWL can averagely improve 4x-5x. Compared with Curling-PCM [14], the lifetime of DCWL can averagely improve 2x-3x. It can achieve 85.28% of the lifetime compared with the ideal case. We also calculate the lifetime of PCM without any wear leveling. PCM would be

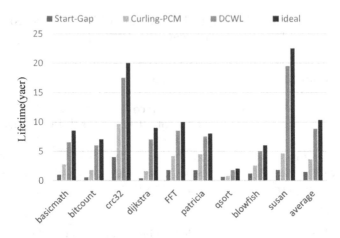

Fig. 5. The lifetime of the PCM

wear-out in a short time, especially for the benchmarks basicmath, diskstra, and crc32.

Compared with no wear leveling, the total number of bit flips is increased in Start-Gap, Curling-PCM and DCWL. Figure 6 shows the extra writes overhead are incurred among these schemes on various benchmarks. Start-Gap incurs approximately 12.11% more writes than no wear leveling. This is caused by periodically moving the empty line. Compared with Start-Gap, our scheme causes a 4.31% increase in the total number of bit flips. However, our scheme still outperforms Start-Gap overall, because of the big improvement in the maximum number of bit flips.

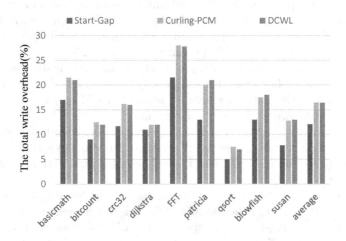

Fig. 6. The total writes overhead

5   Conclusion and Future Work

In this paper, we proposed a novel and effective wear leveling technique, called DCWL, to evenly distribute write activities across the PCM chips for better endurance. The basic idea is to periodically move the hot region across the whole PCM chips. When a move of the hot region is triggered, several small areas in the hot region move to the right. According to experimental results, the proposed technique can greatly improve the lifetime of PCM-based embedded systems, and achieve approximately 85.28% lifetime of the ideal case.

In the future, with the capacity of PCM continues to increase, we can use PCM to store user data that is currently stored in NAND flash. This may require some fundamental changes from the current user data management. Considering the high read speed of PCM, we should have direct PCM read instead of using the traditional structure. The data management of the main memory and the secondary storage memory should be studied.

References

1. Xie, Y.: Modeling, Architecture, and Applications for Emerging Memory Technologies. IEEE Design and Test of Computers 28(1), 44–51 (2011)
2. Lee, B.C., Zhou, P., Yang, J., Zhang, Y., Zhao, B., Ipek, E., Mutlu, O., Burger, D.: Phase-Change Technology and the Future of Main Memory. IEEE Micro 30(1), 143 (2010)
3. Xue, C.J., Zhang, Y., Chen, Y., Sun, G., Yang, J.J., Li, H.: Emerging non-volatile memories: Opportunities and challenges. In: Proceedings of the 9th International Conference on Hardware/Software Codesign and System Synthesis, Taipei, pp. 325–334 (2011)
4. Shao, Z., Chang, N., Dutt, N.: PTL: PCM Translation Layer. In: 2012 IEEE Computer Society Annual Symposium on VLSI (ISVLSI), Amherst, pp. 380–385 (2012)
5. Qureshi, M.K., Srinivasan, V., Rivers, J.A.: Scalable High Performance Main Memory System Using Phase-Change Memory Technology. In: Proceedings of the 36th Annual International Symposium on Computer Architecture, New York, pp. 24–33 (2009)
6. Zhou, P., Zhao, B., Yang, J., Zhang, Y.: A Durable and Energy Efficient Main Memory Using Phase Change Memory Technology. In: Proceedings of the 36th Annual International Symposium on Computer Architecture, New York, pp. 14–23 (2009)
7. Jiang, L., Zhao, B., Zhang, Y., Yang, J., Childers, B.R.: Improving write operations in MLC phase change memory. In: 2012 IEEE 18th International Symposium on High Performance Computer Architecture, New Orleans, pp. 1–10 (2012)
8. Hu, J., Xue, C.J., Tseng, W.C., He, Y., Qiu, M., Sha, E.H.M.: Reducing write activities on non-volatile memories in embedded CMPs via data migration and recomputation. In: 2010 47th ACM/IEEE Design Automation Conference, Anaheim, pp. 350–355 (2010)
9. Hu, J., Tseng, W.C., Xue, C.J., Zhuge, Q., Zhao, Y., Sha, E.H.M.: Write activity minimization for nonvolatile main memory via scheduling and recomputation. IEEE Transactions on Computer-Aided Design of Integrated Circuits and Systems 30(4), 584–592 (2011)

10. Cho, S., Lee, H.: Flip-N-Write: A Simple Deterministic Technique to Improve PRAM Write Performance, Energy and Endurance. In: 42nd Annual IEEE/ACM International Symposium on Microarchitecture, New York, pp. 347–357 (2009)

11. Qureshi, M.K., Karidis, J., Franceschini, M., Srinivasan, V., Lastras, L., Abali, B.: Enhancing Lifetime and Security of PCM-based Main Memory with Start-Gap Wear Leveling. In: Proceedings of the 42nd Annual IEEE/ACM International Symposium on Microarchitecture, New York, pp. 14–23 (2009)

12. Seong, N.H., Woo, D.H., Lee, H.H.S.: Security refresh: Prevent malicious wear-out and increase durability for phase-change memory with dynamically randomized address mapping. In: Proceedings of the 37th Annual International Symposium on Computer Architecture, vol. 38(3), pp. 383–394 (2010)

13. Ferreira, A.P., Zhou, M., Bock, S., Childers, B., Melhem, R., Moss, D.: Increasing PCM main memory lifetime. In: Proceedings of the Conference on Design, Automation and Test in Europe, Dresden, pp. 914–919 (2010)

14. Liu, D., Wang, T., Wang, Y., Shao, Z., Zhuge, Q., Sha, E.H.M.: Curling-PCM: Application-Specific Wear Leveling for Phase Change Memory Based Embedded Systems. In: 18th Asia and South Pacific Design Automation Conference, Yokohama, pp. 22–25 (2013)

15. Chen, C.H., Hsiu, P.C., Kuo, T.W., Yang, C.L., Wang, C.Y.: Age-based PCM Wear Leveling with Nearly Zero Search Cost. In: 49th ACM/EDAC/IEEE Design Automation Conference, San Francisco, pp. 453–458 (2012)

16. Yun, J., Lee, S., Yoo, S.: Bloom Filter-based Dynamic Wear Leveling for Phase-Change RAM. In: Proceedings of the Conference on Design, Automation and Test in Europe, Dresden, pp. 1513–1518 (2012)

17. Kim, J.K., Lee, H.G., Choi, S., Bahng, K.I.: A PRAM and NAND Flash Hybrid Architecture for High-performance Embedded Storage Subsystems. In: Proceedings of the 8th ACM International Conference on Embedded Software, New York, pp. 31–40 (2008)

18. Liu, D., Wang, T., Wang, Y., Qin, Z., Shao, Z.: A block-level flash memory management scheme for reducing write activities in PCM-based embedded systems. In: Proceedings of the Conference on Design, Automation and Test in Europe, Dresden, pp. 1447–1450 (2012)

19. Austin, T., Larson, E., Ernst, D.: SimpleScalar: An Infrastructure for Computer System Modeling. Computer 35(2), 59–67 (2002)

20. Guthaus, M.R., Ringenberg, J.S., Ernst, D., Austin, T.M., Mudge, T., Brown, R.B.: MiBench: A free, commercially representative embedded benchmark suite. In: IEEE International Workshop on Workload Characterization, pp. 3–14 (2001)

Reputation-Based Participant Incentive Approach in Opportunistic Cognitive Networks

Jie Li[1,2,*], Rui Liu[3], Ruiyun Yu[4], Xingwei Wang[5], and Zhijie Zhao[6]

[1] Computing Center, Northeastern University, Shenyang, China
[2] Key Lab of Network Control Systems, Chinese Acad. of Sci., Shenyang, China
lijie@mail.neu.edu.cn
[3] Department of Computing, Hong Kong Polytechnic University, Hong Kong
csrliu@comp.polyu.edu.hk
[4] Software College, Northeastern University, Shenyang, China
yury@mail.neu.edu.cn
[5] College of Information Sci. and Eng., Northeastern University, Shenyang, China
wangxw@mail.neu.edu.cn
[6] Info. and Tech. Center of China Mobile Group Liaoning Co., LTD
zhaozhijie@ln.chinamobile.com

Abstract. Sufficient reputable participants are critical to effective data collections and data disseminations in opportunistic cognitive networks. However, it is difficult to identify reputable or malicious participants in opportunistic networks. Cognitive network technology can be applied to the communication system of opportunistic networks to provide reputation-aware schemes of the participants. Furthermore, keeping participants enthusiasm for activities of networks is also important. In this work, we propose a Reputation-Based Participant Incentive Approach (RBPIA) to motivate reputable participants. RBPIA scores participants using reputation degree according to their sensing data and bid price respectively and encourage them to keep interested in the activities with rewards. Simulations are performed in different scenarios to evaluate efficiency of the approach. The results show that RBPIA can identify participant types well, and remarkably reduce the incentive cost.

Keywords: opportunistic cognitive networks, reputation, incentive, bid price collusion, multidimensional reverse auction.

* This work is supported by the National Natural Science Foundation of China under grant no. 61272529; the National Science Foundation for Distinguished Young Scholars of China under grant no. 61225012 and No. 71325002; the Specialized Research Fund of the Doctoral Program of Higher Education for the Priority Development Areas under grant no. 20120042130003; the Fundamental Research Funds for the Central Universities under grant no. N120417002, no. N110204003 and no. N120104001.Science and Technology Planning Project of Liaoning Province under grant no.2013217004. MOE-Intel Special Fund of Information Technology (MOE-INTEL-2012-06).

J. Wu et al. (Eds.): ACA 2014, CCIS 451, pp. 201–214, 2014.

1 Introduction

Cognitive Networks have already been prototyped for many commercial and civilian applications[1]. Combined with the social intelligence, cognitive networks promise to support services like citizen journalism, mobile social networking, environmental monitoring, and traffic monitoring by integrating ubiquitous sensing, large-scale data collection and cloud computing[2]. Nonetheless, commercialization of sensor network has rarely been successfully deployed in the physical world due to high cost for sufficient number of sensors.

Opportunistic network[3], provides an ideal solution for promoting the evolution of communication among human beings and machines. Smart hand-held devices (e.g., smart phone or PDA) carried by a large number of participants contribute to opportunistic cognitive networks with their sensing parts. The inherent mobility of participants provides unprecedented spatiotemporal coverage and also makes it possible to observe various events. PEIR [4] is an application that uses location data sampled from everyday mobile phones to calculate personalized estimates of environmental impact and exposure. CarTel [5] is a mobile sensor computing system designed to collect, process, deliver, and visualize data from sensors located on mobile units such as automobiles. Reference [6] proposes Bubble-Sensing, a new sensor network abstraction that allows mobile phones users to create a binding between tasks (e.g., take a photo, or sample audio every hour indefinitely) and the physical world at locations of interest, which remains active for a duration set by the user.Reference[7,8]provides efficiently routing schemes in different mobile networks, which is the essence of data collection and dissemination.

Moreover, by including people in the sensing loop, it is now possible to design applications that can dramatically improve daily lives of individuals and communities. In general, there are two main groups of opportunistic cognitive applications, environmental monitoring (air pollution [9], noise [10], traffic [11],data collection[12] and scenery [13]) and social monitoring (social network [14] and user activity [15]).

Participants who submit their collecting data to the system will eventually lose enthusiasm to remain actively in this system without being fairly rewarded. Namely, participants may drop out unless the reward is greater than their expectation. Furthermore, there are some malicious participants who will generate corrupted data when opportunistic cognitive networks are deployed. Malicious participants may supplant normal ones and it may be worse when they collude with each other. In such circumstances, normal participants drop out and malicious ones will control the system without hesitation. Therefore, it's critical to keep sufficient normal participants for collecting reliable sensing data. Also, minimizing incentive cost is essential to participatory sensing systems.

In this paper, we propose the Reputation-Based Participant Incentive Approach (RBPIA) to categorize and motivate participants, while minimizing incentive cost for maintaining sufficient normal participants which always provide accurate sensing data.

RBPIA first analyzes sensing data and bid prices to evaluate the trustworthiness of participants using accumulated reputation degree. Then a multidimensional reverse auction will be performed by RBPIA and reputable participants who bid lower price will win the reward. Furthermore, RBPIA will adjust each participant's bid price and increase winning probability of loser in the next auction round according to their reputation level.

- Establish reputation to evaluate the trustworthiness of participants by participants' reputation degree. The reputation degree is calculated according to sensing data quality and malicious collusion. High reputation degree reflects accumulation of good historical participations and vice versa.
- Design reputation-based incentive approach for participatory sensing systems. RBPIA can greatly decrease incentive cost for maintaining sufficient participants through multidimensional reverse auction where bid price and reputation level are both considered. RBPIA encourages reputable participants in sensing activities by adjusting their bid prices.
- Introduce virtual coupon in RBPIA. The participants who bid lower price will always become winners in reverse auction. However, virtual coupon will be given to the losers to increase winning probability in the next auction round. Moreover, different participants can obtain various amount of virtual coupon according to their reputation.

The remainder of this paper is organized as follows. In Section 2, related works about participatory sensing are illustrated. Section 3 gives detail of RBPIA. In Section 4, RBPIA is evaluated in various simulations. Finally, we conclude this paper in Section 5.

2   Related Work

2.1   Reputation Model

Reputation model has long been studied in a diverse range of disciplines. It is widely used in web site for Comment Rating Environment [16]. As is well known, the online markets such as Taobao and Amazon [17] are much popular. Taobao establishes its own reputation system using reputations to enhance buying and selling experiences [18]. For example, Taobao uses a simple feedback mechanism where a buyer assigns 1 to 5 rating stars to the seller based on his/her satisfaction with the transaction. A seller's overall feedback score is simply the average of all ratings. This approach is simple to implement and understand, but it has some drawbacks. First, negative ratings can be easily drowned by a large pool of positive ratings. Furthermore, it is easy for system administrators to change ratings illegally. There is relevant behavior in recent report. This simple approach is not appropriate in context of participatory sensing systems.

Reputation systems have been used in ad-hoc wireless networks [19, 20, 21, 22]. In [19, 20], the ideas is borrowed from game theory and attempted to address the selfish routing problem in such networks. In [21, 22], Bayesian analysis is used to formulate a similar problem and the resulting reputation systems are shown to counter any misbehaving nodes. Bayesian reputation systems are quite flexible and can be adapted with relative ease in different types of applications and environments [23, 24]. For example, the reputation framework, RFSN, proposed in [25] makes use of Beta reputation for associating a reputation score with each sensor node in a traditional embedded wireless sensor network. However, it takes a less aggressive approach in penalizing participants that contributes corrupted data.

To the best of our knowledge, a few research work is conducted on reputation in participatory sensing systems. Reference [26] implements a noise monitoring system to identify corrupted noise data. However, the system only focuses on the sensing data provided by participants in current monitoring application without considering accumulated reputation of participants. Reference [27] proposes using reputation management to classify the gathered data and provide useful information for campaign organizers and data analysts to facilitate their decisions. However, the author just provides a simple reputation method and cannot adapt to the changeable environment when participatory sensing system deploys in the real world.

2.2 Incentive Mechanism

Incentive mechanism has been widely used in management and economy. In recent years, the mechanism is introduced into computers and networks. Generally, there are two categories of mechanisms in networks: offering rewards and distinguishing services. In the way of offering rewards, the active and well-behaved nodes can obtain some remuneration for their participation [28]. The mechanism of distinguishing services mainly provides different level services to sensors according to their behavior [29]. The mechanism, by its very nature, offers more resources and services to incentive reputable nodes.

Reverse auction is a special form of offering rewards. There are two types of player in an auction: bidder and auctioneer. In a general auction, buyers become bidders and the seller is an auctioneer. By comparison, in a reverse auction there is a single buyer that becomes an auctioneer while many sellers become bidders. In terms of bidding sides, auctions can also be classified as single or double ones. In a single auction, only one side of participants can bid. On the other hand, in a double auction, both sides of participants can bid.

All above mentioned auction types use bids that comprise only of price, so we call it one-dimensional reverse auction. In contrast, a multidimensional reverse auction allows bidders to bid on various attributes beyond the price. Since the auctioneer selects winners based on all bidding attributes, the overall utility of a bid should be computed following various utility functions. General procedures for multidimensional auctions in e-markets have been described in [30]. Recent studies [31] have proposed a motivation system, named the Reverse Auction based Dynamic Price incentive mechanism with Virtual Participation Credit (RADP-VPC).

To the best of our knowledge, no study addresses incentive mechanisms with multidimensional reverse auction in participatory sensing system. RBPIA is the first reputation based incentive system where a multidimensional reverse auction is introduced by taking participants' reputation and incentive cost into account.

3   Reputation-Based Participant Incentive Approach

In this section, we propose the Reputation-Based Participant Incentive Approach (RBPIA) in the context of participatory sensing systems.

3.1   Overview

Fig. 1 depicts the framework of RBPIA. Generally, sensing request is sent to the participants through server in a participatory sensing system. After sensing, each participant uploads sensing data, bid price and personal information (e.g., location) to the server and RBPIA residing in the server processes all data obtained from participants.

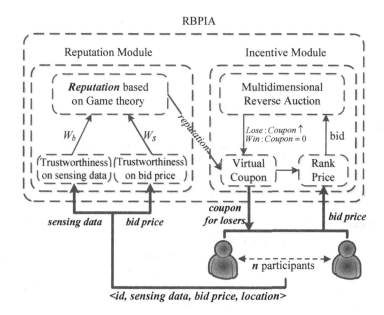

Fig. 1. Framework of RBPIA

Firstly, sensing data and bid prices will be uploaded to the Reputation Module where the Trustworthiness on Sensing Data and the Trustworthiness on Bid Price is produced, respectively. After that, the reputation degree can be successfully derived based on game theory.

Then, a multidimensional reverse auction in the Incentive Module selects winners in terms of Rank Prices which are calculated based on participants' bid prices and virtual coupon they possess.

Finally, the participants with lower Rank Prices win out, get reward and reset their virtual coupon to zero. Nevertheless losers will obtain virtual coupon to raise their winning probability.

3.2 Reputation Module

Trustworthiness on Sensing Data

The number of normal participants is usually larger than that of malicious participants in a target field, so we choose the density-based outlier detection algorithm proposed in [32] to preprocess the sensing data set $S = \{s_1, s_2, \cdots, s_n\}$ received from n participants. The details are illustrated in Eq. 1 and Eq. 2.

$$A = \sum_{i=1}^{n} M_i s_i \tag{1}$$

$$M_i = \frac{\frac{1}{\frac{(s_i - A)^2}{\sum_{i=1}^{n}(s_i - A)^2 + \epsilon}}}{\sum_{j=1}^{n} \frac{1}{\frac{(s_i - A)^2}{\sum_{i=1}^{n}(s_i - A)^2 + \epsilon}}} \tag{2}$$

As shown in Fig. 2, the algorithm is iterative in nature. At first, it defines and initializes $M_i = \frac{1}{n}$. A and M_i are computed in each iteration. M_i^f equals to M_i^{l+1} when the convergence $|M_i^{l+1} - M_i^l| < \eta$ is observed in the $(l + 1)$ th iteration.

It is obvious that tighter convergence could be chosen to produce more accurate result according to specific scenarios. ϵ is a small positive constant for adjustment and more discussion can be found in [33].

As mentioned above, normal participants are usually more than malicious ones in participatory sensing systems. Consequently, the majority of participants who provide similar sensing data will have higher M_i^f. This takes the fact that most participants generate relatively accurate sensing data.

However, in particular circumstances, the number of malicious participants would be larger than that of normal ones in sensing field which will affect overall data accuracy. It may lead to fatal error when making decisions based on such corrupted data provided by malicious ones in participatory sensing system.

After several rounds, a participant will present its trustworthiness through its historical behaviors. The trimmed-mean method [34] is introduced to reflect the long-term trends accordingly. The method is a statistical measure of central tendency and involves the calculation of mean value after discarding given parts of a probability distribution or sample at the high and low end, and typically discarding an equal amount of both.

$W_s = \{w_{s,1}, w_{s,2}, \cdots, w_{s,n}\}$ is computed based on historical M_i^f using the trimmed-mean method which is depicted in Eq. 3.

$$w_{s,i} = \frac{M_{i,[m\sigma]+1}^f + M_{i,[m\sigma]+2}^f + \cdots + M_{i,m-[m\sigma]}^f}{m - 2[m\sigma]} \tag{3}$$

Trustworthiness on Bid Price

To deploy participatory sensing systems with RBPIA in the real world, it is vital to make RBPIA robust against bid price collusion.

In the auctions, participants will bid in terms of their effort. However, collusive participants often bid similar low prices in several initial auction rounds, and will always win in these auctions, which will expel normal participants from the system. After that, they will control the system and bid high prices to boost their profit which will greatly increase the incentive cost. To retain sufficient participants and guarantee fairness of the participatory systems, the k-means algorithm [35] is exploited in the Reputation Module against bid price collusion. The k-means algorithm observes the bid price of each participant and classifies them into different categories to detect collusive ones from the others. The collusive participants will be punished on their trustworthiness value. Based on all bid prices of all participants $B = \{b_1, b_2, \cdots, b_n\}$, the scheme generating $W_b = \{w_{b,1}, w_{b,2}, \cdots, w_{b,n}\}$ is detailed as follows:

a) The k-means algorithm classifies bid prices of all participants B to k clusters and captures the centroids of k clusters in each round. All participants from each cluster whose centroid is lower than the mean of all centroids will be recorded.
b) The scheme only examines successive ζ rounds. The records of ζ rounds will form a list containing all collusive suspects. For participant i, if the frequency of occurrence in the list is greater than or equal to predefined g (say 0.6ζ) during ζ rounds, we set $h_i = h_i + 1$ (h_i is initialized to zero).
c) From round $\zeta+1$, the trustworthiness on bid price of participant i till current round r ($w_{b,i}$) will be produced as shown in Eq. 4.

$$w_{b,i} = ae^{be^{d+ch_i}} + 1 \tag{4}$$

Where coefficient a, b and c are negative numbers, coefficient d is a positive value and e is Euler's Number.

Reputation Based on Game Theory

The trustworthiness of participant i is evaluated by the reputation degree which is a gaming result between $w_{s,i}$ and $w_{b,i}$.

We introduce a joint-weight method based on game theory. The method focuses on discovering compromise of W_s and W_b and minimizing the bias of reputation degree between two weights (i.e., W_s and W_b). Although there are only two weights, the complete method is provided as follow without loss of generality.

Linear combination of q weights is depicted in Eq. 5.

$$W = \sum_{i=1}^{q} \alpha_i W_i^T \qquad (5)$$

The appropriate coefficient α_i balances all weights. A comprehensive weight can be obtained by solving Eq. 6.

$$min\|W = \sum_{i=1}^{q} \alpha_i W_i^T - W_j^T\|_2 \quad j = 1, 2, \cdots, q \qquad (6)$$

After normalization, the reputation degree is computed by α_i and W_i. The reputation degree $RP = \{rp_1, rp_2, \cdots, rp_n\}$ is calculated as Eq. 7.

$$RP = \alpha_s W_s^T + \alpha_b W_b^T \qquad (7)$$

3.3   Incentive Module

To motive participants, a multidimensional reverse auction is introduced in the Incentive Module. The objective of RBPIA is to maintain adequate number of participants for desired service quality while minimizing incentive cost by preventing cost explosion during the multidimensional reverse auction.

Intuitively, participants who bid lower price are more likely to become winners in one-dimensional reverse auction, as shown in Fig. 2. However, the participants who always lose in auction may drop out. As a result, the winners can manipulate subsequent auctions and increase bid price to maximize their profits.

To maintain fair competition and prevent incentive cost explosion, enough participants should participate continuously in reverse auctions of RBPIA. For this goal, the proposed Incentive Module provides a novel winner selection strategy using virtual coupon and reputation degree.

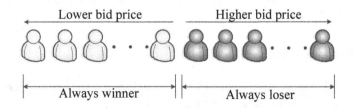

Fig. 2. Winners and losers in one-dimensional reverse auction

A participant (i.e., bidder) i will receive virtual coupon as a reward when they lost in the previous auction round to increase winning probability in the next round. The virtual coupon $D = \{d_1, d_2, \cdots, d_n\}$ can be defined as Eq. 8

$$d_i = \begin{cases} d_i + \gamma \cdot rp_i & i \text{ is a loser} \\ 0 & i \text{ is a winner} \end{cases} \qquad (8)$$

Where γ denotes the amount of virtual coupon and rp_i is a weight created by the Reputation Module. Hence, whenever a participant i loses in an auction round, an amount of coupon γ weighted by reputation degree rp_i is added to virtual coupon d_i. Reputable participants can obtain more virtual coupon.

The virtual coupon d_i is set to zero whenever participant i won or dropped out in the previous auction round. The virtual coupon can be used for decreasing bid price, and thus increase winning probability of participant for current auction round.

We define two types of bid prices: One is actual bid price and the other is Rank Price. The actual bid price b_i is claimed by participant i and the Rank Price p_i can be defined as Eq. 9

$$p_i = b_i - d_i \qquad (9)$$

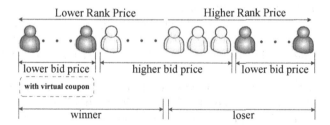

Fig. 3. Winner and loser in multidimensional reverse auction with virtual coupon

In the proposed Incentive Module, the Rank Price p_i is used for selecting winners in each auction round and RBPIA increases the winning probability of the bidder by decreasing Rank Price using virtual coupon.

Even participants who bid higher price can be winners by participating continuously (see Fig. 3). Therefore, RBPIA encourages continuous participation of participants in the system.

4 Performance Evaluation

In this section, we simulate RBPIA in various scenarios to evaluate its effectiveness. The mechanism proposed in reference [30] is also simulated for comparison.

4.1 Simluation Setup

In this work, we simulate a data collection application using RBPIA. A vector of random value is generated for each participant to represent data value monitored at a specific location in a short time period. For ease of comparison, the simulation metrics in [30] is adopted.

Malicious Behavior and Bid Price Collusion

We classify the participants into three categories: normal participant, malicious participant and collusive participant on bid price.

Table 1. Sensing Data and Bid Price Provided By Participants

Participant	Accurate Sensing Data	Bid Price
Normal	90-100%	Normal
Malicious	10-20%	Normal
Collusive	90-100%	Low → High

As shown in Table 1, normal participants upload accurate sensing data in 90-100% of participations and bid according to their true valuation of the sensing data (i.e., the effort for obtaining sensing data).

Malicious participants are supposed to intentionally provide corrupted sensing data (only provide accurate sensing data in 10-20% of participations) and bid normal prices. The bidding behaviors of malicious participants don't follow the utility function.

Collusive participants usually provide accurate sensing data like normal participants, but they collude with each other by initially bidding similar low prices and subsequently bid high price to maximize their profits after they dominate the system.

We run simulations for 50 participatory sensing rounds in three scenarios (marked as scenario A, scenario B and scenario C), and 40 participants are involved in the simulations (see Table 2).

Table 2. Participant Composition In Three Scenarios

Scenarios	Normal	Malicious	Collusive
A	38	2	0
B	20	2	18
C	20	18	2

Note that the setups are used in the following simulations unless they are specified otherwise.

4.2   Simluation Results

Incentive cost

Fig. 4, Fig. 5 and Fig. 6 depict the tendency of incentive cost in 50 participation rounds.

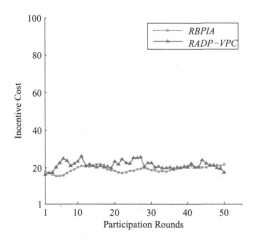

Fig. 4. Incentive cost of RBPIA and RADP-VPC in scenario A

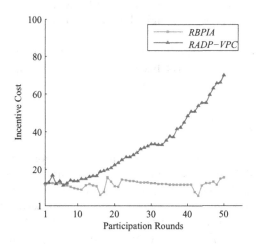

Fig. 5. Incentive cost of RBPIA and RADP-VPC in scenario B

In scenario A, both RBPIA and RADP-VPC mostly select normal participants, and there are no collusive participants in this scenario, so the two schemes both keep low incentive cost.

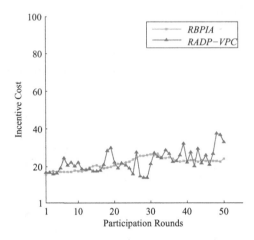

Fig. 6. Incentive cost of RBPIA and RADP-VPC in scenario C

By contrast, as we can see from Fig. 5, incentive cost of RADP-VPC increases dramatically from about round 10 in scenario B due to existence of collusive participants. Such phenomenon means that RADP-VPC cannot cope with bid price collusion. There are almost half of participants are collusive and normal participants will drop out because of low winning probability. Winning prices of participants keep going up since normal participants drop out and collusive participants control the system eventually. Whereas, incentive cost of RBPIA can stay relatively stable even though there are many participants collude with each other on bid price.

Additionally, from Fig. 6, the incentive cost of both RBPIA and RADP-VPC in scenario C stay at a low level because collusive participants account for a small proportion.

5   Conclusion

Sufficient reputable participants are critical to participatory sensing activities such as urban sensing and environmental monitoring. In this paper, we study incentive approaches based on reputation model for participatory sensing. We address the problem of retaining a desired number of active reputable participants in participatory sensing systems to provide adequate level of service quality with low incentive cost. The Reputation-Based Participant Incentive Approach (RBPIA) is proposed for motivating participants in opportunistic cognitive networks. From simulation results, RBPIA perform better than RDAP-VPC which is proposed in literature [30]. In future work, we plan to design an adaptive technique for finding optimal coefficients in the incentive approach.

References

1. Xie, X., Wang, X., Wen, Z., et al.: A QoS Routing Protocol for Cognitive Networks. Chinese Journal of Computers 0936(9), 1807–1815 (2013)
2. Wang, X., Cheng, H., Li, K., Li, J., Sun, J.: A cross-layer optimization based integrated routing and grooming algorithm for green multi-granularity transport networks. Journal of Parallel and Distributed Computing 0673(6), 807–822 (2013)
3. Pelusi, L., Passarella, A., Conti, M.: Opportunistic networking: data forwarding in disconnected mobile ad hoc networks. IEEE Comm. Magazine 44(11), 134–141 (2006)
4. Mun, M., Reddy, S., Shilton, K., et al.: PEIR, the personal environment impact report, as a platform for participatory sensing systems research. In: Proceedings of the 7th International Conference on Mobile Systems, Applications, and Services, MobiSys 2009 (June 2009)
5. Hull, B., Bychkovsky, V., Chen, K., et al.: CarTel: A Distributed Mobile Sensor Computing System. In: Proc. of 11th ACM SenSys 2006 (November 2006)
6. Lu, H., Eisenman, S.B., Campbell, A.T.: Bubble-sensing: Binding sensing tasks to the physical world. In: Pervasive and Mobile Computing (2010)
7. Qu, D., Wang, X., Huang, M.: An Aware Ant Routing Algorithm in Mobile Peer-To-Peer Networks. Chinese Journal of Computers 0736(07), 1456–1464 (2013)
8. Wang, X., Cheng, H., Huang, M.: Multi-robot navigation based QoS routing in self-organizing networks. Engineering Applications of Artificial Intelligence 26(1), 262–272 (2013)
9. Intel Urban Atmosphere, http://www.urban-atmospheres.net/
10. Allen, M., Girod, L., Newton, R., Madden, S., Blumstein, D.T., Estrin, D.: Voxnet: an interactive, rapidly deployable acoustic monitoring platform. In: IPSN 2008: Proceedings of the 2008 International Conference on Information Processing in Sensor Networks, pp. 371–382. IEEE Computer Society, Washington, DC (2008)
11. Hoh, B., Gruteser, M., Herring, R., Ban, J., Work, D., Herrera, J.C., Bayen, A.M., Annavaram, M., Jacobson, Q.: Virtual trip lines for distributed privacy-preserving traffic monitoring. In: MobiSys 2008, Breckenridge, CO (2008)
12. Wang, X., Cai, L., Huang, M., et al.: Spatial Tessellation Based k Coverage Scheme for 3D Wireless Sensor. Mini-micro Systems 35(3), 433–436 (2014)
13. Azizyan, M., Choudhury, R.R.: SurroundSense: mobile phone localization using ambient sound and light. ACM SIGMOBILE Mobile Computing and Communications Review 13(1), 69–72 (2009)
14. Compbell, A.T., Eisenman, S.B., Fodor, K., et al.: CenceMe: Injecting Sensing Presence into Social Network Applications. In: Proc. of Ninth ACM International Symposium on Mobile Ad Hoc Networking and Computing (MobiHoc 2008), Hong Kong (2008)
15. MIT Media Lab: The Owl Project, http://owlproject.media.mit.edu
16. Chen, B.-C., Guo, J., Tseng, B., Yang, J.: User reputation in a comment rating environment. In: Proceedings of the 17th ACM SIGKDD International Conference on Knowledge Discovery and Data Mining, KDD 2011 (2011)
17. Amazon, http://www.amazon.com
18. Li, W., Wu, D., Xu, H.: Reputation in China's online auction market: Evidence from Taobao.com. Frontiers of Business Research in China 2, 323–328 (2008)
19. Buchegger, S., Le Boudec, J.Y.: Performance Analysis of the CONFIDANT Protocol. In: Proceedings of the ACM International Symposium on Mobile Ad Hoc Networking and Computing (2002)

20. Michiardi, P., Molva, R.: Core: a Collaborative Reputation mechanism to enforce node cooperation in mobile ad-hoc networks. In: Jerman-Blažič, B., Klobučar, T. (eds.) Proceedings of the IFIP TC6/TC11 Sixth Joint Working Conference on Communications and Multimedia Security. IFIP, vol. 100, pp. 107–121. Springer, Boston (2002)

21. Buchegger, S., Le Boudec, J.Y.: Coping with False Accusations in Misbehavior Reputation System for Mobile Ad-hoc Networks. EPEL Technical Report Number IC/2003/31 (2003)

22. Buchegger, S., Le Boudec, J.Y.: The Effect of Rumor Spreading in Reputation Systems for Mobile Ad-hoc Networks. In: WiOpt 2003: Modeling and Optimization in Mobile, Ad Hoc and Wireless Networks (March 2003)

23. Josang, A., Ismail, R.: The Beta Reputation System. In: Proceedings of the 15th Bled Electronic Commerce Conference (June 2002)

24. Gelman, A., Carlin, J.B., Stern, H.S., Rubin, D.B.: Bayesian Data Analysis. Chapman and Hall (2003)

25. Ganeriwal, S., Srivastava, M.: Reputation-based Framework for High Integrity Sensor Networks. ACM Transactions on Sensor Networks (TOSN) 4(3) (May 2008)

26. Huang, K.L., Kanhere, S.S., Hu, W.: On the need for a reputation system in mobile phone based sensing. Ad Hoc Netw. (2012), doi:10.1016/j.adhoc.2011.12.002

27. Yang, H., Zhang, J., Roe, P.: Using reputation management in participatory sensing for data classification. In: 2nd International Conference on Ambient Systems, Networks and Technologies, ANT-2011/8th International Conference on Mobile Web Information Systems, MobiWIS 2011 (2011)

28. Yang, B., Garcia-Molina, H.: PPay: micropayments for peer-to-peer systems. In: Proceedings of the 10th ACM Conference on Computer and Communications Security, Washington, D.C., USA, pp. 300–310 (2003)

29. Habib, A., Chuang, J.: Service differentiated peer selection: an incentive mechanism for peer-to-peer media streaming. IEEE Transactions on Multimedia 8(3), 610–621 (2006)

30. Lee, J.-S., Hoh, B.: Dynamic pricing incentive for participatory sensing. In: Pervasive and Mobile Computing (December 2010)

31. Bichler, M.: The Future of e-Markets: Multidimensional Market Mechanism. Cambridge University Press (2001)

32. Bichler, M., Kaukal, M., Segev, A.: Multi-attribute auctions for electronic procurement. In: Proc. 1st IBM IAC Workshop on Internet Based Negotiation Technologies, Yorktown Heights, NY (1999)

33. Chou, C.T., Ignjatovic, A., Hu, W.: Efficient Computation of Robust Average in Wireless Sensor Networks using Compressive Sensing. Technical Report: UNSW-CSE-TR-0915

34. Gompertz, B.: On the Nature of the Function Expressive of the Law of Human Mortality, and on a New Mode of Determining the Value of Life Contingencies. Philosophical Transactions of the Royal Society of London 115, 513–585 (1825), doi:10.1098/rstl.1825.0026

35. MacQueen, J.B.: Some Methods for classification and Analysis of Multivariate Observations. In: Proceedings of 5th Berkeley Symposium on Mathematical Statistics and Probability, pp. 281–297. University of California Press (2009) (retreived)

Semantic Similarity Calculation of Short Texts Based on Language Network and Word Semantic Information

Zhijian Zhan[1], Feng Lin[2], and Xiaoping Yang[1]

[1] School of Information, Renmin University of China, Beijing 100872
[2] School of Opto-electronic and communication Engineering, Xiamen
zhanzj@ruc.edu.cn, linfeng@xmut.edu.cn

Abstract. We first analyzes the deviation when current similarity calculation methods for texts are applied to short texts, and proposes a similarity calculation method for short texts based on language network and word semantic information. Firstly, models the short texts as language network according to the complex-network characteristic of human being's language. Then analyzes the comprehensive eigenvalue of the words in the language network and the word similarity between different texts to obtain the word semantic. Calculate the similarity between short texts combining language network and word semantic. Finally the effectiveness of proposed algorithm is verified through clustering algorithm experiments.

Keywords: language network, text clustering, short texts similarity, word similarity.

1 Introduction

Text Clustering refers to divide text collection into different clusters automatically. Texts in the same cluster are very similar and differentiate in different clusters [1]. Text clustering is the fundamental research for text excavation. Researchers at home and abroad have got an earlier research and development for the algorithm on text clustering and obtain good results. However, there are several principal problems existing in the process of text clustering, include how to define the number of clusters, how to calculate the similarity between texts and how to assess text clustering.

With the rapid development of WEB, short texts such as micro blog, SMS and IM, etc., take more and more importance in people's life. Unlike long texts with rich information, short texts contain poor information. Usually, their lengths don't exceed to 200 words. Short texts generally have explicit themes to transfer the author's intention. Traditional texts similarity calculation methods are to obtain the statistic of word similarity between texts. For long texts, the word number is larger and the method can work effective. But short texts may only contain a few number of words, there may be no common words between them. If the calculation methods of similarity between long texts are applied, we may achieve false results between short texts. Short texts like language that people use in daily life are originated with

J. Wu et al. (Eds.): ACA 2014, CCIS 451, pp. 215–228, 2014.

people's feeling, are uncertain in line with the normal rules of grammar, only if they can express the speaker's meaning. For such short texts with unclear grammar, short length and irregular word order, we can't utilize conventional calculation methods of similarity for long texts. For instance, there're two short texts: "how to download music from internet" and "can I transfer mp3 to my laptop". If only the common words are in statistics, there are few identical words. But the two sentences have a high degree of similarity in fact.

Similarity calculations for short texts have been widely used in many fields. In information retrieval, it's considered as one of the best method to improve the retrieval results [2]. In mail message processing, it can implement mail classification faster [3]. In the interface development of nature language database, it can extend the inquiry interface [4]. Moreover, it also has important applications in health advisory dialogue system [5], property sales [6], telephone sales [7] and smart tour guide [8].

Traditional methods of similarity measure like Vector Space Similarity Measure will cause erroneous results when applied in short texts, because most of them treat texts as a set of words. They calculate the word's number appearing in the text, establish characteristic vector and compute the text similarity using the cosine similarity or Jaccard similarity [9]. Due to fewness of words and brief content of short texts, the method not only ignores the semantics information of the words but also the order information and grammar information. It creates a vector space with very high dimension and necessarily causes a problem of data sparse, finally leads to low computational efficiency.

The innovation of this paper lies in: the first is in accordance with the special characteristics of short text, we introduce the language network model to represents the semantic information of short text; the second is with combine the important features of language network and semantic information of words, we propose a new short text similarity calculation method. Provided the short texts, our method can efficiently and quickly calculate the similarity on the semantic level between them. It can be applied in a wide range.

2   Related Works

With the rapid development of Internet, text resources increase sharply. In fact 80% of Internet resources are texts. In the past few decades, automatically processing of electronic text resources have become the key research of researchers. There's a large quantity of the Internet text resources including Webpage text, email, news messages. With the large number of network texts, researcher's principal interests on text processing are how to mine the needed information [10]. In the early 80s, the major application of text processing is text categorization in knowledge engineering. Experts artificially defined regular knowledge base in first, and then determined the texts to relevant category [11]. In order to avoid the low efficiency caused by excessive artificial involvement in the writing of regular base, in the 90s, researchers proposed many improved method including regular base construction method based on machine learning. The method can get a better result than that based on artificial writing, largely save human resource and improve efficiency [12].

Besides text mining, many other Natural Language Processing application, including data mining, machine learning, pattern recognition, artificial intelligence, statistics, computational linguistics, compute network technology and informatics, also set appropriate requirement for text processing. The text resource on the Internet is massive, heterogeneous and widely distributed. The contents of texts are natural language of human beings and can't be understood by computer directly. The data processed by traditional computer text processing are structured. However, texts are semi-structured or non-structured. In particular, short texts have less content, maybe several sentences, one sentence or several words, even only one word. Consequently, the primary problem is to represent the short text effective in computers to reflect the text characteristic with sufficient information and avoid low computational effectively.

In recent years, the attentions of researchers have been greatly attracted on complex network. Complex network is almost everywhere in our life and their model are widely used in life sciences[13], stress media[14], neural networks[15], space-time game[16], gene controlling network[17] and other self-organized systems. Complex network is composed of nodes and edges, whether it's visual system or not. For example, telephone networks and oil-gas transmission systems are visual and have material nodes and edges. While interpersonal relationship network and social work relationship are invisible. The topology graph of network usually is fully regular or fully random. But many biological networks, technology networks and social networks is between the two [18].

Researchers have demonstrated that human languages also have characteristic of small-world complex network. Common used words severed as nodes and semantic relationship between words as edges, the complex network of human language can be established. Taking it as thinking, we can establish complex network for texts, and obtain the weight and semantic information of characteristic words by computing the comprehensive edge value of each nodes in the language network. As a characteristic word to represent the meaning of the text, it must meet the following four requirements:

1) Distinctly represent the text content ;

2) Clearly distinguish the text meaning from other meanings ;

3) The quantity is small ;

4) The algorithm is not complicated.

Harris believes that the ability to calculate the similarity of text is due to that those element words which represent similar meaning in similar short texts [19]. The thought is confirmed by Firth. Firth supposes that in any language, words with the same meaning appear in different style [20]. Miller further verifies that the words in text are similar to some extend as long as the texts are similar [21]. Thus, a conclusion can be draw that words in similar texts are always similar, since similar texts express similar subject. Instead, if words in texts are similar, the texts are similar. We can firstly compute the similarity of words, and then comprehensively weight them to achieve the similarity of texts. Based on such conclusion, the similarity of short texts can be increased through the improvement of similarity between words and the weighted algorithm.

To address the above problem and after comparing and analysis of other methods for characteristic representation and similarity calculation, the paper proposes an calculation method for the semantic similarity of short texts based on language network and word semantic. The main contributions are as follows:

1) Modeling short texts with language network to provide a proper characterization model for the calculation of semantic similarity.

2) Combining the important features and word semantic information of language network, and presenting the calculation method for the similarity of short texts.

3) Verifying the effectiveness of the proposed method based on classification experiments on several mainstream texts. The experiments have demonstrated that our method is super to the traditional TF-IDF method and the method proposed in [22].

3   Short Texts Similarity Based on Word Semantics

3.1   Important Characteristics of Complex Network

To establish model of complex network with mathematical linguistics and according to the important characteristics of complex networks which are generally accepted in the industry, the graphic definition for complex network is given as below:

Definition1(complex network): Suppose complex network G=(V,E,W) is a graph where $V=\{v_1, v_i \ldots \ldots v_n\}$, is the nodes collection, $E=\{(v_i, v_j), v_i \in V, v_j \in V\}$, is the edges collection and $W=\{w_{ij} | (v_i, v_j) \in E\}$, is the weight collection. The characteristic equation is listed respectively in the following:

1) D_i is the degree of node v_i, defined as:

$$D_i = |\{(v_i, v_j) : (v_i, v_j) \in E, v_i \in V, v_j \in V\}|$$ (3-1)

In complex network, D_i represents the number of nodes which have edge with node v_i. D_i indicates the connectivity of one node with others.

2) Ki is the aggregation degree of node v_i, defined as:

$$K_i = |\{(v_j, v_k) : (v_i, v_j) \in E, (v_j, v_k) \in E, v_i \in V, v_j \in V, v_k \in V\}|$$ (3-2)

In complex network, K_i represents the connectivity between nodes which are v_i-centered. K_i indicates the nodes' aggregation within a local range.

3) C_i is the clustering degree of v_i, defined as:

$$C_i = \frac{K_i}{\binom{D_i}{2}} = \frac{2K_i}{D_i(D_i - 1)}$$ (3-3)

The numerator in the formula is the aggregation degree of v_i, while the denominator is the degree distribution statistics when the graph is complete connected.

4) WD_i is the weigh degree of node v_i, defined as:

$$WD_i = \sum_{(v_i, v_j) \in E} W_{ij} \qquad (3\text{-}4)$$

WD_i is the sum of the weight of all edges which are connected with v_i.

5) WK_i is the weighted aggregation degree of v_i, defined as:

$$WK_i = \sum_{(v_j, v_k) \in E} W_{jk} \qquad (3\text{-}5)$$

WK_i is the sum of the weight of all edges which are vi-centered.

6) WC_i is the comprehensive aggregation degree, defined as:

$$WC_i = \frac{WK_i}{WD_i} \times C_i = \frac{WK_i}{WD_i} \times \frac{2K_i}{D_i(D_i - 1)} \qquad (3\text{-}6)$$

WC_i is proportional to WK_i and K_i, while inversely proportional to WD_i.

7) The aggregation factor of complex network G is defined as:

$$C = \frac{1}{n} \sum_{i=1}^{n} C_i \qquad (3\text{-}7)$$

The aggregation factor is the average of all nodes' clustering degree.

8) The average shortest path of G is defined as:

$$L = \sum_{v_i, v_j \in V} l(v_i, v_j) \qquad (3\text{-}8)$$

$l(v_i, v_j)$ represent the shortest path between any two nodes v_i and v_j. In complex network's graph, there may be more than one path between any two nodes. Given that $l(v_i, v_j)$ is the shortest path, then the average shortest path of the complex network can be defined as the sum of all the shortest paths.

9) BC_i is the clustering factor of node v_i, defined as :

$$BC_i = \sum_{i \neq j \neq k} \frac{l_{jk}(i)}{l_{jk}} \qquad (3\text{-}9)$$

$l_{jk}(i)$ represents the length of the path which is among all the shortest path between v_j and v_k and through v_i. l_{jk} represents all the shortest path between v_j and v_k.

BC_i has strong practical significance and reflects the place flow of v_i toward the complex network. The research has demonstrated that complex network can be regarded as a set of connected sub network. The sub network's connection nodes play a critical role. Consequently, the shortest path between two nodes which belong to two different sub networks is via node v_i.

10) BP_i is the path factor of node v_i, defined as:

$$BP_i = \frac{1}{\sum_{i \neq j \in V} d_{ij}}$$
(3-10)

BP_i is defined to address the situation that the clustering factor may be 0. Since when some key nodes are not in the shortest path, $BC_i = 0$. Nevertheless, those nodes are the key nodes of the complex network. And the clustering factor emphasizes the local connectivity, thus the introduction of BP_i is to enhance the global connectivity.

11) Z_i is the comprehensive eigenvalue of node v_i in complex network, defined as:

$$Z_i = \frac{\alpha \times WC_i + \beta \times BC_i + \eta \times BP_i}{(N-1) \times (N-2)}$$
(3-11)

α、βandηcan be adjusted according to different applications.

3.2   Text Pre-processing

Although the word number is small and the content is brief, current natural language processing technologies can't fully process a short text message. Before building text characteristic model, pre-processing is necessary for short texts, including word separation, removal of stop-word, stemming, etc. For English texts, words are divided by blank space or obvious punctuations, therefore word division can be quickly realized according to such symbols. But there're no clear boundaries between Chinese texts, hence word separation for Chinese texts through algorithm is needed. At present, the algorithms for word separation are mainly distributed into three classes: matching method based on forward, separation methods based on maximum probability and shortest path. The main idea of matching method is to obtain candidate sub-string from text string by lookup in the dictionary. And the separation methods based on maximum probability is to calculate the probability of separation results of Chinese sentence strings and select a separation result with maximum probability. Method based on shortest path constructs graph for text string, calculate the number of the word with shortest path and conduct it as separation result. Chinese word separation is the important basis of Chinese information processing and its result has great impact on the effect of application. The main reason for separation ambiguity in Chinese is polysemy and synonymy in sentences, so the expression can be various.

After word separation for short texts, removal of stop words should be implemented. Stop words refer to the words whose impact on text expression is negligible and valueless for text processing, like "the、a、of、for、in" in English. The most common method for removal of stop words is the maintenance a stop word list. When a word appears in the list after text separation, it should be removed. Stop words are always related to application field. Since the proposed method need semantic analysis for words, after word separation and removal of stop words, there're two steps should be executed as following:

1) Replace people names, address and organization names in short texts with particular strings. Among them, names are substituted with PEO, address is substituted with ADD, and organization names with COM.
2) Mark the property of words in short texts. Words can be divided into different types according to their characteristic and application. Among them, notional word can best represent the meaning of short texts. Thus, it's necessary to distinguish the words that who are nouns, verbs, adjectives or adverbs.

3.3   Language Network Construction

One of important features that distinguish human language from other biological language is that human language has a large number of words. Statistics show that an ordinary foreign high school student's English vocabulary is more than 100 thousand. People can make decision within 100ms that the combination of a word or term is right or wrong. Research has indicated that the reason for human being's literacy skill is the great deal of connection between human languages. Human language has network characteristics as small-world. The words in human language texts are not random and out-of-order, but express a particular subject according to the relationship between words. The number of word is limited, while different word order can produce tens of thousands of texts that hold different meanings. Texts are mostly composited with paragraphs and sentences. The basic component element of a sentence is word. Taking words as nodes, the relationship between words as edges, and the language network can be constructed for the text. When two different words appear in the same sentence, they have grammar relationship, and the edge is generated. Therefore, edge inevitably exists between adjacent words. However, dose grammar relationship exists between non-adjacent words? How to define a specific distance within which two words have edge relation? If only the relation between adjacent words is collected, the relation between long-distant words may be lost and the significance of some useless words in the network maybe rose. So the correlation between words in the sentence should be determined. If the span is too short, much important correlation can't be recorded, whereas much redundancy information will be generated if the span is too long. The paper explores the regulation in [23] that the maximum correlation span is 2, because it's most common and important in language network. For instance, for the sentence "texts similarity calculation process", "texts", "similarity", "calculation" and "process" will be generated through word separation, thus the language network can be built as the Fig.1 shows. The construction of language network for the whole texts can be generated by combination of the same nodes and edges in each sentence.

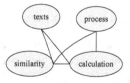

Fig. 1. An example of language network

3.4   Similarity Calculation of Short Texts

After construction of language network for short texts, we can compute the comprehensive eigenvalues of each word node by using formula (3-11) and consider them as an eigenvector to calculate the similarity between short texts. Due to small number of words and brief content of short texts, there are not too many words after preprocessing. Hence, the dimension of the eigenvector can't be high. The next is to consider how to calculate the similarity of short texts. Because those words deliver the most information of short texts, the similarity of short texts can be converted into that of eigenvectors. Moreover, thanks to the variable length of each short text, the dimension of eigenvectors which characterize the short text is also different. Such impact should be eliminated to make the similarity of eigenvectors satisfy the basic measurement standard of similarity.

Suppose v_i and v_j are eigenvectors of two different short text X and Y and $v_i=(w_{i1},w_{i2},\ldots\ldots w_{im})$, $v_j=(w_{j1},w_{j2},\ldots\ldots w_{jn})$. Define the similarity between two vectors as follows:

$$STSim(v_i,v_j) = cf \times VectSim(v_i,v_j) \qquad (3\text{-}12)$$

VectSim(v_i,v_j) denotes the similarity between v_i and v_j and cf denotes the weight factor. If there're many words whose similarity is high in the two short texts and their comprehensive eigenvalues take a large proportion, they will play important roles in each short texts.   Therefore, we can firstly find out the feature words which meet the similarity threshold criteria, and then compute the sum of the comprehensive eigenvalues of the feature words, and finally ratio it with the total comprehensive eigenvalues of the whole text and weight it. The detail calculation formula of the weight factor is defined as following:

$$cf = \frac{1}{2} \times \left\{ \frac{\sum\limits_{k\in\Lambda i} Z_{ik}}{\sum\limits_{k=1}^{m} Z_{ik}} + \frac{\sum\limits_{l\in\Lambda j} Z_{jl}}{\sum\limits_{j=1}^{n} Z_{jl}} \right\} \times \frac{(|\Lambda_i|+|\Lambda_j|)/2}{\max(m,n)} \qquad (3\text{-}13)$$

Where, Z_{ik} is the comprehensive eigenvalue of language network of feature word w_{ik}. In the right term, the numerator denotes the sum of comprehensive eigenvalue of feature words which meet the similarity threshold criteria, and the denominator signifies that of all feature words. The definitions of the collection Λ_i and Λ_j in (3-13) are:

$$\Lambda_i = \{k : 1 \le k \le m, \max\{sim(w_{ik}, w_{jl})\} \ge \mu\} \qquad (3\text{-}14)$$

$$\Lambda_j = \{l : 1 \le l \le n, \max\{sim(w_{jl}, w_{ik})\} \ge \mu\} \qquad (3\text{-}15)$$

If the similarity between the word w_{ik} in the eigenvector v_i and another word $w_{jl}(l=1,2\ldots\ldots n)$ in the eigenvector v_j exceeds the specified similarity threshold, the feature word w_{ik} will be subsumed to collection Λ_i. Select the feature words from eigenvector v_j in collection Λ_j according to the construction process of Λ_i. $|\Lambda_i|$ and

$|\Lambda_j|$ denote the element number of Λ_i and Λ_j respectively. The more the element of the collection is, the more the number of words who meet the similarity threshold criteria is and the greater significance on similarity they will place. $Sim(w_{jl}, w_{ik})$ signifies the semantic similarity between w_{jl} and w_{ik}.

$$\text{VectSim}(v_i, v_j) = \frac{1}{2}(\frac{1}{m}\sum_{k=1}^{m}\max\{Sim(w_{ik}, w_{jl})\} +$$

$$\frac{1}{n}\sum_{l=1}^{n}\max\{Sim(w_{ik}, w_{jl})\}) + \frac{\sum_{k=1}^{\max(m,n)}Z_{ik} \times Z_{jl}}{\sqrt{\sum_{k=1}^{m}Z_{ik}^2 \times \sum_{l=1}^{n}Z_{jl}^2}} \qquad (3\text{-}16)$$

$VectSim(v_i, v_j)$ is determined by the word similarity of vector v_i and v_j and cosine similarity between vectors.

3.5   Basic Flow

Input : two short texts X and Y, similarity threshold μ

Output : similarity value between X and Y

Step1: preprocess X and Y, establish corresponding language network and calculate the comprehensive eigenvalue Z for each node in the network by formula (3-11);

Step2: generate the feature word vectors for X and Y, $v_i = (w_{i1}, w_{i2}, \ldots \ldots w_{im})$ and $v_j = (w_{j1}, w_{j2}, \ldots \ldots w_{jn})$;

Step3: from the word w_{i1} in vector v_i on, seek the word w_{jk} in v_j which has a highest similarity with w_{i1} and record the similarity value θ between w_{i1} and w_{jk}. Compare θ with μ. Place w_{i1} into the collection Λ_i if θ is larger than μ.

Step4: repeat Step3 until all the words in vector v_i has their corresponding largest-similarity word in vector v_j. Record the similarity value and adjust the collection Λ_i.

Step5: calculate the sum achieved in Step3 and Step4, and divide it by the number of words in vector v_i. Take the result as the similarity $Sim(v_i, v_j)$ between v_i and v_j;

Step6: acquire Λ_j and $Sim(v_j, v_i)$ in the same way;

Step7: get $VectSim(v_i, v_j)$ by using the result of Step5 and Step6 and formula 3-16.

Step8: calculate the total of comprehensive eigenvalue of all the words in collection Λ_i and Λ_j, and gain the weight factor cf by formula 3-13;

Step9: compute the similarity value between X and Y by formula 3-12.

4   Experiments and Analysis

We choose experiment data from the partial text classification corpus library gathered and organized by the natural language processing group of Fudan University. The partial corpus library is divided into 10 categories and contains 2706 articles. Each category is subdivided into different categories based on text content as table 1 shows:

Table 1. Abstract of experimental data

category	Number of text	Number of subcategory	the smallest number of text in subcategory	the biggest number of text in subcategory	The average text number in subcategory
Environment	200	6	8	25	33
Computer	200	5	10	22	40
Transportation	214	8	7	20	26
Education	220	6	6	16	37
Economy	325	5	11	14	65
Military	240	8	12	20	30
Sports	350	9	9	22	39
Medicine	204	6	8	20	34
Arts	248	5	7	23	50
Politics	505	10	7	18	50

The experiment firstly implement the processing on text collection using division software ICTCLAS developed by Chinese Academy of Science and then establish language network, calculate the comprehensive eigenvalue Z for each word. Take feature word as feature vector of the text and comprehensive eigenvalue as weight of vector. The similarity between feature words can be obtained suing the method proposed in [21]. Afterwards, combining with the method for text similarity calculation proposed in the paper, compute the similarity of text data collection to get the similarity matrix.

The experiment is carried out in the Windows 7 operating system, hardware configuration of CPU dual core 3.3G, 4G ram, 1T hard disk space. Using Java language, development tools is Eclipse 3.2.

The experiment verifies the effectiveness of the proposed algorithm, and compare the clustering result gained by text similarity matrix based on TF-IDF[10] and that of TSemSim combining with word semantic information proposed in [17]. Clustering experiments are done with CLUTO toolkit① and algorithms like K-Mean(DKM), bipartite K-mean(BKM) and aggregation K-mean(AKM) are achieved.

The experiment adopts F-metric value to measure the computation of text similarity. F-metric value is a comprehensive evaluation index given by precision P and recall R, defined as follows:

$$F = \frac{2RP}{R+P}$$

$$P = \frac{\text{num of correctly returned text}}{\text{num of total calculated text}}$$

$$R = \frac{\text{num of correctly returned text}}{\text{num of text in subcategory}}$$

F-metric value of global clustering is defined as:

$$F = \sum_i \frac{n_i}{n} \max_j (F)$$

In above formula, n_i denotes the text number in each subcategory, n denotes the number of all texts and j is the clustering result after computation. The larger F is, the better the clustering result is.

The first step is to determine the impact that similarity threshold μ places on clustering result. Fig1 shows the impact of μ in the case of DKM clustering algorithm. Seen from the diagram, the clustering effect changes in a parabola trend when μ varies. When μ is in the interval [0.65, 0.7], the clustering effect is best. After analysis, when μ is too small or too large, the number of elements in the selected feature word collectionΛ_i andΛ_j will varies and affect the clustering effect.

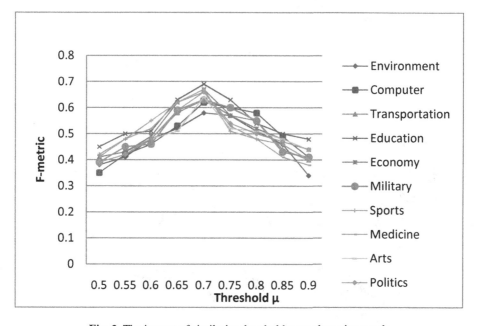

Fig. 2. The impact of similarity threshold μ on clustering result

According to above experimental result, the paper chooses 0.7 as similarity threshold μ. Fig.2 presents the comparison result gained by proposed algorithm, TF-IDF and TSemSim algorithm. We can see from Fig.3 that no matter in the situation of DKM、 BKM or AKM clustering algorithm, the proposed algorithm can achieve better F-metric value than the other two. Thus the proposed algorithm can effectively enhance clustering result.

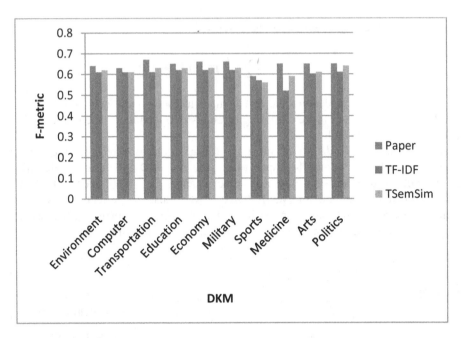

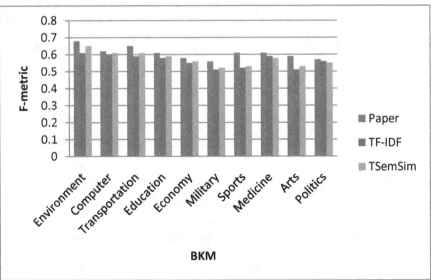

Fig. 3. Comparison result of F-metric gained by proposed algorithm, TF-IDF and TSemSim algorithm in DKM, BKM, AKM clustering algorithm

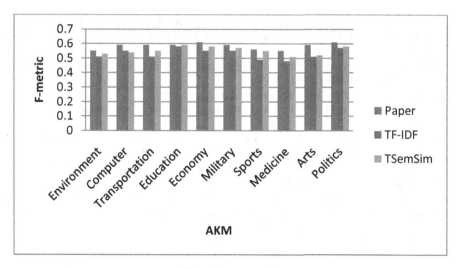

Fig. 3. (*continued*)

5   Conclusion

The paper firstly analyzes the disadvantage of existing measurement method for text similarity based on statistic and semantic analysis and then proposes a new calculation method for text similarity based on language network and word semantic information. Compared with traditional method, the proposed algorithm can decrease the dimension of text representation model and combine the semantic similarity between words to calculate the similarity between texts. Experiments based on classical clustering algorithm are implemented to verify the effectiveness of proposed algorithm.

The further work is to in-depth analyze the influence exerted by the words in different location or with different weight on the similarity calculation result, basing on existing basis of language network and word semantic information analysis. Comprehensively consider other information like the location weight of word and paragraph structure and improve the calculation precision of similarity calculation for texts.

References

1. Fung, B.C.M., Wang, K., Ester, M.: Hierarchical document clustering. In: John, W. (ed.) The Encyclopedia of Data Warehousing and Mining, pp. 970–975. Idea Group (2005)
2. Hall, P., Dowling, G.: Approximate string matching. Computing Survey 12(4), 381–402 (1980)
3. Lamontagne, L., Lee, H.-H.: Textual reuse for email response. In: Funk, P., González Calero, P.A. (eds.) ECCBR 2004. LNCS (LNAI), vol. 3155, pp. 242–256. Springer, Heidelberg (2004)

4. Glass, J., et al.: A Framework for Developing Conversational User Interfaces. In: Fourth International Conference on Computer-Aided Design of User Interfaces, Funchal, Isle of Madeira, Portugal (2004)
5. Bickmore, T., Giorgino, T.: Health dialog systems for patients and consumers. J. Biomed. Inform. 39(5), 556–571 (2006)
6. Cassell, J., et al.: Embodied Conversational Agents (2000)
7. Gorin, A.L., Riccardi, G., Wright, J.H.: How I help you? Speech Communication 23, 113–127 (1997)
8. Graesser, A.C., et al.: AutoTutor: An Intelligent Tutoring System With Mixed Initiative Dialogue. IEEE Transactions on Education 48(4), 612–618 (2005)
9. Salton, G.: The SMART Retrieval System-Experiments in Automatic Document Processing. Prentice Hall Inc., Englewood Cliffs (1971)
10. Dinesh, R., Harish, B.S., Guru, D.S., Manjunath, S.: Concept of Status Matrix in Text Classification. In: The Proceedings of Indian International Conference on Artificial Intelligence, Tumkur, India, pp. 2071–2079 (2009)
11. Mitra, V., Wang, C.J., Banerjee, S.: Text Classification: A least square support vector machine approach. Journal of Applied Soft Computing 2007(7), 908–914 (2007)
12. Fung, G.P.C., Yu, J.X., Lu, H., Yu, P.S.: Text classification without negative example revisit. IEEE Transactions on Knowledge and Data Engineering 2006(18), 23–47 (2006)
13. Strogatz, S.H., Stewart, I.: Coupled oscillators and biological synchronization. Sci. Am. 269(6), 102–109 (1993)
14. Gerhardt, M., Schuster, H., Tyson, J.J.: A cellular automaton model of excitable media including curvature and dispersion. Science 247, 1563–1566 (1990)
15. Hopfield, J.J., Herz, A.V.M.: Rapid local synchronization of action potentials: Toward computation with coupled integrate-and-fire neurons. Proc. Natl Acad. Sci. USA 92, 6655–6662 (1995)
16. Nowak, M.A., May, R.M.: Evolutionary games and spatial chaos. Nature 359, 826–829 (1992)
17. Kauffman, S.A.: Metabolic stability and epigenesis in randomly constructed genetic nets. J. Theor. Biol. (22), 437–467 (1969)
18. Watts, D., Strogatz, S.: Collective dynamics of 'small-world' networks. Nature 393, 440–442 (1998)
19. Harris, Z.: Distributional Structure. Word (10), 146–162 (1954)
20. Firth, J.R.: A Synopsis of Linguistic Theory, 1930–1957. In: Special Volume of the Philological Society. Blackwell, Oxford (1957)
21. Miller, G., Charles, W.: Contextual Correlates of Semantic Similarity. Language and Cognitive Processes 6, 1–28 (1991)
22. Li, Y., McLean, D., Bandar, Z.A., James, D.: Sentence Similarity Based on Semantic Nets and Corpus Statistics. IEEE Transactions on Knowledge and Data Engineering 18(8), 1138–1150 (2006)
23. Ferrer i Cancho, R., Sole, R.V.: The small world of human language. Biological Sciences 268(1482), 2261–2265 (2011)

A New Technology for MIMO Detection: The μ Quantum Genetic Sphere Decoding Algorithm

Jian Zhao[*], Hengzhu Liu[**], Xucan Chen, and Ting Chen

School of Computer, National University of Defense Technology, 410073, Changsha,
P.R. China
zhaojian9014@gmail.com

Abstract. The technology for multiple-input multiple-output (MIMO) detection is a kind of key enabling technology in high-rate wireless communication, whose performance directly affects the data throughput of the whole system. How to improve the MIMO detection technology, so as to increase the detecting rate and reliability, as well as to lower the bit error rate (BER) has become a hot topic in the field of wireless digital communication. Since the original sphere decoding algorithm (OSDA) has a relatively high computational complexity and a relatively long decoding time, in this paper, we present a new technology for MIMO detection: the μ quantum genetic sphere decoding algorithm (μQGSDA), which combines the super-parallelism of μ quantum computing with the global superiority of genetic algorithm (GA), and can be summarized as a multi-dimensional search for a single-dimensional search, thus to avoid a large number of complex matrix operations, as well as to improve the detection efficiency. Simulation experiment results demonstrate that our method has some advantages of good robustness, search capability and convergence rate. What's more, the detection performance of μQGSDA has been greatly improved than OSDA.

Keywords: MIMO Detection, Wireless Digital Communication, μ Quantum Computation, OSDA, μQGSDA.

1 Introduction

Recently, users' demand for system capacity and service quality is continually rising with the integration of internet and multimedia applications in the next generation of wireless digital communication [1]. On the other hand, we couldn't satisfy users' needs without a higher spectral efficiency and link reliability since the bandwidth is a limited resource. Study on information theory shows that: MIMO technology with multiple antennas in both transmitter and receiver of the wireless digital communication system can meet the above requirements very well, which makes it be widely used in the relative fields.

However, the performance of MIMO technology is improved at the cost of the increasing computational complexity of the receiver. Thus, the MIMO detection

---

[*] Student Member, CCF.
[**] Member, IEEE.

J. Wu et al. (Eds.): ACA 2014, CCIS 451, pp. 229–241, 2014.

technology has become a key to MIMO wireless digital communication system. To optimize the MIMO detection algorithm so as to minimize the system computational complexity will be a hot topic of the researches on the next generation of wireless digital communication system [2].

Before giving the main structure of this paper, we introduce a narrowband MIMO wireless digital communication system model under the flat Rayleigh fading channel, and briefly trade off several common technologies for MIMO detection.

1.1   MIMO Wireless Digital Communication System Model

Our MIMO wireless digital communication system model is shown in Fig 1. Consider a narrowband MIMO wireless digital communication system with nTx transmit antennas and nRx receive antennas under the flat Rayleigh fading channel, the nRx*1 dimensional received signal vector is given by:

$$Y = H*S+N \tag{1}$$

Where H denotes the nRx*nTx dimensional channel matrix, whose element h_{ij} is a complex Gaussian random variable with zero mean and unit variance under the independent identical distribution. $S=[s_1, s_2, \ldots , s_{nTx}]^T$ is the nTx*1 dimensional transmitted signal vector. N stands for the nRx*1 dimensional additive complex Gaussian white noise vector, whose components are independent with zero mean and σ^2 variance. Besides, we furthermore assume nRx $\geq$ nTx, and the channel matrix H is quasi-static, that is to say, H can be considered to remain unchanged during one or more data bursts, so that we could accurately obtain H by sending test sequence or other channel estimation methods.

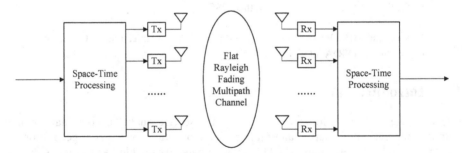

Fig. 1. MIMO wireless digital communication system schematic diagram

1.2   Conventional MIMO Detection Technologies

1)   Maximum-likelihood detection algorithm (MLDA), which solves formula (2), is the optimal detection under the condition of minimum BER. However, its computational complexity is closely related to the size of signal space as well as the number of transmitting and receiving antennas, and grows exponentially with the increase of modulation order as well as the minimum number of transmit and receive antennas, which makes it an NP problem and be severely limited in a high order modulation MIMO system [3].

$$\hat{S} = \arg\min \|Y - H * S\|^2 \tag{2}$$

2)   Serial interference cancellation algorithm (SICA), zero-forcing algorithm (ZFA), minimum mean square error algorithm (MMSEA), which have low complexities but poor BER performance.

3)   OSDA, which can achieve a better performance with a lower computational complexity, thus to solve the problem of MLDA quite well [4]. There are two kinds of search strategies in OSDA: depth-first and breadth-first. The former can provide the optimal BER performance, but its instantaneous throughout and computational complexity vary widely, and still are the exponential functions of antennas number and modulation order. The BER performance of the latter is relatively lower, but its instantaneous throughout and computational complexity are deterministic, and are the linear functions of antennas number and modulation order. So each has advantages and disadvantages, and both have attracted widespread attention. In view of the superior performance of OSDA, ever since it is introduced and applied to MIMO detection, reduction of its computational complexity effectively has been a hot topic in the research of the algorithm. Nevertheless, to the best of our knowledge, so far most of the researches on MIMO detection technologies are merely focus on the optimization of OSDA itself, with some limitations existed inevitably (e.g., [5], [6], [7], [8]). Little attention has been paid to the combination of OSDA and other ideas or intelligent algorithms, and the associated performance tradeoffs and evaluations.

1.3   Outline

The rest of this paper is organized as follows: Chapter 2 briefly reviews the basic principle and flow of OSDA, and then sums up the current problems. Chapter 3 introduces the concept and theory of μ quantum, and presents a new technology for MIMO detection: μQGSDA, and highlight its principle and flow. Chapter 4 compares and analyses μQGSDA with OSDA by carrying out tradeoffs and evaluations of the associated performance through simulation experiments. At last, chapter 5 concludes the whole paper and makes an expectation.

2   Original Sphere Decoding Algorithm

The main idea of OSDA is to decrease the search space of MLDA by certain limitations, so as to achieve the goal of speeding up the search process and reducing the computational complexity. Through constraining the detection to only those points that lie inside a hypersphere with specified radius (r) around the received signal vector Y, thus to avoid the complex search, and the nearest point to vector S is the point of maximum likelihood [9-11]. The corresponding sphere constraint (SC) inequality is

$$\|Y - H * S\|^2 \le r^2 \tag{3}$$

Only imposing SC does not lead to computational complexity reductions, we also need to take a rapid method to determine whether a candidate vector is within the hypersphere, and then find out the closest point to the received signal vector, namely S_{ML}.

Through QR decomposition on channel matrix H, formula (3) can be equivalent to

$$\left\| \hat{Y} - R * S \right\|^2 \le \hat{r}^2 \tag{4}$$

Where $\hat{Y} = Q_1^H * Y$, $\hat{r}^2 = r^2 - \left\| Q_2^H * Y \right\|^2$. R is an nTx*nRx dimensional upper triangular matrix, whose element can be denoted as r_{ij}. Q=[Q_1, Q_2] is an nRx*nRx dimensional unitary matrix, where Q_1 and Q_2 respectively are the first nTx columns and the last remaining columns of Q. Thus, formula (4) can be expanded as

$$\left\| \hat{Y} - R * S \right\|^2 = \left\| \begin{bmatrix} \hat{y}_1 - (r_{11} * s_1 + r_{12} * s_2 + ... + r_{1nTx} * s_{nTx}) \\ \hat{y}_2 - \quad\quad (r_{22} * s_2 + ... + r_{2nTx} * s_{nTx}) \\ \cdot \quad\quad\quad\quad\quad\quad\quad\quad\quad \cdot \\ \cdot \quad\quad\quad\quad\quad\quad\quad\quad\quad \cdot \\ \cdot \\ \hat{y}_{nTx} - \quad\quad\quad\quad ...(r_{nTxnTx} * s_{nTx}) \end{bmatrix} \right\|^2 \tag{5}$$

Formula (5) can be further simplified as

$$\left\| \hat{Y} - R * S \right\|^2 = \left\| \begin{bmatrix} \tilde{y}_1 \quad - \quad r_{11} * s_1 \\ \tilde{y}_2 \quad - \quad r_{22} * s_2 \\ \cdot \quad\quad\quad \cdot \\ \cdot \quad\quad\quad \cdot \\ \tilde{y}_{nTx} - r_{nTxnTx} * s_{nTx} \end{bmatrix} \right\|^2 \begin{matrix} \rightarrow \text{ant-1} \\ \rightarrow \text{ant-2} \\ \vdots \quad \vdots \\ \rightarrow \text{ant-nTx} \end{matrix} \quad \begin{matrix} \\ \text{decoding} \\ \text{sequence} \end{matrix} \tag{6}$$

Where $\tilde{y}_i = \hat{y}_i - (\sum_{j=i+1}^{nTx} r_{ij} * s_j)$, i=1, ... , nTx. As can be seen in Fig 2, if we build a search tree, whose depth is the number of transmit antennas, namely nTx. Then from layer nTx to layer 1, each node in each layer represents the each possible symbol value of the transmitted signal vector.

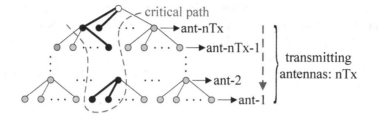

Fig. 2. Construction of the search tree for OSDA with depth-first strategy

Now, we can recursively compute the partial Euclidean distances by traversing down the search tree. For formula (6), assuming:

$$\left\| \tilde{y}_i - r_{ii} * s_i \right\|^2 = e_i(s_i) \tag{7}$$

Where $e_i(s_i)$ is defined as the Euclidean distance increment, corresponding to the length of branch in layer i. The range of results in layer i can be derived from formula (4) and (7):

$$\frac{\tilde{y}_i - \hat{r}}{r_{ii}} \leq s_i \leq \frac{\tilde{y}_i + \hat{r}}{r_{ii}} \tag{8}$$

We define $PED_i(s_i)$ as the partial Euclidean distance, which denotes the cumulative Euclidean distance from the root node to the goal node in layer i:

$$PED_i(s_i) = PED_{i+1}(s_{i+1}) + e_i(s_i) = PED_{i+1}(s_{i+1}) + \left\| \tilde{y}_i - r_{ii} * s_i \right\|^2 \tag{9}$$

To iterate in turn according to formula (9), and each $PED_i(s_i)$ should meet SC, otherwise, the search tree is pruned:

$$PED_i(s_i) \leq \hat{r}^2 \tag{10}$$

Finally, until i=1, when the search tree traversal is finished, the path corresponding to the leaf node with the lowest Euclidean distance is the maximum likelihood solution, record the results and update SC.

Although OSDA can effectively cut down the number of points that the transmitted signal vector symbol to be traversed, and reduce the computational complexity to some extent. However, the indexes such as computational complexity and single decoding time, etc. are unsatisfactory yet, so we still need to seek an improved method [12].

3   u Quantum Genetic Sphere Decoding Algorithm

In order to consider from different viewpoints to further reduce the computational complexity, so as to improve the performance of MIMO detection, we can apply the current widely used intelligent algorithms to the field of signal processing, for MIMO detection can actually be seen as a process of searching the optimal solution [13]. Based on this, we fully absorb the significant advantages of the super parallelism of μ quantum computing as well as the intelligence and the robust of GA, and then introduce the μ quantum state vector expression to genetic coding and present a new technology for MIMO detection: μQGSDA, which achieves a better effect than the conventional MIMO detection methods.

3.1   μ Quantum Bit Coding

In μQGSDA, we adopt the μ quantum bits to store and to express a gene, which can be "0" state or "1" state, or their arbitrary superposition state. That is to say, the expression of a gene no longer contains the determined information, but all possible information. What's more, any operations on a gene will act on all possible information at the same time. All above make this algorithm have a better diversity and convergence than the classical GA.

As can be seen in Fig 3, each individual is composed of chromosome chains, namely, α genetic chain, β genetic chain, and γ genetic chain. Where α genetic chain and β genetic chain denote the signal phase, and determine the evolutionary direction of each gene in the individual. These two real numbers must satisfy the normalization conditions according to the theory of μ quantum computing. So during the crossover and mutation operations, α genetic chain and β genetic chain cannot be destroyed. γ genetic chain denotes the signal amplitude, and can be changed individually.

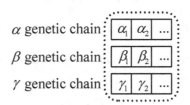

Fig. 3. Individual structure of μ quantum bit

The specific process of initialization coding is shown in the following formula:

$$\mu QL(i, j) = (realL(i, j), imagL(i, j), absL(i, j)) \qquad (11)$$

Where L is the complex matrix corresponding to the signal constellations, μQL is the constellation matrix after the μ quantization. real(•) denotes to calculate the real part, imag(•) denotes to calculate the imaginary part and abs(•) denotes to calculate the plural module value. μQL(i,j)=(•,•, •) denotes that each element in μQL consists of three components, namely, α genetic chain, β genetic chain, and γ genetic chain.

3.2   Search Model and Strategy

The search model and strategy of μQGSDA are similar to those of OSDA, while the difference is the introduction of μ quantum genetic algorithm (μQGA) to the search process in each layer of the search tree. Unlike the traditional quantum genetic algorithm, μQGSDA simplifies the related operations in order to reduce the computational complexity:

➢   Set the upper limit of the evolutional generations as 6.25*M (M is the modulation order of MIMO wireless digital communication system).

➢   Consider there being only limited M points in the whole search space, set the initial population size as 2*M.

3.3   Fitness Function

The fitness function and terminal condition of μQGSDA are shown in formula (9).

3.4   Evolution Operators

1)   Selection operator: when designing the selection operator, in view of the small population size and the relatively simple solution space to be searched, the local-best or premature being not easy to appear, so we directly use the individual fitness value as the basis for selection, choose the individual with the best fitness value, and then spread the prepotency of the individual among the population. While selecting the superior individuals, the current worst individual is also selected, and replaced with a new one.

2)   Crossover operator: as can be seen in Fig 4, crossover operation adopts the two-point crossover strategy, however, two male parents do not simply interchange the selected gene fragment, but respectively keep one genetic chain in the selected gene fragment of each male parents, and exchange the other.

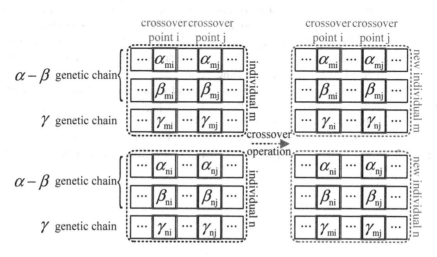

Fig. 4. Crossover operation

3)   Mutation operator: as can be seen in Fig 5, the gene bit to be mutated is selected at first, and then during the mutation operation, the α gene and β gene of this gene bit are randomly generated at the same time, which must also satisfy the normalization conditions of μ quantum computing, while γ gene is randomly generated alone or remains unchanged. In this way, the diversity of new individuals is potentially improved, and thus the population space is enlarged [14].

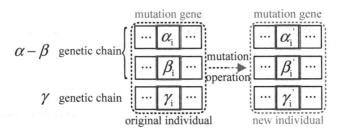

Fig. 5. Mutation operation

3.5   Algorithm Flow

The flow of μQGSDA is shown in Fig 6. The population evolution stage is the just search process, including the operations of selection, crossover, and mutation. The population assessment needs to be iterated layer by layer, and the fitness function in each layer is different in specific parameters, except in the same form. After the completion of the population assessment, the optimal individual must be selected, and determine whether it meets the corresponding terminal conditions or not, if so, exit the search and record the final decoding results, else continue until reach the upper limit of the population evolutional generations. Each time launching the search process of μQGA, the returned results are detected according to the range of solution in each layer obtained by OSDA, if they meet the conditions to continue into the next layer, update the parameters and compute the range of solution in the next layer, and then enter into μQGA to perform the search process, otherwise, determine whether the search process has been completed. Where after, determine whether the whole algorithm is completed according to the results of judgment, if so, quit and return the final decoding results, else enter into the next step. If the results searched by μQGA can neither meet the exit conditions of OSDA, nor meet the conditions of termination to the next layer, reset the search parameters and return to the previous step. The whole μQGSDA cycles time after time on the basis of the above search logic, and finally obtain the maximum likelihood solution.

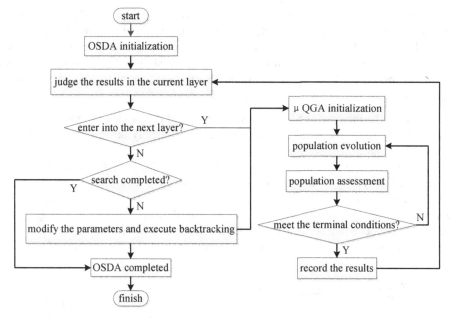

Fig. 6. The flow chart of μQGSDA

4   Simulation Experiment and Results Analysis

The conditions of the simulation experiment and the initial settings of the related parameters are shown in Table 1 and Table 2.

Table 1. The conditions of the simulation experiment

Simulation Experiment Platform			
Processor	Memory	Operating system	Simulation environment
Intel Core i5-3470	3.14GB	Microsoft Windows XP Professional	Matlab 2012b (32bits)

Table 2. The initial settings of the related parameters

Related Parameters Initialization of The Decoder				
Transmit antennas number (nTx)	Receive antennas number (nRx)	Size of data package to be transmitted per antenna	modulation order (M)	channel matrix (H) & noise vector (N)
4	4	100bits	16-QAM	Channel estimation

In order to verify the correctness, validity as well as the superior MIMO detection performance of μQGSDA, we respectively conduct 100 times of simulation experiment on μQGSDA and OSDA with the signal to noise ratio (SNR) ranging from 0 to 20, and then compute the average BER and the average time consuming per decoding apart, the corresponding performance curve and three dimensional heat histogram are shown in Fig 7 (a & b) and Fig 8 (a & b). As can be seen:

1)   With the increase of SNR, the average BER of the two algorithms declines on approximately the same trend, and a zero BER is basically achieved when SNR is around 15.

2)   The average time consuming per decoding of the two algorithms are fairly short, which is closely related to the simple and effective idea of searching layer by layer. Where the average time consuming per decoding performance of μQGSDA is relatively stable, and eventually fluctuates around 0.0026s. While the average time consuming per decoding performance of OSDA fluctuates downward with the increase of SNR, but changes slowly, and is basically stable around 0.0159s in the end.

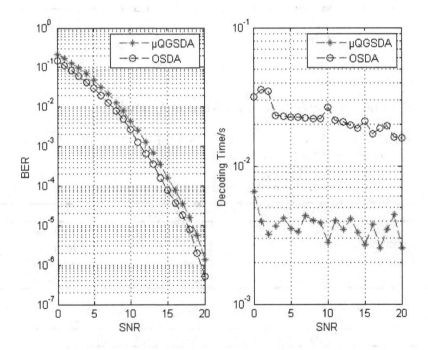

Fig. 7. (a). The average BER performance curve of μQGSDA and OSDA.

Fig 7 (b). The average time consuming per decoding performance curve of μQGSDA and OSDA.

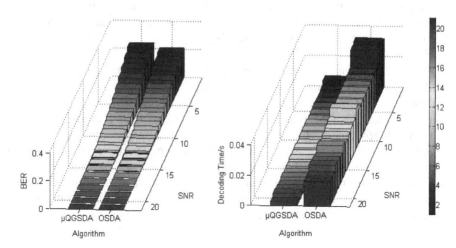

Fig. 8. (a). The average BER performance three dimensional heat histogram of μQGSDA and OSDA.

Fig 8 (b). The average time consuming per decoding performance three dimensional heat histogram of μQGSDA and OSDA.

At last, we contrast the average time consuming per decoding performance of μQGSDA and OSDA with SNR being 15, and the number of the receive & transmit antennas ranging from 1 to 10. Each algorithm cycles 10 times, the simulation experiment performance curve is shown in Fig 9.

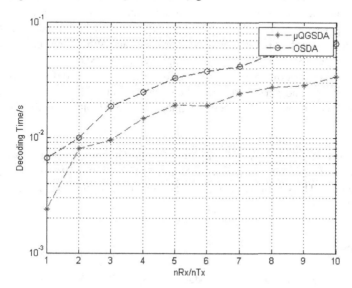

Fig. 9. The performance curve of μQGSDA and OSDA that describes the average time consuming per decoding changing with the number of the receive& transmit antennas

As can be seen: the average time consuming per decoding of the two algorithms grows with the increase of the number of receive & transmit antennas on the same linear trend, and the average time consuming per decoding of μQGSDA is nearly the half of that of OSDA.

The above simulation experiment and results analysis show that: μQGSDA is a kind of deterministic algorithm because of the depth-first search strategy, namely, it is definitely to find out the target results. Because of the introduction of μ quantum computing and GA, OSDA not only keeps its optimal BER performance, but also enhances the robustness, and substantially cuts down the average time consuming per decoding. What's more, as the computational complexity of MIMO detection algorithm is closely related to the number of complex matrix operations, so the summarization from an original multi-dimensional search into a single-dimensional search enables μQGSDA to avoid a large number of complex matrix operations, thus to improve the overall detection efficiency.

5   Conclusion and Expectation

Aiming at the problems of MIMO wireless digital communication system such as how to effectively improve the data detection rate and reliability, and how to reduce BER, as well as the disadvantages of OSDA such as the relatively high computational complexity and the relatively long decoding time, we present a new technology for MIMO detection: μQGSDA, which combines the super-parallelism of μ quantum computing with the global superiority of GA, and can be summarized as a multi-dimensional search for a single-dimensional search, thus to avoid a large number of complex matrix operations, as well as to improve the detection efficiency. Simulation experiment results demonstrate that our method has some advantages of good robustness, search capability and convergence rate. What's more, the detection performance of μQGSDA has been greatly improved than OSDA.

However, the work of this paper is still a lot of deficiencies and defects, remaining to be further improved and perfected. With the development of the fourth generation of wireless digital communication system, technologies for MIMO detection will attract more attention [15].

Acknowledgements. This work is supported by the Doctor Program Foundation of Education Ministry of China, under grant No. 20114307130003. We thank Yanghong TAN and Saihua CHEN from Hunan University in China for their valuable comments to improve this paper.

References

[1] Paulraj, A., Nabar, R., Gore, D.: Introduction to Space-Time Wireless Communications. Cambridge Univ. Press, New York (2003)
[2] Huang, T., Yuan, C., Yang, R., Liu, M.: Relative Technologies and Applications of MIMO. Mechanical Industry Press, Bei Jing (2007)

[3] Lin, Y., He, F.: Theory and Application of MIMO Technology. Pt. Press, Bei Jing (2010)
[4] Shi, F., Wang, H., Yu, L., Hu, F.: 30 Cases Analysis of MATLAB Intelligent Algorithm. Buaa. Press, Bei Jing (2012)
[5] Wang, N., Li, J., Jin, N.: An improved sphere detection algorithm. Journal of China University of Metrology 22(4), 386–402 (2011)
[6] Liu, C.: A Fast Generalized Complex Sphere Decoder for MIMO Systems. Journal of Electronics & Information Technology 30(5), 1189–1192 (2008)
[7] Fu, H., Yao, T., Jiang, X., Chen, S.: A New Fast Sphere Decoding algorithm for Multiple-Antenna Systems. Signal Processing 23(3), 477–480 (2007)
[8] Mao, X., Cheng, Y., Xiang, H.: Hybrid algorithm of depth-first and breadth-first sphere decoding. Journal of Chongqing University of Posts and Telecommunications (Natural Science Edition) 24(5), 535–539 (2012)
[9] Burg, A., Borgmann, M., Wenk, M., Zellweger, M., Fichtner, W., Bölcskei, H.: VLSI Implementation of MIMO Detection Using the Sphere Decoding Algorithm. IEEE Journal of Solid-State Circuits 40(7), 1566–1577 (2005)
[10] Chen, J., Ge, L., Han, H., Shuang, T.: Sphere Decoding Algorithm Performance Simulation and Comparison for MIMO System. Radio Communications Technology 38(6), 38–41 (2012)
[11] Barbero, L.G., Thompson, J.S.: Fixing the complexity of the sphere decoder for MIMO detection. IEEE Trans. Wireless Commun. 7, 2131–2142 (2008)
[12] Yang, C.-H., Marković, D.: A Flexible DSP Architecture for MIMO Sphere Decoding. IEEE Transactions on Circuits and Systems—I: Regular Papers 56(10), 2301–2314 (2009)
[13] Romano, G., Ciuonzo, D., Rossi, P.S., Francesco: Low-complexity dominance-based sphere decoder for MIMO systems. Signal Processing 93(9), 2500–2509 (2013)
[14] Tan, Y., Chen, S., Zhang, G., Xiong, Z.: Adaptive impedance matching using quantum genetic algorithm. Journal of Central South University 20(4), 977–981 (2013)
[15] Sun, Y., Ding, M.: Route Planning Based on Gradient-Field Quantum Genetic Algorithm Model. Journal of Software 8(10), 2511–2516 (2013)

Research on a Kind of Optimization Scheme of MIMO-OFDM Sphere Equalization Technology for Unmanned Aerial Vehicle Wireless Image Transmission Data Link System

Jian Zhao[*], Hengzhu Liu[**], Xucan Chen, Botao Zhang, and Ting Chen

School of Computer, National University of Defense Technology, 410073,
Changsha, P.R.China
zhaojian9014@gmail.com

Abstract. While unmanned aerial vehicle (UAV) is in the mission, the acquired big data information needs to communicate in real-time with the base. Consequently, how to achieve a high-speed and high-quality data transmission via the limited bandwidth and frequency spectrum resource has currently become a hot researching topic in the field of wireless communication and aeronautical telemetry. Aiming at these problems, in this paper, we present a kind of optimization scheme of multi-input multi-output (MIMO) orthogonal frequency division multiplexing (OFDM) sphere equalization technology for UAV wireless image transmission data link system, which combines MIMO technology with OFDM technology, thus to increase the spectrum utilization rate and to improve the system performance while resisting to the multipath effect. What's more, by means of carrying out the collaborative optimization on the original sphere equalization technology (OSET), and by the introduction of the support of the configurable parameters, the system computational complexity is significantly reduced, the detection efficiency as well as the adaptability to complex environment is also improved. Simulation experiment results demonstrate that our method has an approximately optimal bit error rate (BER) performance, a high bandwidth efficiency, a good robustness, a fast convergence rate, and the comprehensive performance is greatly improved than OSET. Furthermore, our method also has a very important reference significance and application value to the development of the equalization technologies of the wireless image transmission data link system based on the UAV platform in our country, as well as to the researches in domestic and foreign related fields.

Keywords: UAV, wireless image transmission data link, MIMO, OFDM, OSET.

1 Introduction

In recent years, with the continuously rapid development of the computer technology, the electronic technology and the communication theory, the concept and idea of

---

[*] Student Member, CCF.
[**] Member, IEEE.

J. Wu et al. (Eds.): ACA 2014, CCIS 451, pp. 242–254, 2014.
© Springer-Verlag Berlin Heidelberg 2014

"information dominance" gradually starts to enter people's horizons, and then is widely adopted and applied around the world. No matter in the military field or in the civilian area, who takes the "information dominance", who takes the first strike and controls the future. At the same time, with the continuous promotion and perfection of the social informatization, the multimedia technology and the radio communication constantly to integrate with each other, besides, the structure of communication system began to tend to three-dimensional and networked, and evolve rapidly from narrowband to broadband. As a result, the existing technologies such as terrestrial communication and satellite communication, etc. have been unable to meet people's growing demand. Therefore, the technology for UAV wireless image transmission data link system has currently become a hot research topic in the field of wireless communication and aeronautical telemetry [1].

Researches on the information theory demonstrate that the selection of the combination of MIMO technology with OFDM technology in the UAV wireless image transmission data link system is able to resist the influence of multipath effect very well, substantially increase the frequency band resource utilization rate, and effectively reduce the front-end design complexity of the transmitter/receiver. However, in the frequency selective Rayleigh fading channel under the condition of dynamic and multipath, the impact of the factors like inter-symbol interference (ISI), etc. on the system performance is very serious. As a result, a feasible equalization technology has become the key to the design of the UAV wireless image transmission data link system.

Although OSET can be able to effectively reduce the number of grid points traversing the symbol vectors, and lower the computation complexity of MIMO-OFDM system to a certain degree. However, the indexes like single decoding time, etc. are unsatisfactory yet, so we still need to seek an improved method.

Before giving the main structure of this paper, we introduce the system model of MIMO-OFDM UAV wireless image transmission data link, and briefly trade off several common equalization technologies for UAV wireless image transmission data link system.

1.1 The System Model of MIMO-OFDM UAV Wireless Image Transmission Data Link

Our system model of MIMO-OFDM UAV wireless image transmission data link is shown in Fig 1. The collaborative communication between each UAV, and the collaborative communication between UAVs and the base are all achieved through the corresponding data link. In order to meet the technical index requirements of UAV wireless image transmission data link better, so as to transmit the more high-resolution images and video in real-time under the limited bandwidth resource and the poor communication environment, MIMO-OFDM technology is adopted in this paper to guarantee the reliability and the validity of the data link. Consider a MIMO-OFDM wireless data communication system in the frequency selective Rayleigh fading channel under the condition of dynamic and multipath, whose transmitting antennas number is nTx, and receiving antennas number is nRx, then the nRx dimensional received signal vector can be expressed as:

$$Y = H*S + N \qquad (1)$$

Where, H denotes the $nRx * nTx$ dimensional channel matrix, whose element h_{ij} is a complex Gaussian random variable with zero mean and unit variance under the independent identical distribution. $s = \left[s_1, s_2, \cdots, s_{nTx} \right]^T$ is the nTx dimensional transmitted signal vector. N stands for the nRx dimensional additive complex Gaussian white noise vector, whose components are independent with zero mean and σ^2 variance. Besides, we further assume the channel matrix H is quasi-static, namely, H can be considered to remain unchanged during one or more data bursts, so that we could accurately obtain H by sending pilot frequency test sequence or other channel estimation methods.

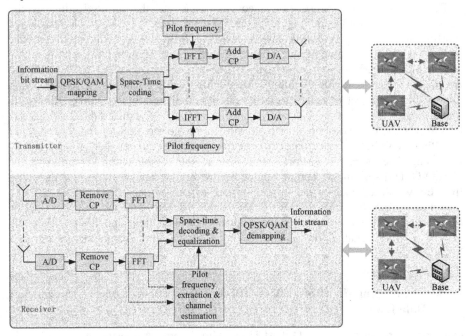

Fig. 1. The system principle diagram of MIMO-OFDM UAV wireless image transmission data link

1.2   Conventional UAV Wireless Image Transmission Data Link System Equalization Technologies

1)   Maximum likelihood (ML) equalization technology: with the minimum BER, this technology is the optimal receiving scheme which regards the additive complex Gaussian white noise vector as an unknown quantity, and takes 2^{M*nTx} (where, M is the modulation order, and assume $nRx \geq nTx$) kinds of possible transmitted symbol into formula (2) one by one for computation, and then select the result with the minimum additive complex Gaussian white noise vector power as the ML output.

However, its computational complexity is closely related to the size of signal space as well as the number of receiving/transmitting antennas, and grows exponentially with the increase of modulation order as well as the minimum number of transmit and receive antennas, which makes it an NP problem and be severely limited in a high order modulation system [2].

$$\hat{S} = \arg \min \|Y - H * S\|^2 \tag{2}$$

2)   Zero-forcing (ZF) equalization technology, and minimum mean square error (MMSE) equalization technology: as representatives of the linear equalization technologies, these two technologies are able to separate the same frequency signals very well under the condition of high signal to noise ratio (SNR), besides, they have a relatively low computational complexity but a relatively poor BER performance [3].

3)   OSET: proposed by Fincke and Pohst in 1985, this technology searches within a pre-set limited spherical region to reduce number of the grid points to be searched, so as to shorten the search time and realize the approximately optimal detection of MIMO-OFDM system with a relatively low computational complexity, rather than searching exhaustively just like ML. OSET can be divided into two kinds of search strategies, namely, depth-first and breadth-first. The former can provide the optimal BER performance, but its instantaneous throughout and computational complexity vary widely, and still are the exponential functions of antennas number and modulation order. The BER performance of the latter is relatively lower, but its instantaneous throughout and computational complexity are deterministic, and are the linear functions of antennas number and modulation order. So each has advantages and disadvantages, and both have attracted widespread favor and attention within the circle. In view of the superior performance of this technology, ever since it is introduced and applied to MIMO-OFDM detection in UAV wireless image transmission data link system, reduction of its computational complexity effectively has always been a hot topic in the research of the related fields. Nevertheless, to the best of our knowledge, so far most of the researches are merely focus on the optimization and improvement of a certain aspect of the sphere equalization technology, with some limitations existed inevitably (e.g., [4-6]). Little attention has been paid to the collaborative design and optimization of multiple parameters of OSET, and to the related attempt to tradeoff and evaluate the comprehensive performance of the system.

1.3   Outline

The next chapter briefly introduces the basic concepts, principles and connotations of MIMO-OFDM technology, including the concepts and principles of MIMO technology, the concepts and principles of OFDM technology, and the necessity analysis for the combination of MIMO technology and OFDM technology. Subsequently, chapter 3 detailedly elaborates solutions and countermeasures of the collaborative improvement and optimization in aspects of initial search radius, detection order, and search strategies, etc. on OSET, and highlights its principle and flow. Through simulation experiments, chapter 4 compares and analyzes the optimized

MIMO-OFDM sphere equalization technology with the conventional methods and OSET, and carries out tradeoffs and evaluations on the overall performance of the UAV wireless image transmission data link system. At last, chapter 5 concludes the whole paper and makes an expectation.

2   The Basic Principle of MIMO-OFDM Technology

2.1   The Basic Principle of MIMO Technology

Currently, science and technology continuously get rid of the stale and bring forth the fresh, and the demand for UAV wireless image transmission data link system broadband high-speed data communication service is constantly growing, what's more, the limited link resources are faced with the communication data big bang difficulties, so how to transfer more information with the limited bandwidth resource while restraining the radio interference very well has become a huge challenge in UAV wireless image transmission data link system development. Researches on the communication theory show that MIMO technology with multiple antennas in both transmitter and receiver of the wireless digital communication system can expand the spatial degree of freedom, exponentially increase the capacity and the spectrum efficiency of the communication system, lower BER, and improve the transmission quality of the wireless signal without increasing the spectral bandwidth. Its system principle block diagram is shown in Fig 2.

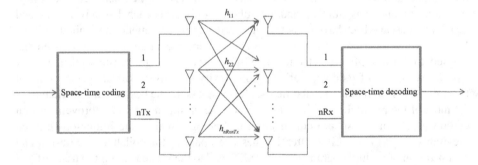

Fig. 2. MIMO system principle block diagram

The key of MIMO technology is space-time signal processing, namely, to combine the time domain and the space domain for signal processing via multiple antennas distributed in space, so as to economize the random fading and the possibly existing multipath propagation to increase the data transmission rate. Furthermore, MIMO technology is able to provide spatial multiplexing gain and spatial diversity gain for the system:

1)   Spatial multiplexing gain: while signal is propagating in a rich scattering environment, it is just like passing through a plurality of independent parallel data channels simultaneously in the same space, which not only enhances the reliability, but also increases the transmission rate, thereby significantly expands the system capacity.

The implementation of spatial multiplexing gain requires that the separation distance between the transmitting antennas and the receiving antennas is further than their correlation distance (usually more than 10 times of signal wave length), in order to guarantee each subchannel of the receiving/transmitting end being independent fading non-correlated channel, so as to realize the spatial diversity reception of the signal.

2)   Spatial diversity gain: in the wireless channel, the probability of multiple copies of the same signal propagated via the independent fading link or branch being simultaneously in deep fading is very small. In order to improve the reliability of the wireless link, we can combine those copies of the signal at the receiving end according to certain rules to improve the reliability of the channel and to lower BER.

Laboratory studies show that: the spectrum efficiency of MIMO technology in the indoor environment can get as high as 20-40 bit/s/Hz, while that of the traditional wireless communication technologies in the mobile cellular is merely 1-5 bit/s/Hz, and only 10-12 bit/s/Hz even in the point to point fixed microwave system [7]. However, the performance indexes of MIMO technology in the aspects of resisting to the frequency selective fading, etc. are unsatisfactory yet, so we still need to seek a combination scheme with other technologies to get a more excellent system performance.

2.2   The Basic Principle of OFDM Technology

April in 2003, IEEE802.11 wireless local area network (LAN) physical layer interface standard was put forward by institute of electrical and electronic engineers (IEEE), and then the broadband wireless LAN air interface standard below 11 GHz frequency band was set on the basis of IEEE802.11 standard, which specified OFDM technology as one of the two kinds of standard transmission mode [8].

OFDM technology is a kind of special multicarrier digital modulation technology, which can also be understood as a kind of multiplexing technology, whose system principle block diagram is shown in Fig 3. The operation of OFDM technology is based on data block, and input data carries out serial to parallel conversion after constellation mapping, and then the original data symbols are concurrently modulated to mutually orthogonal subcarriers, which is able to overcome the frequency selective fading or narrowband interference introduced by multipath delay very well. By means of adding cyclic prefix (CP), the sustainable length of data symbols on each subcarrier is made to relatively increase, so that ISI introduced by the time dispersion of the wireless channels can be effectively reduced. After CP is removed, frequency domain equalization is realized by fast Fourier transform (FFT), and the influence of channel interference can be simplified to the product of a complex propagation constant and a subchannel transmission signal, so the complexity of channel equalization is greatly simplified, which is difficult to realize in the traditional single carrier system with the same bandwidth. Moreover, the frequency band is divided into several disjoint subband by the traditional frequency division multiplexing (FDM) technology to transmit data stream, and each subchannel is separated by a set of filters in the receiving end. This technology is simple and direct but a waste of resources, what's worse, its frequency band utilization rate is relatively lower, too. While OFDM technology allows the frequency spectrum of the subcarriers to overlap with each other, and maximizes the use of frequency spectrum resources. However, there are also some disadvantages in OFDM:

1)   Being susceptible to frequency deviation. The frequency spectrum of the subcarriers overlaps with each other in OFDM system, which proposes a more stringent requirement on the orthogonality between them. However, because of the time-varying characteristics of the wireless channels, the phenomenon of frequency deviation will occur while the wireless signal is being in the transmission process. For example, the Doppler frequency shift or the frequency deviation between the transmitter carrier frequency and the receiver local oscillator will all possibly destroy the orthogonality between the subcarriers in OFDM system, and thereby result in the generation of inter-channel interference (ICI) between the subcarrier signals.

2)   The sending signal has a relatively high peak-to-average power ratio (PARA), which requires a wider dynamic range for the transmitter power amplifier, and simultaneously asks for a smaller phase noise coefficient of the tuning unit as well as other analog devices in the receiver. As a result, the system cost increases.

Consequently, simply adopting the roadmap with single OFDM technology cannot obtain the ideal solution, either.

2.3   The Necessity Analysis for the Combination of MIMO Technology and OFDM Technology

In UAV wireless image transmission data link system, multipath effects and frequency selective fading are two key issues which must also be considered in the signal transmission process except for the necessity of fully increasing bandwidth resource utilization rate. Easily leading to the generation of ISI, multipath effects are often regarded as a harmful factor by the traditional receiver. While MIMO technology is just generated aiming at multipath channels, and the multipath components produced during propagation can be utilized to some extent, so the influence of multipath effects can be seen as a favorable factor instead. However, MIMO technology is still unable to avoid frequency selective fading, while solve the problem of frequency selective fading happens to be one of the advantages of OFDM technology. Thus, the combination of OFDM technology and MIMO technology is bound to be the inevitable trend of the development of wireless radio communication technology and space telemetry technology [9].

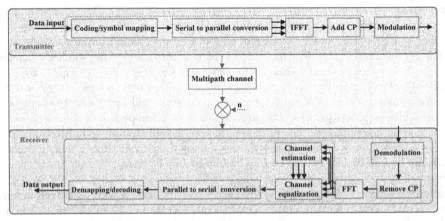

Fig. 3. OFDM system principle block diagram

3   The Solutions and Countermeasures of the Optimization on Sphere Equalization Technology

OSET is able to achieve the ML performance and to keep the calculation efficiency at the same time. Hence, it is a kind of very effective method for MIMO-OFDM detection. However, for the unequal symbol energy constellation graph like quadrature amplitude modulation (QAM), there is a large amount of computation. In order to further reduce the computational complexity of OSET, in this paper, by means of carrying out the collaborative improvement and optimization in aspects of initial search radius determination, pretreatment ranking, and search strategies, etc. on OSET, and by the introduction of the support of configurable parameters, the comprehensive effectiveness of UAV wireless image transmission data link system is further improved. The idiographic flow is shown in Fig 4.

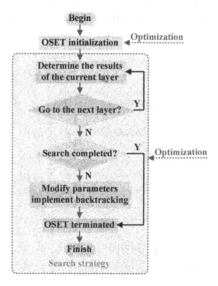

Fig. 4. OSET optimization scheme flow diagram

1)   Determination of the initial search radius. Take the 64-QAM constellation diagram for example, as can be seen in Fig 5, the core of the efficiency of OSET lies in its selective search process, that is to say, we only need to search the area within the range of predetermined conditions, and then search for the closest transmitted symbol vector s around the received symbol vector y. If the initial search radius r is selected too small, just like r_1 shown in the figure, the expected solutions will not be obtained; If the initial search radius r is selected too big, just like r_3 shown in the figure, although the expected solutions can be obtained, however, the search time will also be increased at the same time, resulting in a decrease in the overall efficiency of the system; The best initial search radius is supposed to be r_2 shown in the figure, but it

turns out to be that the determination of the initial radius being the best or not is essentially an NP problem. Consequently, the way to select an appropriate initial search radius has been a key issue in the improvement and optimization of OSET. There are two main methods frequently-used to determine the initial search radius:

➢   Select the initial search radius according to the probability distribution of the additive complex Gaussian white noise vector variance, namely:

$$r^2 = \alpha(2N_t)\sigma^2, (1 \le \alpha \le 200) \tag{3}$$

This method has a relatively low complexity, but can not guarantee the transmitted symbol vector located within the hypersphere, thus there is a possibility of search failure.

➢   Adopt ZF technology for pre-detection, and take the Euclidean distance between its results and the received signal as the initial search radius. This method ensures that there is at least one mapping point of the transmitted signal within the initial hypersphere, thus there is no possibility of search failure, therefore, in this paper, we adopt this method to determine the initial radius, so as to improve and optimize OSET.

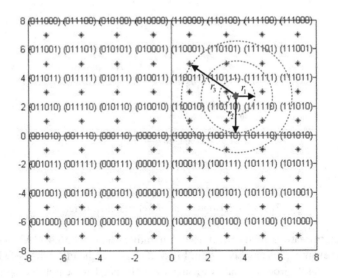

Fig. 5. OSET initial search radius selection schematic diagram (64-QAM)

2)   Pretreatment ranking. Determine the reliability of the transmitted signal by adopting the initial estimate value of ZF equalization technology as a reference. While calculating the candidate set of each dimensional symbol vectors, rank the possible coordinate values in it according to the size of the upper and lower boundary, and synchronously update all upper and lower boundaries according to each updated search radius. Thereby, enhance the convergence rate and shorten the detection delay of OSET.

3)   Search strategies. There are two search strategies in the tree search process of OSET: Fincke-Pohst (FP) strategy and Schnorr-Euchner (SE) strategy. The main distinction between the two strategies is the order to enumerate the candidate nodes. When FP strategy visits the nodes located on the next layer, it is in accordance with the order of the signal constellation, which is to enumerate the signal constellation points in turn from left to right. While SE strategy ranks the signal constellation points located on the next layer according to the order of ascending metric values, and enumerates the signal constellation points according to this order when it visits nodes. SE strategy carries out the search using the zig-zag method, and the first point acquired is the point with the minimum metric value located on the current layer (BaBai point), so if the search fails, then the rest nodes located on that layer can be immediately skipped, thus the computational complexity is greatly reduced [10]. SE strategy starts its search from the node with the minimum branch metric value, so it can find out the ML solution with a higher speed as well as a lower computational complexity than FP strategy. Hence, in this paper, we adopt SE strategy to carry out improvement and optimization on OSET.

4)   Support to the configurability of the system. Including the configurability of search methods (K-best breadth-first strategy and depth-first strategy), the configurability of antenna array (upper limit to 16 * 16), the configurability of the number of subcarriers (upper limit to 128), and the configurability of modulation mode (upper limit to 64-QAM). Accordingly, UAV wireless image transmission data link system can carry out adaptive adjustment at any time according to the actual environment and other changes of conditions to acquire a more excellent performance.

4   Simulation Experiment and Result Analysis

The conditions of the simulation experiment and the initial settings of the related parameters are shown in Table 1 and Table 2.

Table 1. The conditions of the simulation experiment

Simulation experiment platform			
Processor	Memory	Operating system	Simulation environment
Intel Core i5-3470	3.14GB	Microsoft Windows XP Professional	Matlab 2012b (32bits)

Table 2. The initial settings of the related parameters

Related parameters initialization				
Transmit antenna number (nTx)	Receive antenna number (nRx)	Number of subcarriers	Modulation type	Channel matrix (H) & noise vector (N)
4	4	100000	16-QAM	Channel estimation

In order to verify the correctness, validity as well as the superior MIMO-OFDM detection performance of the collaborative optimized OSET, in this paper, we respectively conduct the simulation experiment on ZF equalization technology, MMSE equalization technology, and the collaborative optimized OSET with SNR ranging from 0 to 30, and then respectively compute the average BER under the three technologies, the corresponding performance curve is shown in Fig 6. As can be seen:

1)   With the increase of SNR, the average BER of ZF equalization technology and MMSE equalization technology both decline on the parabolic trend, and the average BER performance of MMSE equalization technology is about 2dB better than ZF equalization technology.

2)   The collaborative optimized OSET is still able to continually maintain the approximately optimal ML detection performance in terms of the average BER index, with 11dB better than MMSE equalization technology and 13dB better than ZF equalization technology.

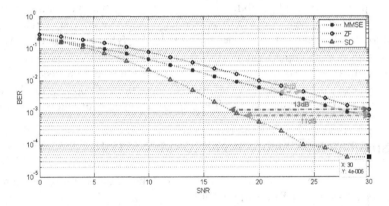

Fig. 6. The average BER performance curve of ZF equalization technology, MMSE equalization technology, and the collaborative optimized OSET

At last, we contrast the average time consumed per decoding performance of the collaborative optimized OSET and OSET with SNR being 15, and the number of the receive & transmit antennas ranging from 1 to 10. Each algorithm cycles 20 times, the simulation experiment performance curve is shown in Fig 7. As can be seen: with the increase of the number of receive & transmit antennas, the average time consumed per decoding of the two technologies both increase on the linear trend, and the average time consumed per decoding of the collaborative optimized OSET is approximately the half of that of OSET.

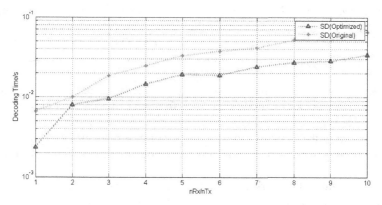

Fig. 7. The performance curve of the collaborative optimized OSET and OSET that describes the average time consumed per decoding changing with the number of the receive & transmit antennas

The above simulation experiment and result analysis show that: the innovative technology roadmap combining MIMO technology with OFDM technology makes UAV wireless image transmission data link system be able to enhance the capacity of resistance to multipath interference and to fully improve the bandwidth utilization rate. Besides, because of the collaborative improvement and optimization in the three aspects of the determination of initial search radius, pretreatment ranking, and search strategies on OSET and the introduction of the support of configurable parameters, OSET has enhanced its robustness, lowered its computational complexity, and greatly reduced the average time consumed per decoding on the basis of maintaining its approximately optimal BER performance.

5   Conclusion and Expectation

Aiming at the problems of UAV wireless image transmission data link system under the condition of informatization such as how to improve the transmission efficiency, detection speed and reliability of the big data information, so as to lower BER, and the disadvantages of OSET such as the relatively high computational complexity and the relatively long average time consumed per decoding, etc.. In this paper, we present a kind of optimization scheme of MIMO-OFDM sphere equalization technology for UAV wireless image transmission data link system, which combines MIMO technology with OFDM technology, thus to increase the spectrum utilization rate and to improve the system performance while resisting to the multipath effect. What's more, by means of carrying out the collaborative optimization on OSET, and by the introduction of the support of the configurable parameters, the system computation complexity is significantly reduced, the detection efficiency as well as the adaptability to complex environment is also improved. Simulation experiment results demonstrate that our method has an approximately optimal BER performance, a high bandwidth efficiency, a good robustness, a fast convergence rate, and the comprehensive performance is greatly improved than OSET. Furthermore, our method also has a very important reference significance and application value to the development of the equalization technologies of the wireless image transmission data link system based on the UAV platform in our country, as well as to the researches in domestic and foreign related fields.

However, the work of this paper is still a lot of deficiencies and defects, the aspects of lowering PARA and simplifying the front-end design complexity of the transmitter/receiver, etc. still remain to be further improved and perfected [11]. With the development of the wireless radio communication system and the space telemetry system, MIMO-OFDM sphere equalization technology will attract more attention.

Acknowledgement. This work is supported by the Doctor Program Foundation of Education Ministry of China, under grant No. 20114307130003.

References

[1] Siebert, S., Teizer, J.: Mobile 3D Mapping for Surveying Earthwork Projects Using an Unmanned Aerial Vehicle (UAV) System, Automation in Construction (2014)

[2] Han, J., Chen, Y.: Multiple UAV Formations for Cooperative Source Seeking and Contour Mapping of a Radiative Signal Field. Journal of Intelligent & Robotic Systems 74(1-2), 323–332 (2014)

[3] Zhao, X., Choi, J.: Design of a MIMO antenna with low ECC for a 4G mobile terminal. Microw. Opt. Technol. Lett. 56(4) (2014)

[4] Liu, T.-H., Chiu, C.-N.: On fast preprocessing schemes for the real-valued spatially multiplexed MIMO detectors. Int. J. Commun. Syst. 27(2) (2014)

[5] Moradi, M., Falahati, A.: Antenna Power Cutback Manipulation to Optimize Relay Power Allocation over MAMR Networks Employing Zero Forcing Scheme. Wireless Personal Communications 73(3), 1215–1225 (2013)

[6] Ashrafinia, S., Naeem, M., Lee, D., He, J.: Discrete Artificial Bee Colony for Computationally Efficient Symbol Detection in Multidevice STBC MIMO Systems. In: Advances in Artificial Intelligence, vol. 2013 (2013)

[7] Qi, Q., Chakrabarti, C.: Parallel High Throughput Soft-Output Sphere Decoding Algorithm. Journal of Signal Processing Systems 68(2), 217–231 (2012)

[8] Hu, C.-C., Chiu, Y.-S.: Robust joint optimization for MIMO AF multiple-relay systems with correlated channel uncertainties. AEUE - International Journal of Electronics and Communications (2013)

[9] Guan, Y., Xu, T., Leuken, R., Qian, M.: Parallel Channel Estimator and Equalizer for Mobile OFDM Systems. Circuits, Systems, and Signal Processing 33(3), 839–861 (2014)

[10] Nex, F., Remondino, F.: UAV for 3D mapping applications: a review. Applied Geomatics 6(1), 1–15 (2014)

[11] Ramiro, C., Roger, S., Gonzalez, A., Almenar, V., Vidal, A.M.: Multicore implementation of a fixed-complexity tree-search detector for MIMO communications. The Journal of Supercomputing 65(3), 1010–1019 (2013)

Author Index